# Collins | English for Exams

## Cambridge English Qualifications

# B1 Preliminary
# for Schools
# 8 practice tests

Published by Collins
An imprint of HarperCollins Publishers
Westerhill Road
Bishopbriggs
Glasgow
G64 2QT

HarperCollins Publishers
Macken House
39/40 Mayor Street Upper
Dublin 1
D01 C9W8
Ireland

First edition 2020

10 9 8 7

© HarperCollins Publishers 2020

ISBN 978-0-00-836754-1

Collins® and COBUILD® are registered trademarks of
HarperCollins Publishers Limited

collins.co.uk/elt

HarperCollins does not warrant that any website
mentioned in this title will be provided uninterrupted,
that any website will be error-free, that defects will be
corrected, or that the website or the server that makes it
available are free of viruses or bugs. For full terms and
conditions please refer to the site terms provided on the
website.

If you would like to comment on any aspect of this book,
please contact us at the given address or online. E-mail:
collins.elt@harpercollins.co.uk

Author: Peter Travis
Series editor: Celia Wigley
For the Publisher: Lisa Todd and Sheena Shanks
Editor: Alison Silver
Typesetter: Jouve, India
Illustrations: Jouve, India
Photographs and map illustration on page 58:
Shutterstock.com
Printer: Printed and bound by Ashford Colour Press
Ltd.
Audio recorded and produced by ID Audio, London
Cover designer: Gordon McGilp
Cover illustration: Maria Herbert-Liew
Sample Answer sheets (pages 217–9): Reproduced
with permission of Cambridge Assessment English ©
UCLES 2019

The Publishers gratefully acknowledge the permission
granted to reproduce the copyright material in this book.
Whilst every effort has been made to trace the copyright
holders, in cases where this has been unsuccessful, or if
any have inadvertently been overlooked, the Publishers
would gladly receive any information enabling them to
rectify any error or omission at the first opportunity.

All exam-style questions and sample answers in this
title were written by the author.

### About the author

**Peter Travis** has taught English in various European
countries including Greece, Portugal and the UK and
authored course books and workbooks for major ELT
publishers. Peter is co-founder of Flo-Joe, the award-
winning portal for Cambridge English exams and runs
other popular ELT websites. Peter is also the author of
Collins Practice Tests for Cambridge English: First (FCE)
and Collins Practice Tests for B1 Preliminary.

# Contents

# How to use this book

## Who is this book for?

This book will help you to prepare for the *Cambridge Assessment English B1 Preliminary for Schools* exam. The exam is also known as the *PET for Schools* exam. The exam was updated for 2020 and this book has been written for the new exam. This book will be useful if you're preparing for the exam for the first time or taking it again. It has been designed so that you can use it to study on your own, however, you can also use it if you're preparing for the *B1 Preliminary for Schools* exam in a class.

The book contains:

- **Tips for success** – important advice to help you to do well in the exam
- **About** *B1 Preliminary for Schools* – a guide to the exam
- **How to prepare for the test** – advice to help you to succeed in each paper
- **Practice tests** – eight complete practice tests
- **Mini-dictionary** – definitions of the more difficult words from the practice tests
- **Audio scripts** – the texts of the audio for the Listening and Speaking papers
- **Sample answer sheets** – make sure you know what the answer sheets look like
- **Answer key** – the answers for the Reading and Listening papers
- **Model answers** – examples of good answers for the Writing and Speaking papers
- **Speaking paper: Additional practice by topic** – more sample questions to help you prepare for the Speaking paper
- **Audio** – all the recordings for the practice tests as well as model answers for the Speaking papers are available online at **www.collins.co.uk/eltresources**

## Tips for success

- **Start studying early** – The more you practise, the better your English will become. Give yourself at least two months to revise and complete all the practice tests in this book. Spend at least one hour a day studying.
- **Time yourself** when you do the practice tests. This will help you to feel more confident when you do the real exam.
- **Do every part** of each practice test. Don't be afraid to make notes in the book. For example, writing down the meaning of words you don't know on the page itself will help you to remember them later on.

## Using the book for self-study

If you haven't studied for the *B1 Preliminary for Schools* exam before, it is a good idea to do all the tests in this book in order. If you have a teacher or friend who can help you with your speaking and writing, that would be very useful. It is also a good idea to meet up with other students who are preparing for the exam or who want to improve their English. Having a study partner will help you to stay motivated. You can also help each other with areas of English you might find difficult.

Begin preparing for the *B1 Preliminary for Schools* exam by getting to know the different parts of each paper, what each part tests and how many marks there are for each part. Use the information in the **About B1 Preliminary for Schools** section to find out all you can. You can also download the *B1 Preliminary for Schools Handbook* from the Cambridge Assessment English website for more details. You need to know how to prepare for each of the papers in the best way possible. The **How to prepare for the test** section in this book will be useful. Try to follow the advice as it will help you to develop the skills you need.

In the practice tests in this book, you will see certain words highlighted in grey. These are the more difficult words and you can find definitions of these in the *Mini-dictionary* at the back of the book. The definitions are from *Collins COBUILD* dictionaries. It's a good idea to download the *Cambridge B1 Preliminary Vocabulary List* from the Cambridge Assessment English website. This is a list of words that you should understand at B1 level. Search 'B1 Preliminary Vocabulary List 2020' online. Look through the list and make a note of the words you don't know. Then look up their meaning in a dictionary. Knowing these words will help you to do better in the exam. You could use the Collins online dictionary: www.collinsdictionary.com

## Preparing for the Writing and Speaking papers

When you are ready to try the practice tests, make sure you do the tasks in the Writing papers as well as the Speaking papers. You can only improve your skills by practising a lot. Practise writing to a time limit. If you find this difficult at first, start by writing a very good answer of the correct length without worrying about time. Then try to complete the tasks faster until you can write a good answer within the time limit. Learn to estimate the number of words you have written without counting them. Study the model answers at the back of the book. This will give you a clear idea of the standard your answers need to be. Don't try to memorise emails, articles or stories for the Writing paper or answers to the questions in the Speaking paper. If you work your way through the book, you should develop the skills and language you need to give good answers in the real exam.

The Speaking paper in this book has accompanying audio so that you can practise answering the examiner's questions. You will be Candidate B, so if you hear the examiner ask Candidate B a question, this means you should answer by pausing the audio on your computer and answering the question. In Parts 3 and 4 of the Speaking paper, you are expected to have a conversation with Candidate A. Again, you will be Candidate B and will respond to Candidate A's statements or questions. This experience will not be 100% authentic as Candidate A cannot respond to your statements or questions, however, this book and the audio have been designed to give you an excellent opportunity to practise answering questions through the eight practice tests. Once you have finished the Speaking paper you can listen to the model answers for Candidate B that have been provided for you. Another option is that you record your answers and then compare these with the model answers.

Please note that there are two versions of the Speaking Test audio:

- The first version contains the pauses for you to practise answering the questions in the Speaking tests. This is when you have to answer the questions for Candidate B. The scripts for this audio can be found from page 186 onwards in your book. For example, you'll see on page 186 that Test 1 Speaking audio track is labelled 'Track 05'. Look for Track 05 when you search for the audio online.

- The second version of the audio contains the Model Answers for the Speaking tests. These are for you to listen to, to see how a good student might answer the questions in the Speaking test. The scripts for this audio can be found from page 234 onwards in your book. You'll see that these audio files are labelled with an 'a' at the end, for example Track 05a, etc. Look for Track 05a when you search for the audio online.

At the back of the book you'll find more sample questions for the Speaking paper. These provide another opportunity to practise answering questions that an examiner might ask you. There are 16 topics and all the questions have been recorded. Try answering these questions as fully as possible. Don't just give a 'yes/no' answer but try to give a reason or an example in your answer. Finally, read as much as possible in English; this is the best way to learn new vocabulary and improve your English.

# About B1 Preliminary for Schools

The *Cambridge B1 Preliminary for Schools* test is an intermediate-level English exam delivered by Cambridge Assessment English. It is for school students who need to show that they can deal with everyday English at an intermediate level. In other words, you have to be able to:

- read simple textbooks and articles in English
- write emails and articles on everyday subjects
- understand factual information
- show awareness of opinions and mood in spoken and written English.

The exam is one of several offered by Cambridge Assessment English at different levels. The table below shows how *B1 Preliminary for Schools* fits into the Cambridge English Qualifications. The level of this exam is described as being at B1 on the Common European Framework of Reference (CEFR).

| | CEFR | Cambridge English Scale | Cambridge qualification |
|---|---|---|---|
| Proficient user | C2 | 200–230 | C2 Proficiency |
| | C1 | 180–199 | C1 Advanced |
| Independent user | B2 | 160–179 | B2 First for Schools |
| | B1 | 140–159 | B1 Preliminary for Schools |
| Basic user | A2 | 120–139 | A2 Key for Schools / A2 Flyers |
| | A1 | 100–119 | A1 Movers |
| | Pre A1 | 80–99 | Pre A1 Starters |

The *B1 Preliminary for Schools* qualification is for school students studying general English. Cambridge Assessment English also offers a *B1 Preliminary* qualification. These two qualifications follow exactly the same format, the level of the exams is the same and the candidates are tested in the same skills. However, the content of the exams is a bit different. The 'for Schools' version is specifically designed to suit the interests and experiences of school-age candidates. If you're an adult learner, it would be better for you to take the *B1 Preliminary* qualification and use the *Collins Practice Tests for B1 Preliminary* to prepare for the exam.

There are four papers in **B1 Preliminary for Schools** (each is worth 25% of the total mark):

- Paper 1: Reading (45 minutes)
- Paper 2: Writing (45 minutes)
- Paper 3: Listening (approximately 30 minutes)
- Paper 4: Speaking (12–17 minutes)

## Timetabling

You usually take the Reading, Writing and Listening papers on the same day. The Speaking test may take place on a different day and it may be before or after the other papers. If you're studying on your own, you should contact your exam centre for dates. The exam is paper based. You can also take the exam on a computer in some countries. For more information, see: https://www.cambridge-exams.ch/exams/CB_exams.php

## Paper 1 Reading (45 minutes)

### What is it?

The Reading paper tests how well you can understand general English texts. It includes different types of texts about lots of different subjects.

### Skills needed

In order to do well in the Reading paper, you must be able to:

- read real-world texts such as emails, notices and articles and understand the main ideas; understand details about the writer's opinion and their reason for writing; and scan texts of different lengths to find a particular piece of information.
- answer questions within the given time.

The Reading paper has six parts:

**Part 1** has five short real-world texts, for example, notices, messages, emails and signs, and five multiple-choice questions with three options, A, B or C. You have to read each text and choose the correct answer. (Total marks: 5)

**Part 2** has five short descriptions of people and eight short texts. You have to match each of the descriptions with the correct text. (Total marks: 5)

**Part 3** has a longer text and five multiple-choice questions with three options, A, B or C. You have to understand details about the text as well as the writer's attitude or opinion on a particular issue and their purpose for writing. (Total marks: 5)

**Part 4** has a longer text with five sentences removed. Following the text are eight sentences, which include the five that have been removed. You have to find the missing sentences. (Total marks: 5)

**Part 5** has a shorter text with six gaps followed by six multiple-choice questions. You have to fill the gaps by choosing the correct word from four options, A, B, C or D. (Total marks: 6)

**Part 6** has a short text with six gaps. You have to fill the gaps by deciding what the missing word is. (Total marks: 6)

## Paper 2 Writing (45 minutes)

### What is it?
The Writing paper tests how well you can write an answer to a question using a good range of vocabulary and grammatical structures.

### Skills needed
In order to do well in the Writing paper, you must be able to:
- understand the instructions and identify the key points that you have to include in your answer.
- use a good range of B1-level vocabulary and grammatical structures.
- write emails, articles and/or stories.
- write a well-organised text that is easy for the reader to follow.
- rephrase information given in the instructions.
- write your answers within the word limits given in the instructions.
- write your answers within the given time.

The Writing paper has two parts.

**Part 1** tests how well you can communicate information clearly. You will need to write a short email (100 words). The instructions ask you to include four important points in your message. (Total marks: 20)

**Part 2** tests how well you can communicate, organise your ideas and use a range of language. This part gives you a choice of two different tasks: an article or a story. Your answer must be about 100 words. For the article, you read an announcement from a magazine or website. For the story, you are given a sentence which you have to use at the beginning of your answer. (Total marks: 20)

In each part, marks are awarded in the following ways:
- five marks if you include all the necessary information.
- five marks if you express your message clearly.
- five marks if you organise your message so a reader can follow it easily.
- five marks if you use a good range of grammatical structures and vocabulary.

## Paper 3 Listening (about 30 minutes)

**What is it?**
The Listening paper tests how well you can understand conversations, talks and recorded messages.

**Skills needed**
In order to do well in the Listening paper, you must be able to:
• understand main ideas and details.
• understand a speaker's opinion and attitude.
• answer questions within the given time.

The Listening paper has four parts.

**Part 1** has seven short extracts from monologues (= a speech by one person) or dialogues (= speech by two people) such as conversations, recorded messages or radio programmes, and seven questions. For each question, you have to listen and choose the correct answer from three options, A, B or C. The options are pictures. (Total marks: 7)

**Part 2** has six dialogues and six questions. You have to listen and choose the correct answer to a question from three options, A, B or C. (Total marks: 6)

**Part 3** has a longer monologue and six questions. You have to listen and complete six gaps in a text. (Total marks: 6)

**Part 4** has an interview and six questions. You have to listen and choose the correct answer from three options, A, B or C. (Total marks: 6)

## Paper 4 Speaking (12–17 minutes)

**What is it?**
The Speaking paper tests your ability to use spoken English. You take the Speaking test with another candidate (your partner) or sometimes in a group of three. You can't take it alone. There are two examiners: one asks you and your partner(s) questions, the other (the assessor) has the marksheets. They both listen carefully and give you marks. If you are taking the exam in a pair, it lasts about 12 minutes; if you are taking it in a group of three it lasts about 17 minutes.

You can only take the exam in a group of three if there is an uneven number of candidates in the session; the group of three is always the last to be examined in the session. You can't choose to take the exam in a group of three and you can't take the exam on your own.

Depending where you take the exam, you may already know the person you take the exam with, or you may meet them for the first time when you go into the exam. It doesn't make any difference to how well you do in the exam. The examiners listen to each of you very carefully.

**Skills needed**
In order to do well in the Speaking test, you must be able to:
• talk about everyday subjects and express your opinions.
• ask and answer questions during a conversation.
• speak clearly for about a minute.
• speak using a good range of B1-level vocabulary and grammatical structures.

The Speaking paper has four parts.

In **Part 1** the examiner asks you questions about your personal details, daily routine, past experiences, future plans, etc. (Time: 2 minutes)

In **Part 2** the examiner asks each candidate to talk in turn. He/She will give you a photo and ask you to describe it. You have to talk for about a minute. The examiner then gives your partner a different photo. Your partner also has to talk for about a minute. (Time: 3 minutes)

In **Part 3** the examiner describes a situation and gives you and your partner instructions to talk about it. He/She also gives you a picture showing you the situation and different things to discuss. You have to make suggestions to your partner and reply to his/her suggestions, talk about different possibilities and agree about the situation. (Time: 4 minutes)

In **Part 4** the examiner asks you and your partner questions related to the theme in Part 3. You have to talk to the examiner and each other and discuss the questions. (Time: 3 minutes)

## Marks and results

After the exam, all candidates receive a Statement of Results. Candidates whose performance ranges between CEFR Levels A2 and B2 (Cambridge English Scale scores of 140–170) also receive a certificate.

The Statement of Results shows the candidate's:

* score on the Cambridge English Scale for their performance in each of the four language skills (reading, writing, listening and speaking).
* score on the Cambridge English Scale for their overall performance in the exam. This overall score is the average of their scores for the four skills.
* grade – this is based on the candidate's overall score.
* level on the CEFR – this is also based on the overall score.

The certificate shows the candidate's:

* score on the Cambridge English Scale for each of the four skills.
* overall score on the Cambridge English Scale.
* grade.
* level on the CEFR.
* level on the UK National Qualifications Framework (NQF).

For *B1 Preliminary for Schools*, the following scores will be used to report results:

| Cambridge English Scale Score | Grade | CEFR level |
| --- | --- | --- |
| 160–170 | A | B2 |
| 153–159 | B | B1 |
| 140–152 | C | B1 |
| 120–139 | Level A2 | A2 |

Grade A: Cambridge English Scale scores of 160–170

Candidates sometimes show ability beyond Level B1. If a candidate achieves a Grade A in their exam, they will receive the *Preliminary English Test for Schools* certificate stating that they demonstrated ability at Level B2.

Grades B and C: Cambridge English Scale scores of 140–159

If a candidate achieves a Grade B or Grade C in their exam, they will receive the *Preliminary English Test for Schools* certificate at Level B1.

CEFR Level A2: Cambridge English Scale scores of 120–139

If a candidate's performance is below Level B1, but falls within Level A2, they will receive a *Cambridge English* certificate stating that they demonstrated ability at Level A2.

Scores between 102 and 119 are also reported on your Statement of Results, but you will not receive the *Preliminary English Test for Schools* certificate.

For more information on how the exam is marked, go to: http://www.cambridgeenglish.org

Working through the practice tests in this book will improve your exam skills, help you with timing for the exam, give you confidence and help you get a better result in the exam.

Good luck!

# How to prepare for the test

## Developing your English skills

The practice tests in this book will enable you to have a clear understanding of what is required in the exam and the opportunity to get lots of practice before the big day. However, in addition to your knowledge of the exam, your success will also be dependent on your general English skills. Here are some suggestions on how to develop your Reading, Writing, Listening and Speaking skills. Several of the points here will also give you useful tips on how to build your vocabulary skills.

## Top 10 tips for Reading skills

1. It's important that you read as much and as widely as possible. This will result in you developing your vocabulary and help you become familiar with the different types of texts you are likely to come across in the exam. Read newspapers, magazines, blogs and articles. There is no need to try to understand every word. Focus on getting a general understanding.

2. Read for pleasure. Consider buying a 'reader'. These are simplified short stories of famous novels that are written for English students at various levels. See the Collins website for the Agatha Christie and Amazing People readers.

3. You will regularly come across words you don't understand. Try the following strategy:

   a) If you can understand the sentence without knowing the meaning of a particular word, move on and continue reading.

   b) If a particular word (or words) stops you understanding the general meaning of a sentence, and that sentence stops you understanding the paragraph, look up the word in a dictionary.

4. Use 'key' words and phrases that appear before and after unknown words to help you guess their meaning. For example, imagine you don't know the meaning of the underlined word in this sentence: *The students had different* <u>excuses</u> *for not doing their homework, such as 'My dog ate it' or 'My mum washed it in the washing machine'.* You should be able to guess from what follows the word that 'excuses' means reasons for not doing something.

5. Look at parts of words such as prefixes and suffixes to guess the meaning of unknown words. A prefix is one or more letters, e.g. *un-, dis-, pre-, co-, under-* that go at the beginning of a word, e.g. *unhappy, disorganised.* A suffix is one or more letters, e.g. *-ful, -less, -ation, -y, -ment, -hood* that go at the end of a word, e.g. *enjoyment, neighbourhood.* If you learn the meanings of common English prefixes and suffixes, you will be able to guess the meaning of many unknown words. For example, the prefixes *un-* and *dis-* give a word a negative meaning.

6. Remember there are different ways of reading depending on why you are reading.

   **Skimming** is when you read a text quickly, paying attention only to the most important ideas. In this way, you can often quickly find the important sections that many questions are based on. This will save you a lot of time. To practise skimming, read the title of a text; this often gives you an idea of what the text is about. In the same way, paragraph headings may help you to find the topic of each paragraph. Read the last two or three sentences of the introductory paragraph. They often include the main idea of the text. Read the first and last sentence of a paragraph. They usually include the main idea of the paragraph. Read the first two or three sentences of the conclusion. They often say in a few words what the text was about.

   **Scanning** is when you read a text quickly in order to find specific key words or ideas. For example, if you're reading through a TV guide to look for a particular programme you want to watch, you'll scan the text for key words to help you find what you're looking for. To practise both skimming and scanning, look at an English magazine or newspaper and **scan** the articles to find one you're particularly interested in. Then **skim** the text in the way suggested above.

7. Test yourself on how a text is structured. Find one that interests you in a magazine or newspaper or print it off if it's online. Cut it up into the individual paragraphs before you read it. Then try putting it back together, using the content of each one, linking words and any other clues to help you.

8. Working with a 'study buddy' is a great way to help you develop your reading skills. Decide on a text you both want to read. Look at the heading and maybe the first sentence. Then stop and talk about:

   a) what the text might be about

   b) which words or expressions the text might include

   c) what the purpose of the text might be, for example, to explain, to persuade, etc.

   Then read the text to see if you're correct. Finally, why not write two or three questions on the text to test your partner's comprehension?

9. Test your own understanding of a text. As you read, underline any numbers you come across or key words. When you've finished, try to explain what each one means in the context of the text.

10. Write a short review of a text you have read. On a single piece of paper, write the title of the text, a short summary of what the text is about, another short paragraph on your opinion of the content and finally a list of any new vocabulary you found useful.

## Top 10 tips for Writing skills

1. Keep a daily diary in English. This is an excellent opportunity to get some practice in using tenses: past tenses to talk about what you did the day before or future tenses to describe your plans for the day ahead. You could also decide to focus on a different subject each day, such as sports news one day and what you're eating or a hobby or an interest on another day. This will give you the chance to use some new topic-based vocabulary in your entries.

2. If you're feeling brave, you could use a blog to make your diary public. Tell your friends, relations or teacher that this is a project to help you develop your English writing skills and that you will be very happy to receive feedback from anyone who can help. It can be motivating to write something knowing that other people will be reading your work.

3. Sometimes it can be difficult to know what to write about. Don't make things even more difficult for yourself by worrying about making mistakes in your use of English. Start by getting your thoughts or ideas down on paper quickly in note form first. Think about how these notes can best be organised, then write a first draft. Read it through and check your use of English, then complete a second draft where you focus more on accuracy.

4. Practise writing different text types. If you read a book or see a film, try writing a short review. This will give you the opportunity to use vocabulary to describe books or films. If something interesting happens to you one day, write a short story. This will give you the chance to practise tenses. You could even write instructions for a recipe, as this can help you to order information.

5. Do you have a friend who is also studying English? Why not agree to write your emails to each other in English? You don't have to do this all the time but just writing them occasionally will help you get used to writing in another language.

6. If you're lucky enough to have someone who can mark your written work, check to see what kind of mistakes you sometimes make. Do you sometimes get your tenses mixed up? Do you have problems putting words in the correct order? Are there any words you often spell incorrectly? Getting to know the areas of English you find challenging is very useful. Make a list of things to look out for when you next do any writing as this can help you avoid similar mistakes in the future. Read through your work focusing on each area in turn before handing it in to your teacher for feedback.

7. Pay attention to how you organise your ideas. Focus on using linking words to help you signpost the direction of your writing. If it's a story, make sure you use words such as *first*, *then*, *at the same time* or *finally*. If you're giving an opinion, you might want to use words or expressions such as *on the one hand*, *however*, *in contrast* or *as a result*. These words and expressions will help you to organise your ideas clearly and help the reader follow your ideas or opinions easily.

8. As you write longer pieces, don't forget to organise your work into paragraphs. Each paragraph should deal with a different subject. To help get an understanding of how writers use paragraphs, note how they are used when you're reading English texts.

9. Avoid repeating yourself. Try not to use the same word again and again in your writing. Make your work more interesting by using lots of different words to avoid repetition. For example, if you're writing an article and you've used the word *film*, use a different word like *movie* next time. If you're describing your experience of watching football and have used the word *game*, try using *match* a little later. Get into the habit of using words like *it, this, these, that,* etc. to avoid using the noun again.

10. Keep a record of your written work. There will be times when you think your English isn't improving. Reading some of your early attempts at writing will show you just how much progress you've made and will help you stay focused on your studies.

## Top 10 tips for Listening skills

1. Whatever it is you decide to listen to, spend a few minutes beforehand thinking about the topic. If it's a news item, have you heard it already in your own language? Do you know what the general content is going to be? Think about what you're likely to hear and make notes. As you listen, check to see if any of your points are mentioned.

2. Use recordings to practise listening rather than live, spoken English, which you can't play back and listen to a second or third time. Podcasts and videos are excellent resources for this and many of them come with transcripts.

3. Don't set yourself the goal of understanding everything too quickly. The first time you listen, try to get an overall idea of the topic and the main points the speaker is making. Be prepared to listen several times, because you will understand more and more each time.

4. Each time you listen, make a note of key words. These can help you identify the topic. For example, if you hear the words *sightseeing*, *beach* and *hotel* it's likely that the person is talking about holidays.

5. As you listen again, make a note of signposting words. If you hear *for instance*, you know the speaker is going to give examples. If you hear words or expressions like *however*, *on the one hand* or *although*, these will signpost when the speaker is giving alternative opinions or facts.

6. Try to become familiar with a wide range of accents. Videos on YouTube and podcasts are a good resource for this as you will hear a range of speakers from all over the world.

7. Try to listen to English every day, even if it's just 15 minutes each time. If you have a smartphone or computer this will give you easy access to English. Download English-language podcasts or radio programmes that you can store on your phone or computer. At first, practise listening for only a minute or two at a time. As your comprehension gets better, listen for longer.

8. You can help yourself to understand a news item by reading about a news story in a magazine or newspaper first and then listening to the same item on the news. This will help you with key vocabulary and also help you predict what you are likely to hear during the news report.

9. Working with a 'study buddy' is a great way to help you develop your listening skills. Here's a fun way to practise listening together. You need a short text, no longer than 100 words. One of you should read the text at normal speed, not too slowly. The other person should write down all the words they hear. This should be repeated several times until you have what you believe is the same as is written on your partner's sheet. You can then compare what you have written with your partner.

10. Here's another way to do some listening practice with a 'study buddy'. Each of you can probably understand different parts of a listening text better than the other person. Your partner might be able to help you understand sections that you find difficult and vice versa. As the expression goes, 'two heads are better than one'!

**Top 10 tips for Speaking skills**

1. Take every opportunity you can to practise speaking. Even in your English classes, you won't spend very much time speaking English. It helps to practise as much as possible and you can do many of the things in this list of tips on your own, so take every opportunity you have to practise them.

2. You probably feel a bit nervous about speaking in English, especially if people correct you every time you make a mistake. Remember that speaking in English is not just about being accurate. It's also important to focus on becoming more fluent, and this means allowing yourself to make mistakes. Give yourself the opportunity to practise both fluency and accuracy when speaking in English.

3. For fluency practice, record yourself speaking for short periods of between 30 and 60 seconds. Talk about anything you like. You could start by describing your room, or talking about your best friend – what do you like about him or her? The important thing to remember is to keep talking. Don't worry about making mistakes as the focus is on fluency, not accuracy. As there's nobody around to correct you, you may start to feel more confident about speaking in English.

4. When you do exercises like this, play the recording back and count how many words you say in the time you were speaking for. Then try again a few days later. Do this again and again. As your English develops, you should notice you're able to say more words in the same amount of time. This will give you an idea of your speech rate, which will improve as you become more fluent.

5. While you listen to yourself speaking, make a note of where the pauses occur. Fluent speakers pause in logical places, such as *My name's Paolo* ... (pause) ... *I come from Italy* ... (pause) ... *I live with my parents in Milan* ... (pause) .... Someone who is less fluent will pause at various points, often because they don't know a word or are trying to work out how to form a sentence. For example, *My name's Christine* ... (pause) ... *I* ... (pause) ... *come from France* ... (pause) ... *I live* ... (pause) ... *in Paris* ... (pause) *with my* ... (pause) ... *parents* ... (pause) ....

6. Try recording a daily diary, in the same way as described above for Writing. You could do this in the morning to talk about what your plans are, or at the end of the day to describe what you did. You could do this for fluency practice but it's also a good opportunity to focus on accuracy, such as in using tenses.

7. Use photographs from magazines to give you practise in describing pictures. Try describing the picture first in your own language. Then try again in English. Which words don't you know? Look them up and try again. This is an excellent way of developing your vocabulary.

8. Learn the phonetic alphabet. This will help you to work out how a word is pronounced. A good learners' dictionary includes a definition of the word and also shows you how the word is pronounced. You can use the list of pronunciation symbols (the phonetic alphabet) in the dictionary when you are learning how to pronounce the word in English. Alternatively, most online dictionaries, such as www.collinsdictionary.com include audio files for each word so you can listen to the pronunciation of new words online.

9. Find out which pronunciation problems are common for people who speak your mother tongue. For example, it's sometimes difficult for Japanese people to say the /l/ and /r/ sounds in English for words like *led* and *red*. Spanish speakers sometimes put an /e/ sound before a word beginning with /s/ and say things like *eSpain* rather than *Spain*. It's helpful to know what these problems are so you can identify any of your own problems with pronunciation.

10. If you want people to understand you when you speak, you have to stress words correctly. If you stress the wrong syllable, people might not understand you. For example, in the following nouns, the underlined syllable is stressed:

    cele<u>bra</u>tion

    ad<u>ver</u>tisement

    pho<u>tog</u>raphy

However, in the verb form, a different syllable is stressed:

c̲elebrate

a̲dvertise

ph̲otograph

Knowing how to pronounce words with more than one syllable is important and you should use a good dictionary to check the stress of new words when you learn them.

**Top 10 tips for building your vocabulary**

1. Keep a record of new words. You can organise this in your notebook with pages for topics, such as 'Health', and add new words as you find them.

2. Learn different categories of vocabulary. For example, make a note of synonyms (words that have the same meaning, such as *hard/difficult*, *easy/simple*), and antonyms (words that have an opposite meaning, such as *hot/cold* or *happy/sad*).

3. Learn the common prefixes and suffixes in English. (See 'Reading' above.) You can add these to your records of new words.

4. Learn 'chunks' as well as individual words. Some words are often used with other words together in set expressions, such as *believe in* or *talk about*. There are lots of phrasal verbs like *get on* and *turn off*, and phrases like *See you soon* and *Best wishes*. Make a point of learning these chunks as they are extremely common and very useful.

5. Decide which words are worth recording and which ones are less important. For example, unless you are interested in a particular topic, such as football, it might not be worthwhile making a note of all the words you come across in an article on this subject. Words like *penalty*, *referee* or *foul* are important if football is a topic you're keen on, but if not, focus on learning more general vocabulary.

6. Try to use new words in your writing. If you follow the tip above and keep a daily diary, decide how you can use new words in your diary entries.

7. Test yourself with flashcards. It's simple to make a flashcard where you have the English word on one side of the card and the translation on the other side. You can make them even more effective by highlighting any stressed syllables or including an example sentence.

8. Always remember to review the vocabulary you learnt in previous weeks. The more you test yourself on these new words, the easier it will be to remember the words when you need to use them.

9. One of the most effective ways of learning new words is to read as much as possible. There is no need to record every new word you find, though you might want to make a note of any interesting words or expressions. If you just read for pleasure you will see the same words again and again and you will find that you learn them naturally.

10. Buy a good learner's dictionary. This is essential for your studies because it will help you not only with the meanings of words but also with pronunciation.

# Dealing with exam questions

You will save yourself a lot of time and avoid making mistakes if you can approach each of the tasks in the exam with a clear understanding of what you are being asked to do *and* the best ways to do it. Here are some suggestions for each part of the exam. Make sure you try these when doing the practice tests in this book.

## Reading

In Parts **1**, **3**, and **5** the questions are multiple choice. When answering multiple choice questions:

- decide which answer options are clearly incorrect. Usually, you can ignore an option that has information that is the opposite of the facts in the text or has information that does not answer the question.

- find evidence for your answer in the text. For example, if you think option A is correct, find the part of the text where the answer is and underline it.
- don't just select an answer because it contains the same word as in the text. This will often be a distractor (an answer written to take your attention away).
- you will often find that the correct answer may contain a word that means the same as the word in the text.

In **Part 2** you will often find that **some** of the text indicates a correct answer. However, there may be something that means the answer is wrong, such as the wrong date or time.

In **Part 4** you should look out for key words that help you to decide which of the sentences listed is the missing one for a gap. Linking words like *however*, *for example* or *in addition* can be a sign that the sentence is the one you're looking for. Also, pronouns such as *these*, *it* or *they* might be talking about a noun in the previous sentence, so be careful and look for these.

In **Part 6** some gaps need a 'grammar' word. These are words such as determiners (e.g. *a, the, much, many*), prepositions (e.g. *on, at, in*) and conjunctions (e.g. *and, but, because*). Make a list of all the types of grammar words you find in these practice tests and learn them so you understand how they are used. Work with a 'study buddy' and make your own text with gaps. To do this, find a short text and cross out some grammar words. Then create four answer options for each gap. Some gaps need words that are part of an expression. For example, a text might have the expressions *at least* and *spend time*, with *at* and *spend* in the text, so *least* and *time* go in the gaps. Focus on the words around the gap and decide if the missing word is part of an expression. Make a list of vocabulary 'chunks' like these and not just individual words. Leave the gaps you don't know to start with and come back to them later. Cross out the answer options that you know are wrong so you have fewer options to choose from.

## Writing

In **Part 1** begin by reading the task carefully and making a note of who you are writing to. If it's a friend, your email will be informal. However, if you are writing to someone like a teacher you should avoid using informal language.

There are four notes linked by lines pointing to text in the **Part 1** email question. These notes are the content points and they tell you what you need to write about in your email answer. You must make sure you answer each of these content points. Quite often the first content point will be to reply with a friendly opening sentence. The next three content points may tell you to agree, disagree, give an opinion, explain, suggest, recommend, describe or ask something. If you answer each of the content points successfully you will immediately receive five marks for content. In addition, doing this should also mean your email is the correct length, at approximately 100 words.

There are many set expressions that are used in emails. If you can remember these, you will find it easier to start your piece of writing and bring it to an end. Here are some examples you could use if you are writing to a friend. Add new ones when you learn them.

| Section of email | Expressions |
|---|---|
| Beginning | *How are you?*<br>*I hope you're well.*<br>*Thanks for your email.*<br>*It was great to hear from you.* |
| Commenting on information you have received | *I'm sorry to hear …*<br>*I'm / I was so pleased to hear …*<br>*It's / It was great to hear …* |
| Ending | *Write back soon.*<br>*Best wishes,*<br>*See you soon.*<br>*Take care.* |

In **Part 2** you choose one of the two tasks: an article or a story.

The **Part 2 article** task will always ask you to write about something you have experience of, so spend a minute or two thinking about your answer. It usually contains two questions which you need to write about in your answer. Think about the kind of vocabulary you might include in your answer. For example, if the question asks you to describe your favourite film, try to show your ability to use appropriate words or expressions such as *actor, actress, director, thriller, horror film,* etc. During your studies, keep a list of topic vocabulary like this.

In the **Part 2 story** task your story has to begin with the sentence you are given. If you have trouble thinking of something to write about in a story, it's a good idea to use question words to help you think of ideas. Ask yourself questions beginning with *Where, When, Who* and *Why*. Imagine you have to write a story with the opening sentence *It was late and I was lost*. Ask yourself questions like these: *Where was I? When was it? Who was I with? Why was I there?* If you answer these questions, you will set the scene for your story. Then ask yourself, *What happened?* If you give details of what happened, you will describe the events.

Timing is very important in the exam and you should pay attention to this when preparing for the Writing paper. Begin by allowing yourself a little extra time for each question but as you get closer to the exam day make sure you are able to complete the questions within the time limit. Don't forget to allow yourself a few minutes at the end to read through your work. Here are some suggested timings:

| Time | What you should do |
| --- | --- |
| **Part 1: 25 minutes** | |
| 3 minutes | Read the instructions carefully. Underline the key words in each of the four points. |
| 5 minutes | Make notes and plan your answer. |
| 15 minutes | Write your answer. Make sure you answer all four points. Think about how you can express the ideas in the points using different words and/or structures. |
| 2 minutes | Check your spelling and look for mistakes in your grammar. |
| **Part 2: 20 minutes** | |
| 2 minutes | Read the instructions carefully. Decide which question you are going to answer. If you choose the article, underline the key words in the instructions. |
| 2 minutes | Make notes and plan your answer. Think about a good beginning, middle and end. |
| 14 minutes | Write your answer. |
| 2 minutes | Check your spelling and look for mistakes in your grammar. |

## Listening

The instructions for the Listening paper are always the same, but of course the listening tasks are different. When you do the practice tests in this book, make sure you know what you have to do in each of the four parts in the Listening paper. In the exam and in the practice tests you will hear each recording twice, so if there is something you don't understand the first time, listen for it again the second time. Always make sure you read the questions carefully because they give you lots of information about what you will hear. If you have time, underline the key words in the questions before the audio starts.

In **Part 1**, read the question first, then look at the pictures. They will give you an idea of what each question is about. It is very likely that you will hear each of the pictures mentioned, but only one of them will be the correct answer. For example, you may hear words like *but, however* or other key words that will help you decide which of the three pictures is correct.

In **Part 2**, read the questions and options carefully. This will help you get an idea of what the people will be talking about and you can guess what the answers might be.

In **Part 3**, read the sentences before the recording starts and try to guess what the missing words might be. For example, are there words before or after the gap that indicate the missing word might be a date or a number? Is it likely the missing word is a noun?

In **Part 4**, read through all the questions and options. This will give you a good idea of what the interview is about and the kind of things that are discussed. As you listen the first time, put a question mark next to the option you think is possibly correct. Make sure you listen carefully the second time for evidence that your choice is correct.

Take care in **Parts 1**, **2** and **4** not to choose an answer just because you hear a word that also appears in the question. These are often 'distractors' and will not be the correct answer. The correct answer will often contain a synonym of a word or expression that is on the recording.

## Speaking
In **Part 1**, the examiner asks you and your partner questions in turn. It is a chance for him/her to get to know more about you. You don't have to give very long answers but you should also say more than 'Yes' or 'No'. The examiner will make it clear if he/she wants you to say a bit more or will tell you when to stop if you are talking for too long. You don't need to worry about this.

When you answer Part 1 questions, give a reason for your answer or an example. If the examiner asks *Do you enjoy studying English?* say why you do or don't enjoy it. For example, *Yes, I do. I love listening to music and I can understand the words better in some songs.* If the examiner asks *What kind of food do you like to eat?* don't just reply *Indian food* or *pizza*. Think of a meal you have eaten and explain why you enjoyed it. For example, *I enjoy Indian food. I often go to an Indian restaurant near where I live and I always order something spicy to eat.*

In **Parts 1** and **4**, try not to repeat the same words and phrases all the time. Use different words when you can. For example, the following expressions all mean *I like* or *I don't like*:
- I'm (not) fond of ...
- I'm (not) keen on ...
- I enjoy ...
- I can't stand ...

Remember that **Parts 3** and **4** are conversations. You will do better in the exam if you ask your partner questions and respond to the things your partner says. This means you have to listen to your partner carefully because it will help you to keep the conversation going.

Time yourself when you practise talking about a photo for the **Part 2** task, to give an idea what it feels like to talk for one minute. By timing yourself, you will learn not to speak too fast or too slowly and you will be able to give a complete answer within the time. In the exam, the examiner will encourage you to say more if you haven't said enough or will tell you to stop talking when you have said enough.

Practise using a structure for your description. Here is a suggestion:
- Begin by saying what the photo is about. For example: *This is a photo of a birthday party. It looks like a children's birthday party.*
- Talk about the people in the photo and what they are doing. For example: *There are several children and two adults. The children are sitting at a table and the adults are serving them food...* (You could continue by describing what some of them are wearing or what you think they are eating or doing.)
- Say what you think of the scene. For example: *It's similar to the birthday parties I went to when I was young.*

## Dos and don'ts
Finally, here is a list of things to remember to do *and* not to do on the day of the exam.

## Dos
- Make sure you are thoroughly familiar with the order of the exam before the exam day.
- Make sure you get to the place where the exam is being held in plenty of time.
- Remember to take a pen, pencil and eraser, and perhaps a bottle of water in case you get thirsty.
- Try to calm your nerves and increase your confidence by thinking of a time in the past when you did something well.

- Read the instructions on the exam paper carefully and do exactly what you are asked to do.
- Answer the easier questions first.
- In multiple choice questions ignore the answers which you know are wrong.
- Be prepared to change your answers if you think your first choice is wrong.
- Read the texts in the Reading paper first quickly from the beginning to the end before answering any questions as this will help you gain a general understanding of the text.
- Try to find the points in the text which show your answers in the Reading texts.
- Give yourself time to plan, write and then check what you've written in the Writing paper.
- Make sure you answer all four content points in the Writing Part 1 email question.
- Remember to use a good range of language in your writing.
- Check your work carefully for spelling, grammar and punctuation mistakes.
- In the Speaking test, always ask the examiner if you don't understand. He/She will repeat the instruction so you understand. You won't lose marks for this.
- Remember to listen carefully to your partner in the Speaking exam as you need to show you can communicate with other people during conversations.

## Don'ts

- Avoid spending time talking with people about the exam beforehand. This may make you feel nervous.
- Avoid leaving questions in the Reading and Listening papers without an answer. If you really don't know the answer, guess it. You won't lose marks if you're wrong.
- Avoid wasting time trying to work out the meaning of unknown words. Try to guess the meaning from the context.
- Avoid giving short one- or two-word answers in the Speaking exam. Always try to give a reason, an example or just some added detail to give the examiner an idea of your use of English.
- After the exam, try not to talk to other students about your answers. This will often result in you feeling you've done something wrong when you probably haven't!

Good luck!

# Test 1

# Test 1 READING

## Part 1

### Questions 1–5

For each question, choose the correct answer.

---

**1**

> **To:** Christine
>
> **Subject:** Homework
>
> Are you having problems understanding the homework? It's more difficult than normal. Fancy coming round? We can work on it together. I'll see if my sister will help us!
>
> Nancy

**A** Nancy thinks the homework is hard.

**B** Nancy's sister has offered to help.

**C** Christine normally has problems with the homework.

**2**

> **Please note the school swimming pool will be closed until further notice for repairs. Swimming classes will be held in the public pool.**

**A** There are no swimming classes at the moment.

**B** Classes will take place in another swimming pool.

**C** Please pay attention to notices around the swimming pool.

**3**

> Hi Tessa,
>
> I'm away this weekend with my parents. My brother's not joining us so there's room in the car.
>
> Would you like to come? We can share a room as there are two single beds.
>
> Karen

**A** Tessa can have her own bed.

**B** Tessa can have her own room.

**C** Karen's brother will be joining them later.

**4**

**BOAT HIRE**

River boats can be hired for £10 per hour. Return late and a second hour is charged.

A You pay for another hour if you're late back.

B It is cheaper to pay for a second hour.

C Boats must be returned before the hour is complete.

**5**

**School Play**

The performance starts at 7.00 p.m. Please make sure you are in your seats by 6.45 p.m. or you may not be able to enter.

A You may not be able to see the play if you arrive before 7.00 p.m.

B Doors open at 6.45 p.m.

C Please arrive at least 15 minutes before the performance begins.

# Part 2

## Questions 6–10

For each question, choose the correct answer.

---

The young people below all want to buy a book.
On the opposite page there are descriptions of eight books.
Decide which book would be the most suitable for the people below.

**6**

Victoria has some homework about the Internet. She wants an introduction to the subject and would like to be able to learn how it started.

**7**

Guillermo has been studying English for a year and has to do a grammar test. He would like to buy a book that explains grammar points and also provides exercises to practise.

**8**

Roberta is learning to play the guitar. She knows how to read music and would like something with popular songs she can try to play.

**9**

Andrey is interested in modern art and would like to buy a book that explains what makes a good painting and how to understand a work of art.

**10**

Antoinette is thinking of doing an English course during her school holiday. She would like to go to an English-speaking country and is looking for a book that will give her and her family some advice.

# Recommended Books

## A Tune In

*Tune in to the Guitar* is the latest in our series of books looking at the history of different musical instruments. There are audio files on the Internet too! Find out when the earliest guitar appeared and the different types of guitar that are available, and read stories from some of the world's top guitarists.

## B Art in the UK

If you have an interest in art and are planning to visit some of the world-famous galleries in London, this guide will be very useful. You'll get news of the latest exhibitions, reviews from experts and discounts on entry tickets. New! Go to our website to visit our online gallery.

## C Making Sense

If you've seen any of our other titles on understanding the world around us, you'll know our latest title, *Making Sense of Modern Art*, will be an important addition to your bookcase. You'll learn what to focus on the next time you study a piece of art and what makes a great piece of art so special.

## D English Alive

As thousands of students go abroad to start an English course, *English Alive* will give you all the information you need to make sure you make the best decisions, whether that's choosing a school or the kind of accommodation that is available.

## E Heads Up

*Heads Up* is a series of self-study grammar practice books for students studying English. With books aimed at everyone from beginners to advanced students, each one gives a clear explanation of grammar points and lots of exercises to help you learn each point.

## F Camberley Study Guides

Most of us would be completely lost without our access to the world wide web. Our latest study guide will give you a complete introduction to this fascinating subject, explaining where it all began. The author also predicts how it might develop in the future.

## G Do it!

This latest book from Keyhole Publishers is for anybody interested in taking their musical skills to the next level. Our latest title looks at the guitar and is aimed at those who can read music and would like to put their skills to the test by playing well-known tunes.

## H Get Ready for English

A complete course for beginners of English. This book will give you an understanding of basic grammar and vocabulary to help you start your journey in learning this wonderful language. Each book comes with a CD-ROM and extra activities on the Internet.

## Part 3

## Questions 11–15

For each question, choose the correct answer.

---

# Teenagers and Sleep
*Mary Atwood wonders whether*
*teenagers need extra time in bed*

Research in America suggests that teenagers are having to go to school too early and that the school day should start later. Not getting enough sleep is known to be bad for our health, particularly amongst youngsters, and a study at a school in the UK showed that when teenagers were required to attend school at 10.00 a.m. rather than 8.30 a.m. their grades increased and they suffered fewer health problems.

It is a scientific fact that teenagers have different needs when it comes to sleep. In fact, it's been claimed that teenagers require two hours more sleep a night than adults: nine hours a night rather than seven. It is argued that having less than this results in their mental ability not being as good as it could be. And it's not simply due to going to bed too late either. It's also true that because of changes the human body goes through during the day, teenagers feel sleepy later and are likely to need to go to bed later than adults.

So what does a lack of sleep mean for young people? To begin with it can stop them concentrating for periods of time, so they can have difficulty focusing on subjects at school. But it's not just their studies that can leave them struggling if they don't get enough sleep. Equally important is the effect on their general mental health – it has also been shown lack of sleep can leave them feeling depressed. This plus the timetables students have to follow at school has led experts to ask schools to think about starting the school day later. One or two have even argued that teenagers would perform best if the school day started at 11 a.m. or even 12.00 noon.

However, the problems of changing the timetables would create problems elsewhere. The school day usually fits in with the working hours of parents, so starting and finishing later could easily cause problems for families. Of course it would also cause difficulties for teachers. And then there are always those people who disagree with the science and think all this simply encourages teenagers to be lazy. What do you think?

---

**11** Mary explains that

    **A** teenagers are suffering at school because they get up too late.

    **B** teenagers can manage with less sleep than adults.

    **C** teenagers with too little sleep are late for school.

    **D** a later start to the day can result in better marks at school.

**12** What does science show about teenagers?

    **A** They shouldn't go to bed late.

    **B** They need to sleep longer than adults.

    **C** They have more trouble sleeping at night than adults.

    **D** Some are having two hours less sleep than they need.

**13** Mary says that experts

    **A** think a lack of sleep can stop teenagers paying attention at school.

    **B** believe problems at school are more important than their general health.

    **C** agree when lessons should start.

    **D** say school timetables are too long.

**14** If the timetables started later

    **A** it might create problems for children.

    **B** everyone would be happier.

    **C** children would become lazy.

    **D** it would have an effect on other people.

**15** What would be a good introduction to this article?

| **A** Why are school children going to bed so late? | **B** Parents want changes to the school timetable. |
| --- | --- |
| **C** A later start might mean better results for your child. | **D** Teachers disagree with the latest research. |

**Part 4**

## Questions 16–20

Five sentences have been removed from the text below.
For each question, choose the correct answer.
There are three extra sentences which you do not need to use.

---

# School PE Lessons
*What do we need to do to make*
*classes more popular?*

Encouraging young people to take up physical exercise is really important. [ 16 ] But reports out recently show that only half of girls who were questioned by researchers enjoy doing sport at school. [ 17 ] And the reasons? Because of their dislike of the clothes they are asked to wear and the lack of facilities to do their hair afterwards. As more girls than boys fail to take part in physical activity, this is seen as a problem that needs dealing with.

Many of the girls questioned said they disliked wearing the skirts that are often part of PE kits and that the kit should be more comfortable to wear. The girls wanted to have the chance to say what the PE kit should look like. They suggested clothing that covered more of their bodies, such as leggings and high-necked shirts. [ 18 ]

Another key issue the girls reported was not having the facilities available to do their hair after they have taken part in exercise. The girls being interviewed wanted private spaces where they could get changed. They also felt schools should supply hairdryers or somewhere they could plug their own one in so they can style their hair. [ 19 ] They could use this time to do their hair and make sure they looked the same as they did before the class.

The researchers argue that since girls worry a great deal about how they look during their teenage years, it is important that schools take these issues seriously. [ 20 ] Some teachers feel sport should be a way of taking teenagers' minds off how they look. It should help them see the value of keeping physically fit, enjoying team sports and perhaps achieving sporting success and not worrying about what their hair looks like.

---

**A**   They also thought the materials used should be more comfortable to wear.

**B**   Unfortunately, most girls don't agree with this suggestion.

**C**   And a quarter of them actually avoid taking part.

**D**   However, not everyone agrees with the suggestions.

**E**   Girls had the following problems with PE classes.

**F**   PE classes are one way of getting young people to do this.

**G**   And the teachers completely agree.

**H**   They also requested 15 minutes at the end of the PE class.

# Part 5

## Questions 21–26

For each question, choose the correct answer.

---

### Tour de France

The Tour de France is probably the most **(21)** ............ cycling race in the world. It was first held in 1903 and has **(22)** ............ place most years since then. Cyclists follow a route around France, even starting or heading out for a **(23)** ............ time to another country such as Belgium, Germany, Italy or Spain. However, since 1975 the race has always finished in Paris on the Champs Elysées.

Only the very best cyclists in the world **(24)** ............ this competition, around 200 of them, and they ride as part of a team, with about 20 teams in all. The modern Tour de France consists of 21 day-long stages over a 23-day **(25)** ............ and covers a distance of about 3,500 kilometres on roads and up mountains. The race is **(26)** ............ by millions of people throughout the route as well as millions more on TV.

---

| 21 | **A** great | **B** famous | **C** best | **D** biggest |
|---|---|---|---|---|
| 22 | **A** started | **B** made | **C** set | **D** taken |
| 23 | **A** narrow | **B** small | **C** brief | **D** moment |
| 24 | **A** enter | **B** play | **C** run | **D** have |
| 25 | **A** time | **B** period | **C** age | **D** length |
| 26 | **A** held | **B** caught | **C** looked | **D** watched |

## Part 6

### Questions 27–32

For each question, write the correct answer.
Write **one** word for each gap.

---

# Alexander Graham Bell
## *by Matthew Holding*

I've been researching Alexander Graham Bell for my school
project. He was a British inventor **(27)** ..................... is
famous for inventing the telephone. Bell was born in Scotland
in 1847 and moved to Canada **(28)** ..................... his family
in 1870. Bell moved to the USA in 1871 and began his career
**(29)** ..................... a teacher of deaf people. While he was
teaching Bell developed the basic ideas for the telephone, and on
10 March 1876 experiments he carried **(30)** .....................
with his assistant Thomas Watson proved successful. His
invention was introduced to the world and Bell was later given
the Volta Prize in 1880, which **(31)** ..................... worth
50,000 French francs. He used this to open a laboratory in
America. He died in 1922 in his hometown of Baddeck, Canada,
where today people can visit **(32)** ..................... Alexander
Bell National Historic Site to see further examples of his work.

---

# Test 1 WRITING

## Part 1

You **must** answer this question.
Write your answer in about **100 words** on the answer sheet.

---

### Question 1

Read this email from your English-speaking friend Carole and the notes you have made.

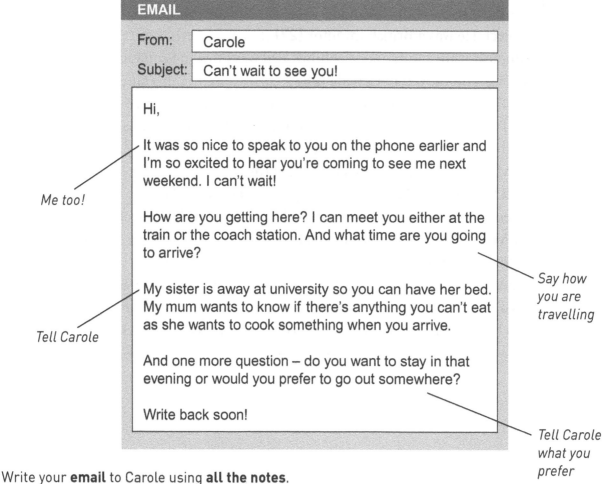

**EMAIL**

From: Carole

Subject: Can't wait to see you!

Hi,

It was so nice to speak to you on the phone earlier and I'm so excited to hear you're coming to see me next weekend. I can't wait!

*Me too!*

How are you getting here? I can meet you either at the train or the coach station. And what time are you going to arrive?

*Say how you are travelling*

My sister is away at university so you can have her bed. My mum wants to know if there's anything you can't eat as she wants to cook something when you arrive.

*Tell Carole*

And one more question – do you want to stay in that evening or would you prefer to go out somewhere?

Write back soon!

*Tell Carole what you prefer*

Write your **email** to Carole using **all the notes**.

## Part 2

Choose **one** of these questions.
Write your answer in about **100 words** on the answer sheet.

---

## Question 2

You see this notice in an English-language magazine.

**Articles wanted!**

**HAVE YOU GOT A FAVOURITE PLACE?**

Is your favourite place somewhere big, like a town or city, or somewhere small like a room in your house?

Why do you particularly like this place?

**Write an article answering these questions and we will put it in our magazine.**

Write your **article**.

## Question 3

Your English teacher has asked you to write a story.

Your story must begin with this sentence.

*I looked out of the window at the people passing by.*

Write your **story**.

# Test 1 LISTENING

## Part 1

### Questions 1–7

For each question, choose the correct answer.

---

**1** What date is the school closed?

A

B

C

**2** Where is Sam meeting his friends?

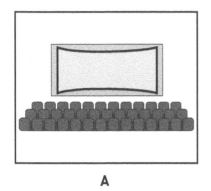

A

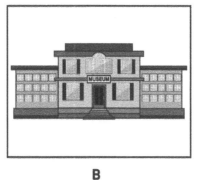

B

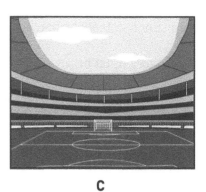

C

**3** What has stopped working?

A

B

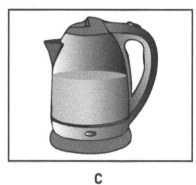

C

**4**   How much is the school trip?

A                               B                               C

**5**   When does the art class normally start?

A                               B                               C

**6**   When is the dance performance?

A                               B                               C

**7**   Where is the boy going to buy his dad a shirt?

A                               B                               C

# Part 2

02

## Questions 8–13

For each question, choose the correct answer.

---

**8** You will hear two friends talking about doing homework.
What does the girl say about studying?

   **A** The library is a quiet place to do this.

   **B** She doesn't like listening to music when she's studying.

   **C** She finds it easy to concentrate when she's studying.


**9** You will hear two friends talking about doing an after-school activity.
The girl says the boy

   **A** will have to pay for the activity at school.

   **B** would be better doing it somewhere else.

   **C** should speak to his friends.


**10** You will hear two friends talking about a holiday.
The boy says

   **A** last year their hotel was flooded.

   **B** it was lucky that it didn't rain last year.

   **C** he'd like nice weather.


**11** You will hear two friends talking about a video game.
What does the girl say about the game?

   **A** She can't afford to get it.

   **B** The graphics are good.

   **C** She got it for her birthday.


**12** You will hear a girl and her father talking about her plans for the weekend.
What is the girl worried about?

   **A** being able to buy a dress

   **B** not finishing her homework

   **C** getting home from the party


**13** You will hear two friends talking about one of their teachers.
The boy says the teacher

   **A** makes them read too many novels.

   **B** keeps the class quiet.

   **C** talks too much in the lesson.

# Part 3

03

## Questions 14–19

For each question, write the correct answer in the gap. Write **one** or **two words** or a **number** or a **date** or a **time**.

You will hear a teacher talking about an end-of-year party.

## End-of-year party

The party starts at 7.00 p.m. and ends at **(14)** ……………….. p.m.

The person collecting you must park in the school car park, not on the **(15)** ………………..

Those using the bus service should meet in the **(16)** ………………..

Inform the school **(17)** ……………….. by Friday about what you would like to eat.

The school band performance lasts for **(18)** ………………..

Please stay in the **(19)** ……………….. while you are waiting to be collected.

# Part 4

04

## Questions 20–25

For each question, choose the correct answer.

___

You will hear an interview with a woman called Sylvia Evans, who helps students with their career choices.

**20** What does Sylvia say about hairdressers?

    **A** Their friends always ask them for advice.

    **B** You'll learn which shampoo is the best.

    **C** They are unlikely to lose their job to technology.

**21** Sylvia says that when a customer enters a hairdresser's

    **A** the shop needs to look fantastic.

    **B** they want to feel confident you can make them look good.

    **C** they should be welcomed with a smile.

**22** What does Sylvia say about a hairdresser's salary?

    **A** You shouldn't expect to earn much.

    **B** It can be higher if the customers like you.

    **C** You will often need to request a pay rise.

**23** Sylvia says

    **A** employers prefer you to have more than one skill.

    **B** it's best to focus on getting a hairdressing qualification.

    **C** you won't get work without any qualifications.

**24** In addition to qualifications, Sylvia says you should

    **A** be happy to take advice from others.

    **B** be confident enough to tell the boss if you have a problem.

    **C** find jobs to do when the shop isn't busy.

**25** What does Sylvia say about having a career in hairdressing?

    **A** You get the chance to enter competitions.

    **B** You have the chance to work for yourself.

    **C** A lot of people continue working for the same business.

# Test 1 SPEAKING

1A

1B

Audio scripts and Model answers on pages 183–249.

07–08

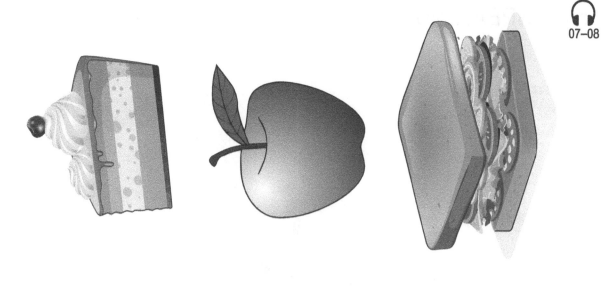

Some things a girl could buy to eat on a journey

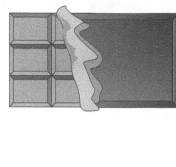

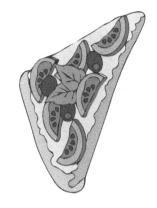

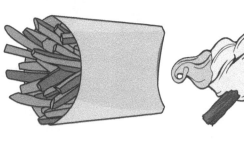

Audio scripts and Model answers on pages 183–249.

# Test 2

# Test 2 READING

## Part 1

### Questions 1–5

For each question, choose the correct answer.

---

1

**Basketball match**

Come to Room 215 at 1.00 p.m. on Friday for information about the transport we've arranged for Saturday's game

A  There's a basketball match at 1.00 p.m.

B  There's a meeting on Friday.

C  People must arrange their own transport to the game.

2

Hey Charlotte

My sister's ill and can't go to the cinema this evening so do you want her ticket? If you can't come, text me and I'll see if Janet wants to come.

Beth

A  Janet wants to go to the cinema.

B  Beth has a spare ticket.

C  Charlotte should text Janet.

3

**School Party**

Snacks, dancing and music. Tickets £5. Money will go towards buying new plants for the school gardens.

A  Have fun and help us develop the school garden.

B  Plants for sale at the school party.

C  Come to our party in the garden.

**4**

Hi Ben

I'm going to be home late from work. Could you put the chicken in the oven when you get back from school? I should be back in time to do the rest.

Love, Mum

**A** Mum won't be home for dinner.

**B** Mum wants Ben to start preparing dinner.

**C** Mum wants to rest when she gets home.

**5**

## School Trip

The coach will now be waiting outside the school gate at 9.00 a.m., not Jarvis Street. Don't be late!

**A** The coach will be parked on Jarvis Street.

**B** The coach might be late.

**C** Arrive no later than 9.00 a.m.

## Part 2

### Questions 6–10

For each question, choose the correct answer.

---

The young people below all want to take part in organised football activities.
On the opposite page there are descriptions of eight football activities.
Decide which activity would be the most suitable for the people below.

**6**

Emma is 13 and wants to play football on a Saturday morning. She plays for her school but as it's the summer holiday there aren't any matches. She wants to join a group for girls.

**7**

Josh is 11 and wants to play football with others of his age. He also has friends who would like to play and they want to enter competitions. He is available on a Sunday morning.

**8**

Leonora is 9 and wants to learn how to play football. She has never played before so wants to join a beginners' class. She's free Monday to Friday from 4.00 p.m.

**9**

Martin is 15 years old and is a keen footballer. He wants to keep fit over the summer and would like to take part in training events as well as play matches against other teams. He is free at weekends.

**10**

Frank is 14 and hopes to be a professional footballer. He wants the chance to show his skills to local clubs. He is on holiday from school and available any time except Saturday afternoon.

# Football activities

**A Cranfield United Summer Camp**

We are once again excited to open our training ground to all 11–16 year olds who want to try some of the strength and fitness exercises practised by top professional footballers. And as usual we'll be organising games each week. Join us every Saturday from 1.00–4.00 p.m.

**B Weekend Soccer**

This summer, join us on our 'Weekend Soccer School'. These take place every Sunday from 10.00 a.m. till 1.00 p.m. at the Welcome Leisure Centre. Our indoor football sessions are designed for boys and girls from six to ten years old. We play inside and all children must wear suitable trainers.

**C St Peter's Community Forum**

We're pleased to announce our under 11's summer activity programme starts again next week with lots for young people of all ages to try. We have football and basketball for children new to the sport as well as other organised activities. Come along and join us on weekday afternoons from 3.00 p.m.

**D Strafford High School**

If you're between 8 and 11, join other children your age in our weekend football sessions. We have a trainer from a local club who will organise 15-minute games between teams. All abilities welcome and you're guaranteed to have fun. Open to boys and girls every Tuesday from 6.00 p.m.

**E Manor Hall Community Centre**

Are you between 10 and 13 years old? Are you interested in playing football against other teams? Why not come along to Manor Hall Community Centre on Sunday at 9.00 a.m. and take part in our five-a-side football competition? Bring your mates if you'd like to make a team with them.

**F Shenfield Sports Centre**

Shenfield Sports Centre will be hosting an event for clubs in the area to watch young players in action and to answer any questions you may have on wanting a career in football. The event is open to anyone between the ages of 14 and 16 and takes place on Sunday at 1.00 p.m.

**G Celcius Leisure Centre**

Join us at Celcius Leisure Centre for our summer football programme for 11- to 14-year-olds. Beginners or more experienced players are welcome and will be supported by our qualified sports team. We are running all-girls teams, with games taking place every Saturday from 9.00–11.00 a.m.

**H Football Skills UK**

Join us on our popular weekend football camps. A fun way for boys and girls aged 8–12 to learn all about football. Practise important ball skills, keep fit and enjoy making new friends. Weekend camps start Friday and end Sunday evening and run each week over the summer holiday.

**Part 3**

## Questions 11–15

For each question, choose the correct answer.

# The Giraffe
*Katie Hepworth talks about her
love of giraffes*

Giraffes are definitely my favourite creature in the animal kingdom. My earliest memory is of my mum reading me a story about a giraffe and I was so in love with the idea that such a wonderful creature existed, I kept asking her to buy me one. I would have been amazed to know that in later life I would spend hours with them every day.

I work in a safari park in the UK and I spend a lot of my time taking care of the giraffes. Visitors to the park have their own favourites of course, with the monkeys being the ones most people like. But I sometimes think the giraffes are the ones they'll never forget after their visit. Visitors always look amazed when they see the giraffes and watch with interest as they move around the park.

I often give talks to visitors about the giraffe and it's true to say that some of the facts about them are surprising. It's hard to believe that despite their long necks, giraffes have the same number of bones in their neck as we do. And it upsets visitors a little when they hear that the animals use their long necks when fighting each other. So I avoid showing videos of this if children are present.

Unlike creatures that have to compete with other animals for food and water at ground level, giraffes have the advantage of being able to reach to the top of trees for their food. In their natural environment, they are less likely to suffer from a lack of water compared to other animals. Their favourite tree, the acacia, is able to obtain a good amount of water through its roots, with the result that the giraffe can get its daily supply from the leaves.

It's really sad to have to tell visitors that, like many of the other animals in the safari park, giraffes also are in danger of disappearing in the wild, where they belong. Once they could be found in wide areas of Africa, but they are now only found in a limited number of places and in much smaller numbers. This is mainly due to people cutting down trees for farming as well as the burning of wood from trees for fuel.

**11** When Katie was a child

    **A** her mum bought her a toy giraffe.

    **B** she couldn't believe a giraffe existed.

    **C** she would have been surprised about her future.

    **D** she decided then she had to work with giraffes.

**12** What does Katie say about visitors to the safari park?

    **A** The monkeys are the most popular.

    **B** They sometimes forget to see the giraffes.

    **C** They all have the same favourite creature.

    **D** The giraffes don't interest some people.

**13** What does Katie say about the talks she gives?

    **A** Visitors don't believe some of the facts she tells them.

    **B** Visitors are surprised by some of the things she tells them.

    **C** Visitors aren't surprised when she tells them about a giraffe's neck.

    **D** She sometimes sells gifts and has a present for children.

**14** In their natural environment, giraffes

    **A** prefer to be on level ground.

    **B** are in competition with other animals for food.

    **C** dislike other animals.

    **D** are in a better position than other animals to get water.

**15** What would Katie be likely to say?

    **A** | The best place for giraffes is in a safari park. |     **B** | Giraffes are in danger of losing their natural environment. |

    **C** | Giraffes can be found in large parts of Africa. |     **D** | Giraffes are causing problems for farmers. |

## Part 4

### Questions 16–20

Five sentences have been removed from the text below.
For each question, choose the correct answer.
There are three extra sentences which you do not need to use.

# Memory palace
*Danny Stephens has some suggestions for improving your memory*

We have two sides to our brain, the right and the left side. The right side is often used when we're being creative. **16** When we want to do this, we tend to rely on the left side of the brain. If you want to improve your memory, one trick is to try bringing the right side of the brain into use.

**17** A memory palace can simply be a place you know well, such as your house or flat, the route to your local shops, your school or your college. Because you know this place so well, it's easy to plan your journey through it knowing where everything is and what comes next.

**18** For example, let's use a shopping list to see how it works. With your memory palace organised, you simply place one of the items from your shopping list in each place. Let's imagine your memory palace is the walk to your nearest supermarket and the first thing on your shopping list is a pair of trainers. So, imagine a pair of trainers waiting at your front door, jumping up and down waiting to go out. It's good to make the picture in your head funny to help you remember.

The next stop is the gate to your house and the next item is a bunch of bananas. So, imagine a row of bananas hanging from your gate, each wearing a pair of sunglasses! And so on. As you follow the route to the supermarket, place one of the items at one of your easy-to-remember places on the journey. **19**

It might be hard to see how this can be used to remember some of the subjects you might be studying. **20** For example, maybe you have to remember a list of dates, the steps necessary in making something or some historical events. Just remember to get that right side of your brain working to come up with scenes that are easy to remember, and put them in a familiar place.

**A**  Now imagine you have to remember something.

**B**  However, some things can't be remembered this way.

**C**  But why not try?

**D**  But what if it doesn't work?

**E**  Using your imagination like this will make it easy to remember.

**F**  However, we don't often use this side to help us remember things.

**G**  On the other hand, the right side works in a different way.

**H**  One method of doing this is to create a memory palace.

## Part 5

### Questions 21–26

For each question, choose the correct answer.

---

### Teeth

Baby teeth, also known as 'milk' teeth, start to grow before we are born and will usually **(21)** ............ when we're about 6 to 12 months old. Most of us will have around 20 milk teeth, which will start to **(22)** ............ out when we're 5 or 6 years old. In the UK, that's when the tooth fairy will come to collect them, in Spain and Latin America it's Perez the Mouse!

The outside of our new, adult teeth is **(23)** ............ 'enamel' and is the hardest part of our body. However, **(24)** ............ to our bones, which can repair themselves over time, damage to enamel is **(25)** ............ and is usually the reason for yellow-coloured teeth or a visit to the dentist. So, **(26)** ............ care of our 32 adult teeth is a serious business. Don't forget that one-third of each tooth is hidden inside the gum, and gums need care and attention too.

---

| 21 | **A** come | **B** appear | **C** present | **D** deliver |
|----|------------|--------------|---------------|---------------|
| 22 | **A** make | **B** set | **C** lose | **D** fall |
| 23 | **A** called | **B** named | **C** picked | **D** shown |
| 24 | **A** different | **B** compared | **C** other | **D** opposite |
| 25 | **A** finished | **B** always | **C** permanent | **D** complete |
| 26 | **A** watching | **B** doing | **C** making | **D** taking |

## Part 6

### Questions 27–32

For each question, write the correct answer.
Write **one** word for each gap.

---

# Cliff Diving
## *by Jess Andrews*

We're on holiday in Spain where we've just watched a cliff diving competition. **(27)** ..................... events take place all around the world. **(28)** ..................... were judges giving scores for the dives, just like you see in Olympic events like gymnastics. I've been reading about it and cliff diving has a long history. In 1770, a king called Kahekili jumped from a cliff and then told his soldiers to do the same in order to prove how brave **(29)** ..................... were! You might have seen people **(30)** ..................... TV cliff diving in a place called La Quebrada in Acapulco, Mexico. The dives there can be **(31)** ..................... high as 35 metres. Depending on **(32)** ..................... high the jump is, the divers will enter the water at really fast speeds. To avoid getting injured, they have to make sure they enter the water in exactly the right position.

# Test 2 WRITING

## Part 1

You **must** answer this question.
Write your answer in about **100 words** on the answer sheet.

---

### Question 1

Read this email from your English-speaking friend Robert and the notes you have made.

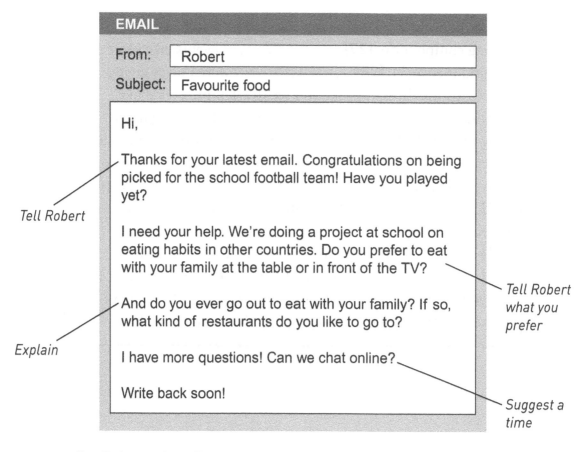

**EMAIL**

From: Robert

Subject: Favourite food

Hi,

Thanks for your latest email. Congratulations on being picked for the school football team! Have you played yet?

*Tell Robert*

I need your help. We're doing a project at school on eating habits in other countries. Do you prefer to eat with your family at the table or in front of the TV?

*Tell Robert what you prefer*

And do you ever go out to eat with your family? If so, what kind of restaurants do you like to go to?

*Explain*

I have more questions! Can we chat online?

Write back soon!

*Suggest a time*

Write your **email** to Robert using **all the notes**.

## Part 2

Choose **one** of these questions.
Write your answer in about **100 words** on the answer sheet.

---

## Question 2

You see this notice in an English-language magazine.

> **Articles wanted!**
>
> **HAVE YOU GOT HOBBY OR INTEREST?**
>
> Have you had this hobby for a long time?
>
> Do you do it at home or do you have to go somewhere?
>
> **Write an article answering these questions and we will put it in our magazine.**

Write your **article**.

## Question 3

Your English teacher has asked you to write a story.

Your story must begin with this sentence.

*I decided to open the smallest present last of all.*

Write your **story**.

# Test 2 LISTENING

## Part 1

### Questions 1–7

For each question, choose the correct answer.

---

**1**   What time did the girl's mum make the appointment at the dentist?

A

B

C

**2**   How has the boy's father been going to work this week?

A

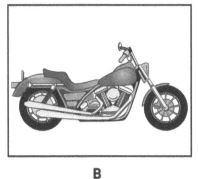

B

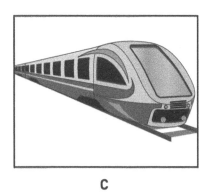

C

**3**   Which event is cancelled?

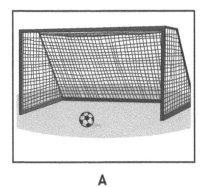

A

B

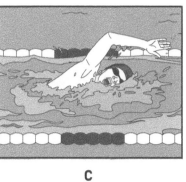

C

**4** What does the woman say will be very busy at the weekend?

|   A   |   B   |   C   |
|-------|-------|-------|

**5** How many cakes does the girl want to order?

|   A   |   B   |   C   |
|-------|-------|-------|

**6** What has the mother stopped drinking recently?

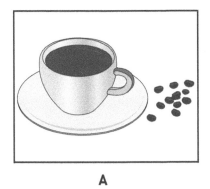 

|   A   |   B   |   C   |
|-------|-------|-------|

**7** When does the teacher say he can meet the parents?

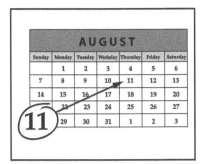 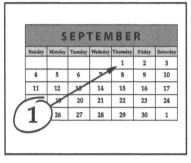

|   A   |   B   |   C   |
|-------|-------|-------|

# Part 2

10

## Questions 8–13

For each question, choose the correct answer.

---

8   You will hear two friends talking about a new shop.
    What does the girl want to go shopping for?

   **A**   There is something special she wants to buy.

   **B**   She needs to get a birthday present for someone.

   **C**   She wants to see if she can buy something in a sale.


9   You will hear two friends talking about a football match.
    What does the boy say about the evening?

   **A**   They need to be quiet while they're watching the game.

   **B**   His mum has bought some snacks.

   **C**   His dad won't be there.


10   You will hear two friends talking about the school holiday.
     The girl says

   **A**   they have to go to school on Friday.

   **B**   she wants to plan some activities for the holiday.

   **C**   she always gets bored on holiday.


11   You will hear a boy and his mother talking about the evening meal.
     The mother explains to her son that

   **A**   she can't cook because she's working late.

   **B**   she doesn't want the chicken to get cold.

   **C**   she has the spices for the meal.


12   You will hear two friends talking about a mobile phone.
     What is wrong with it?

   **A**   It won't connect to the Internet.

   **B**   It won't switch on.

   **C**   There's a fault with the battery.


13   You will hear two friends talking about a fast-food restaurant.
     What is the boy's opinion of it?

   **A**   The online reviews weren't very good.

   **B**   It's quite cheap.

   **C**   It's a bit too far from school.

## Part 3

11

### Questions 14–19

For each question, write the correct answer in the gap. Write **one** or **two words** or a **number** or a **date** or a **time**.

You will hear a man talking about activities at a youth centre.

# Kilbury Youth Centre

Please bring **(14)** ……………….. if you are going on the indoor skiing trip.

The workshop on playing the guitar will take place in the **(15)** ………………..

Make sure the room is **(16)** ……………….. when you leave.

No more than **(17)** ……………….. in a team for the quiz.

We need club **(18)** ……………….. to help with the barbecue.

Meet next Wednesday to help us deliver the **(19)** ………………..

# Part 4

12

## Questions 20–25

For each question, choose the correct answer.

___

You will hear an interview with a woman called Moira O'Neil, who helps students studying in the UK find a family to live with.

**20** Moira says the young students she deals with

    **A**  have never been abroad before.

    **B**  will remember the family for the rest of their lives.

    **C**  don't feel safe being on their own.

**21** Most of the families Moira works with

    **A**  have younger children.

    **B**  don't have lives that are very busy.

    **C**  are single.

**22** What does Moira say about students who are vegetarians?

    **A**  They are not happy to have pets in the house.

    **B**  They don't mind if the family eats meat.

    **C**  Most like to live with other vegetarians.

**23** Moira says that families should

    **A**  try to learn the student's language.

    **B**  offer more than food and accommodation.

    **C**  make sure they know what the student wants from the family.

**24** What can the family do to make the student feel at home?

    **A**  Invite the student to a family celebration.

    **B**  Give students a map of the local area.

    **C**  Allow the student to eat in their room.

**25** Moira says a family offering accommodation

    **A**  will need to have a computer the student can use.

    **B**  will need to provide somewhere for the student to work.

    **C**  should expect the student to keep their room clean and tidy.

# Test 2 SPEAKING

13–14

1A

1B

Audio scripts and Model answers on pages 183–249.

15–16

Things for a walking trip with the school

Audio scripts and Model answers on pages 183–249.

# Test 3

# Test 3 READING

## Part 1

### Questions 1–5

For each question, choose the correct answer.

---

1

| To: All quiz teams |
| --- |
| Subject: Youth Centre Quiz Night |
| Let us know the names of the people in your team before Friday. A maximum of six players in each team. Not yet in a team? We'll find you one!<br><br>Sally |

A  No more than six players in a team.

B  All teams are now full.

C  Tell us the name of your team.

2

**Please keep valuable items in your locker or hand them in to your teacher at the start of the gym class.**

A  Do not bring valuable items to school.

B  Do not give valuable items to your teacher.

C  Valuable items must be kept in a locker.

3

Dance lessons for
13- to 16-year-olds. The first
Wednesday every month at the
leisure centre.
All abilities welcome.
Call: 997 5532

A  dance lessons for experienced teenagers

B  dance lessons once a month

C  dance lessons every Wednesday

**4**

Hi Mum

Can you take me and
Sarah into town
after school? We
want to look at
dresses for the
party. If you
can't, let me know
and we'll ask
Sarah's mum.

Love Megan

**A** Sarah and Megan are in town.

**B** Megan wants a lift to the shops.

**C** Megan's mum should call Sarah's mum.

**5**

Make sure your table is
clean when you've finished
and empty your plate in the
bin as you leave.

**A** Don't leave the table in a mess.

**B** Leave your plate by the bin.

**C** Please empty the bin when full.

## Part 2

## Questions 6–10

For each question, choose the correct answer.

---

The young people below all want to go somewhere for a meal.
On the opposite page there are descriptions of eight places to eat.
Decide which place would be the most suitable for the people below.

**6**

Sarah is 15 and doesn't have much time to get something to eat for lunch before going back to school. She doesn't eat meat and she would like a sandwich and a cold drink.

**7**

Kelvin is planning his 14th birthday and would like to take his friends for a meal on Thursday. He needs somewhere that's easy to get to and somewhere they can also do some kind of activity.

**8**

Juan and his friends have just finished their final year at school and would like to go out to celebrate this weekend. He wants somewhere they can eat and also listen to music.

**9**

Martina is helping her dad plan a surprise birthday meal for her mum this Wednesday evening. Some relatives who are coming are vegetarians, and she'd love it if the restaurant could supply a cake.

**10**

Paula finishes school at 5.00 p.m. and is looking for somewhere to buy a takeaway meal. She likes Italian food and she wants something she can warm up when she gets home.

# Places to eat

### A   Java Lounge

Open seven days a week, the Java Lounge welcomes small and larger groups celebrating that special event. Our menu includes meals for all tastes, including a range of vegetarian options. Call us if it's a special occasion and you'd like us to prepare one of our delicious home-baked birthday or anniversary cakes.

### E   The Lounge Cafe

Our popular meeting place for young people will be opening its doors again this weekend to welcome food lovers and those who enjoy a good dance. Our live music event this week features Sam Costa, one of the area's top DJs. Live music Friday and Saturday only.

### B   Cafe Blanc

Looking for somewhere special to eat and enjoy time with friends or relations? Our vegetarian menu has proved very popular with locals. We open from 9.00 a.m. to 5.00 p.m. and provide you with the very best in service from the moment you walk through the door.

### F   Sam's Cafe

Quality food to take away. Everything is prepared the same day and is made with healthy ingredients. Choose from our delicious hot meals, or if you're in a hurry take away one of our sandwiches, cakes and a hot or cold drink. Open daily from 10.00 a.m. to 4.00 p.m. Vegetarian options are always available.

### C   The Apollo

If you're interested in getting something to eat and having fun at the same time, then the Apollo could be just right for you. Enjoy ice-skating with your friends before sitting down to one of our delicious burgers. Convenient location in the centre of town, just opposite the train and bus stations. Open seven days a week.

### G   Sasha's

If you fancy pizza or pasta tonight, have a look at the menu at Sasha's. Take away one of our quality hot pizzas with a wide range of ingredients. Or why not try a ready meal that you can pop in the microwave when you get home? Open all day from 5.00 p.m. to 11.00 p.m.

### D   Broadway 10

Come and visit us for coffee and cake. We'll be serving our usual homemade cakes from 10.00 a.m. to 4.00 p.m. And if you're a music fan, while you're here why not look though our collection of cheap second-hand CDs. You're certain to find something you like.

### H   The Burger Bar

The Burger Bar is one of the town's most popular fast-food restaurants and our food never disappoints. Choose how you want your burger from a choice of beef, lamb or chicken, and enjoy our great chips. Choice of cold drinks and milkshakes too. Sorry, no takeaway service available due to lack of staff.

## Part 3

### Questions 11–15

For each question, choose the correct answer.

---

# Get focused!

*Kerry Allen offers tips on getting a study space organised*

We sometimes get letters from teenagers asking how best to organise their study time at home. Of course, we all work better if we have a space where we feel comfortable and are able to concentrate. In this article we'll focus on using your bedroom to study. It's the most obvious place, especially if you don't have to share. If you're lucky enough to have your own room, here are our top suggestions.

So, our most important tip is keep it tidy! Teenagers are well-known for having untidy bedrooms. This really won't help you to concentrate, so get yourself a basket and put clothes for washing in there and hang up those you plan to wear again. Your room will look great and you'll feel ready to work!

If possible, create a study space away from your bed, in the opposite corner or on the other side of your room, or it may disturb your sleep. Of course it's best to have a study desk to work at. This should be big enough for a laptop if you have one and a book and notepaper. Apart from items like these, keep the desk free of things you don't need as, again, an untidy desk won't help you work.

Have a space nearby for all your study materials, such as course books, pens and pencils. Keep these organised so you can find what you want easily. Avoid having things nearby that don't help you focus. For example, is it a good idea to have your mobile phone close by? Unless you're using it for your studies it might actually stop you concentrating.

Also, remember that this is also the room you use to sleep. It's really important that this isn't disturbed so, at the end of every work session, switch off all devices such as laptops or PCs. Even better, clear your desk of everything to do with work so you are able to return the room to what looks like a bedroom rather than a study. This will help you get a good night's sleep and get you ready for another day.

---

**11** What does Kerry say about the bedroom?

    **A** It usually has more space than other rooms.

    **B** It's the room most people would think of using.

    **C** People don't like to share one.

    **D** It needs to have comfortable furniture.

**12** Kerry says teenagers

    **A** should put all the clothes they've worn in a basket.

    **B** find it hard to concentrate.

    **C** often have messy bedrooms.

    **D** should do their own washing.

**13** How should the space be organised?

    **A** Create a place to study by the bed.

    **B** Get a second-hand desk for free.

    **C** Keep a limited number of items on the desk.

    **D** Make the bedroom feel big.

**14** What does Kerry say about your study area?

    **A** Never have your mobile phone close to you.

    **B** Some items might disturb you while you're studying.

    **C** Ask for help if you can't focus.

    **D** Organising the space is easy.

**15** What would be a good introduction to this article?

    **A** Organise your room for study and sleep.

    **B** The bedroom isn't really the best place to focus.

    **C** Keep technology out of your bedroom.

    **D** Why students use bedrooms to study.

**Part 4**

**Questions 16–20**

Five sentences have been removed from the text below.
For each question, choose the correct answer.
There are three extra sentences which you do not need to use.

# Plogging

*Children join their teachers to clean up
the streets*

Caroline Adams, the head teacher at Holmere Junior School, was tired of seeing litter blowing around in the school playground. She knew the children were worried about the environment as they had talked a lot about reports on the TV of the problems that litter brings. **16** She called a meeting of teachers and got plans for her idea started.

Caroline spoke to the teachers about setting up a 'plogging' group. The word itself comes from the Swedish word 'plogga' meaning to pick up, and of course from 'jogging'. Her school had won several awards for its interest in environmental issues and this idea fitted with the school's values. **17** After meetings with parents, a small group of volunteer children were invited to join the teachers on their first plogging run.

The ploggers follow a set route, about two miles around the area where their school is. Teachers organise different groups depending on whether the children want to jog or walk and each group is accompanied by two adults. **18** They each get a pair of strong gloves, plastic rubbish bags and litter pickers. The school has also produced colourful T-shirts for the children to wear during the activity. **19** Plastic bottles and paper can be picked up, while things like broken glass must be left where it is.

**20** As well as keeping the streets around the school free of litter, it's also an opportunity to do some exercise. The school has appeared in the local newspaper and other schools are said to be planning a similar activity themselves. Most importantly of all, the ploggers are getting the message out that dropping litter is not acceptable and will hopefully reduce the amount of waste people throw away without thinking first.

A    But there is still a lot of litter outside the school gates.

B    Her suggestion was welcomed by the teachers and then, later, the pupils.

C    Teachers make it clear what kind of items the children should collect.

D    However, the parents are happy for the children to take part.

E    So she decided to do something about it.

F    The activity has proved to have more than one benefit.

G    Some people were worried about safety issues.

H    The children are all given the tools they need for plogging.

## Part 5

### Questions 21–26

For each question, choose the correct answer.

---

### Greetings Cards

Sending greetings cards goes back many years to the ancient Chinese, who sent messages to each other to **(21)** ............ the New Year.  The early Egyptians were also known to have sent **(22)** ............ messages to each other. It took a little while longer before the custom **(23)** ............ in other parts of the world.  Europeans started sending homemade cards in the 15th century and the oldest known greetings card can be **(24)** ............ in the British Museum in London. The Germans would print New Year's messages from pieces of wood, and Valentine's cards (25) ............ from paper appeared around the same time. The arrival of postage stamps in the 19th century and developments in printing technology meant sending greetings cards **(26)** ............ more popular. In 1856, a company in America became an important commercial producer of Christmas cards.

---

| 21 | **A** call | **B** celebrate | **C** party | **D** approve |
|---|---|---|---|---|
| 22 | **A** alike | **B** close | **C** like | **D** similar |
| 23 | **A** came | **B** visited | **C** arrived | **D** delivered |
| 24 | **A** seen | **B** looked | **C** watched | **D** met |
| 25 | **A** worked | **B** made | **C** done | **D** built |
| 26 | **A** went | **B** changed | **C** turned | **D** became |

## Part 6

### Questions 27–32

For each question, write the correct answer.
Write **one** word for each gap.

---

### Cave Paintings of Altamira
*by Alice Simpson*

We've been learning about cave paintings at school today. Some
of **(27)** .................... date from 10,000 to 20,000 years ago,
with some going back even further in time. We looked at photos
of the ones in Altamira in Spain. They were discovered by a
young girl **(28)** .................... was with her father, Marcelino
Sanz de Sautuola, the owner of the land where the cave was
situated. He **(29)** .................... previously found prehistoric
items in the caves and on a later visit he **(30)** ....................
accompanied by his daughter, Maria. **(31)** ....................
was Maria who noticed paintings of bison on the ceiling in
part of the cave. Her father was sure they were examples of real
prehistoric art and published a report. **(32)** ....................
first many experts doubted they were thousands of years old,
but experts later accepted they were real prehistoric paintings.

---

# Test 3 WRITING

## Part 1

You **must** answer this question.
Write your answer in about **100 words** on the answer sheet.

---

## Question 1

Read this email from your teacher Mrs Horton and the notes you have made.

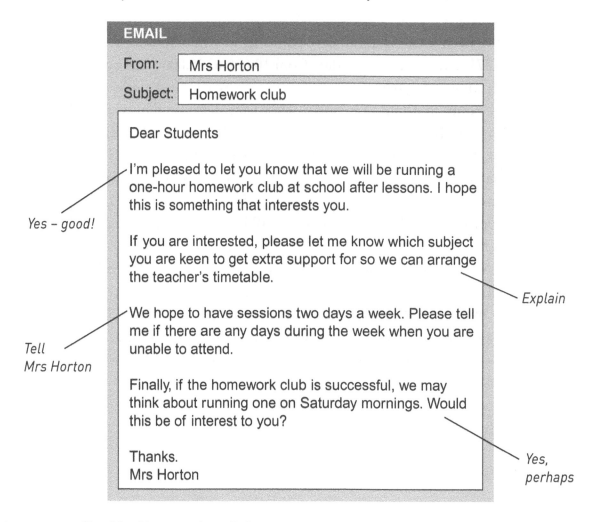

EMAIL

From: Mrs Horton

Subject: Homework club

Dear Students

I'm pleased to let you know that we will be running a one-hour homework club at school after lessons. I hope this is something that interests you.

*Yes – good!*

If you are interested, please let me know which subject you are keen to get extra support for so we can arrange the teacher's timetable.

*Explain*

We hope to have sessions two days a week. Please tell me if there are any days during the week when you are unable to attend.

*Tell Mrs Horton*

Finally, if the homework club is successful, we may think about running one on Saturday mornings. Would this be of interest to you?

Thanks.
Mrs Horton

*Yes, perhaps*

Write your **email** to Mrs Horton using **all the notes**.

## Part 2

Choose **one** of these questions.
Write your answer in about **100 words** on the answer sheet.

---

## Question 2

You see this notice in an English-language magazine.

| Articles wanted! |
| --- |
| **HAVE YOU GOT A FAVOURITE TV PROGRAMME?** |
| What is it about? |
| What do you like about it? |
| **Write an article answering these questions and we will put it in our magazine.** |

Write your **article**.

## Question 3

Your English teacher has asked you to write a story.

Your story must begin with this sentence.

*I read the email and couldn't believe it!*

Write your **story**.

# Test 3 LISTENING

## Part 1

### Questions 1–7

For each question, choose the correct answer.

---

**1** Which day is the school play taking place this year?

A

B

C

**2** Where was the cat found?

A

B

C

**3** What did the boy do on holiday?

A

B

C

**4** Which book does the woman think was too long?

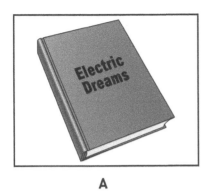
A

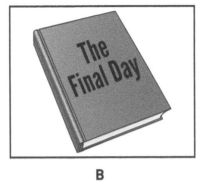
B

C

**5** Which item did the mother forget to buy?

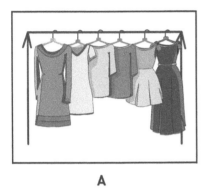
A

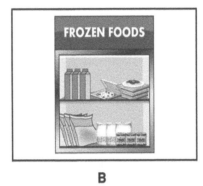
B

C

**6** When does the film begin?

A

B

C

**7** Where will Mr Taylor be if anyone needs him?

A

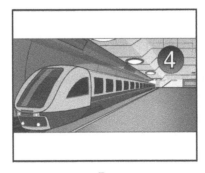
B

C

# Part 2

18

## Questions 8–13

For each question, choose the correct answer.

---

8 You will hear two friends talking about seeing a doctor.
The girl explains that

   **A** her mum is concerned about her toe.

   **B** she finds it difficult to move.

   **C** she hurt her foot on a piece of equipment.


9 You will hear a boy talking to his mother about travelling to school.
What does the mother say the boy should do?

   **A** take an umbrella

   **B** arrange to meet a friend

   **C** wear something to keep dry


10 You will hear two friends talking about going to the cinema.
Which film does the boy want to see?

   **A** Long Shot

   **B** Shark Attack

   **C** The Banker


11 You will hear a girl talking to her father about decorating her bedroom.
The girl says

   **A** decorating is a waste of money.

   **B** she's not going to make a decision yet.

   **C** she wants a room like her friend's.


12 You will hear two friends talking about meeting someone at the station.
What does the boy decide to do?

   **A** go into town on his own

   **B** take a taxi to the station

   **C** go with his dad


13 You will hear two friends talking about a TV show.
What does the girl say about the show?

   **A** She'd heard it was good.

   **B** It is on too late.

   **C** Her mum and dad liked it.

## Part 3

19

### Questions 14–19

For each question, write the correct answer in the gap. Write **one** or **two words** or a **number** or a **date** or a **time**.

You will hear an announcement about a school trip.

---

### The School Trip

The journey will take about **(14)** ....................

The school will provide everyone with a **(15)** .......................
for the trip.

We will be doing the tour in **(16)** ..................... to make it
easier to manage.

If it rains, lunch will be held in the park
**(17)** .......................

Please get back to the park **(18)** ..................... before we
leave.

Please speak to Mrs Evans if you have problems
**(19)** .....................

# Part 4

## Questions 20–25

For each question, choose the correct answer.

---

You will hear an interview with a man called Tony Owen, who is a school's exam officer.

**20** What does Tony say about exams?

    **A** It's not surprising that we feel nervous.

    **B** Being nervous can make us perform badly.

    **C** Most students have a positive experience of them.

**21** Tony says in order to pass exams

    **A** a little bit of luck can help.

    **B** you should always guess if you don't understand.

    **C** revise with another person if it helps.

**22** Before you leave the house on exam day, Tony says you should try to

    **A** make sure you don't leave without anything important.

    **B** find a plan of the test centre.

    **C** find out if your train is cancelled or if there are traffic jams.

**23** What does Tony suggest doing in the exam?

    **A** Ask the examiner to repeat the instructions.

    **B** Find ways to relax before you begin.

    **C** Don't think about passing or failing.

**24** Tony says that during the exam

    **A** don't leave before you've answered all the questions.

    **B** try to get the difficult questions answered first.

    **C** start with questions you can answer easily.

**25** After the exam Tony suggests that you

    **A** keep away from certain people.

    **B** talk about the difficult questions with others.

    **C** help people who haven't done well.

# Test 3 SPEAKING

1A

1B

Audio scripts and Model answers on pages 183–249.

23–24

## A birthday present for an 8-year-old boy

Audio scripts and Model answers on pages 183–249.

# Test 4

# Test 4 READING

## Part 1

### Questions 1–5

For each question, choose the correct answer.

---

**1**

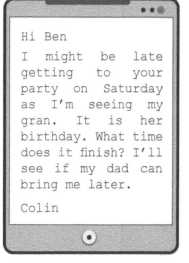

Hi Ben
I might be late getting to your party on Saturday as I'm seeing my gran. It is her birthday. What time does it finish? I'll see if my dad can bring me later.

Colin

**A** Colin can't go to Ben's party.

**B** Colin has to see his grandmother on Saturday.

**C** Colin will see Ben later.

**2**

**School Security**

Students must wear their identity card at all times.

Entry to school is not permitted without one.

**A** You must have your identity card to get into the building.

**B** You need permission to not wear your identity card.

**C** Students without identity cards must get permission before entering the building.

**3**

**FOR SALE**

New and used computer games. Used ones tested and work perfectly.
For selected games, buy two and get one free.

**A** special offer if you buy three games

**B** some games are second-hand

**C** you can test the games out first

**4**

Hiya Tony

I've phoned the leisure centre – it costs £20 for one hour to book the football pitch. That's £2 each if all ten of us play. Let me know if you think that's fair.

Mark

A  Mark wants to know if £2 each is reasonable.

B  They must have ten players to book the pitch.

C  Mark wants to know if they have ten players.

**5**

The library PCs are being updated and are not available today. Laptops for use today can be booked from student services.

A  Students can't use PCs in the library this week.

B  There are no computers available today.

C  Student services will help students borrow a laptop.

# Part 2

## Questions 6–10

For each question, choose the correct answer.

---

The young people below all want to find a job during their summer holiday.
On the opposite page there are advertisements for eight jobs.
Decide which job would be the most suitable for the people below.

**6**

Benjamin is 13 and wants to work with animals, especially learning how to care for horses. He is free at the weekend and doesn't mind hard work.

**7**

Carla is 15 and wants to help out with a summer camp for young people. She is free all summer, Monday to Friday, and is happy to spend time away from home.

**8**

Karenne, 16, wants to earn money for a holiday. She is looking for work serving customers in a shop as she has some experience in doing this.

**9**

Mati is 14 years old and is very keen on sport. He would like to be able to volunteer at a sporting event. He is free on Saturday mornings.

**10**

Lisa, 15, needs work experience for her school. She is very creative and would love to be involved in anything to do with design. She can work at the weekend.

# Job advertisements

**A Volunteers urgently needed**

How would you like to spend a few Saturdays over the summer helping us organise our weekly runs? We urgently need people 13 years and over to hand out water during the run and give out prizes at the end. The runs take place in Marshgate Park at 8.30 a.m. and 10.00 a.m.

**E Garden Centre**

Looking for voluntary work over the summer? Join us in your local garden centre. You'll be expected to help dig, plant trees and other plants and water them. You may be required to help customers with their enquiries, even if it's just finding a more experienced worker for help.

**B Hayden Scouts**

Would you like to spend your summer working with other young people on outdoor activities? Hayden Scouts are looking for helpers between the ages of 14 and 16 to support our young people during their summer camp. These are four-day events and run from Tuesday to Friday. Food and accommodation provided.

**F Carlton Youth Club**

Help kids in your area get the most from their summer holiday. Come along to our youth club this summer to create a positive environment during out-of-school time. You'll work with children aged six and over on homework and games. Activities take place every afternoon from 12.00–4.00 p.m.

**C Summer work**

Give people the time of their lives this summer by working at Crowden Park! Choose from various activities, such as serving food in our café or helping to keep the park clean and tidy. Work the whole summer holiday or sign up for part-time hours.

**G Grange's Department Store**

Grange's are currently looking for young people age 14–16 to help with our shop window display team on Saturday afternoons. You'll get the opportunity to learn how best to create an attractive display and gain valuable work experience.

**D Leydon Community Association**

Leydon will once again be running its weekend summer programme and urgently needs volunteers to help us with some of our activities. We particularly need youngsters to help with our horses. You will gain useful skills in horse care and help us keep their accommodation clean and tidy.

**H Clara's**

Are you looking for the opportunity to earn some cash over the summer and gain some useful work experience? We are looking for young people to serve customers in our shop every Saturday over the summer holiday. We are very interested in hearing from people who have done similar work in the past.

## Part 3

### Questions 11–15

For each question, choose the correct answer.

# My phone and me
## by Kieran Lewis

I was 11 when my mum and dad bought me my first mobile phone. I had tried for ages to get one and going to a new school at 11 years old was the perfect opportunity to persuade them! My new school was a bus ride away compared to the school I was leaving, which was just around the corner. Both mum and dad thought they would worry less about my safety knowing I had a phone, so we went shopping to get one.

For the first month or two mum and dad would check how I was using it all the time. I didn't get it out at the dinner table, they told me not to use it when I went to bed and, of course, to be careful about personal safety online. It would sometimes annoy me to be told not to do things that I wouldn't have done anyway, but I knew they were only saying these things because they loved me, so I tried to be understanding. They have trusted me as I've got older, though I'm still not allowed to bring it to the dinner table.

I'm now 16 and I can't imagine life without a mobile phone. I sometimes think older people who complain about teenagers always being on their phone need to understand us better. We have grown up with this technology. It's such a valuable tool for communication, shopping, fact-finding – even education. It's often how we deal with the world around us. Of course, if the Internet crashed and we couldn't use it, we'd survive. But you could say the same thing about TVs, cars and all the other technology that older people use all the time, even though using them is sometimes seen as a problem.

So, if I could say one thing to older people it would be 'live and let live'. Trust us to know what we're doing and to realise when it's time to put the phone down and do some exercise. By the way, we are able to communicate face to face and we do so, often when you're not looking! We know you are only thinking about our best interests, but please trust us to make the right decisions.

**11** Kieran explains that he got a mobile phone because

   **A** he had his 11th birthday.

   **B** his new school was further away.

   **C** his new school told him he needed one.

   **D** he felt safer having one.

**12** Kieran says his parents

   **A** told him not to take his phone to bed.

   **B** made him do things he didn't want to do.

   **C** showed they cared about him.

   **D** didn't trust him.

**13** What does Kieran say about the mobile phone?

   **A** It has been with young people all their lives.

   **B** Young people couldn't live without one.

   **C** They cost a lot of money.

   **D** Old people don't understand how to use them.

**14** Kieran asks older people to

   **A** try communicating with younger people more.

   **B** realise young people know what is best for themselves.

   **C** stop complaining about younger people.

   **D** try doing some exercise.

**15** What would be a good introduction to this article?

   **A**
   | Kieran Lewis explains how best to use your mobile phone. |
   |---|

   **B**
   | Give teenagers the chance to make the right decisions, says Kieran Lewis. |
   |---|

   **C**
   | Kieran Lewis thinks we should help older people understand the phone better. |
   |---|

   **D**
   | Young people should listen more to the older generation, says Kieran Lewis. |
   |---|

## Part 4

### Questions 16–20

Five sentences have been removed from the text below.
For each question, choose the correct answer.
There are three extra sentences which you do not need to use.

# The painting that destroyed itself
## *How Banksy surprised the art world*

It might have been a comment on the millions of pounds spent on art works, or a way to get the artist's name in the press. **16** Banksy, the famous British street artist, had one of his paintings for sale in Sotheby's auction house. 'Girl with a balloon' had originally appeared painted on a wall in London. **17** The painting on sale was also a copy and was in a frame that had also been supplied by the artist.

The fact that it was such a well-known picture, and painted by a very famous person, meant it was clearly expected to sell for a lot of money. And it certainly did. The person who bought it, who chose not to be named, paid an enormous $1.4 million dollars for it. **18** The fact that it sold for so much was big news and would probably have been reported in newspapers around the world. But what happened next was even more surprising and made sure the art world would get to know about it.

The sale of the painting had finished when suddenly an alarm went off and, in front of everyone's eyes, the painting started to slip down the frame and slice itself into little pieces. It was actually destroying itself until it stopped half-way down. Banksy had previously put the painting in a frame with a 'shredder' inside. **19** Nobody knows if Banksy was present in the room and started the shredder or whether the auction house knew this was going to happen.

If his reason for doing this was to get his name in the newspapers, it certainly worked. **20** However, if it was an attack on the high sums of money spent on art, his plan may not have worked. Experts believe that the half-destroyed painting is probably worth a lot more now thanks to how famous it became after the sale.

**A** He said the reason was to destroy it were it ever sold.

**B** Either way, the sale of a painting in London hit the headlines.

**C** However, his paintings had not sold well before.

**D** This was a record for a work by a British street artist.

**E** The story was indeed reported around the world.

**F** The person who bought it isn't too unhappy.

**G** It had been copied many times by Banksy and by other artists.

**H** On the other hand, nobody knows whether Banksy saw it happening.

# Part 5

## Questions 21–26

For each question, choose the correct answer.

---

### Surveillance Cameras

Countries around the world have been making use of surveillance cameras for many years. You will see them high up on buildings on **(21)** ............ every street corner, especially in and around shopping **(22)** ............, to record criminal activity. They are also often found on roads to **(23)** ............ people to drive more carefully and to use as evidence if they drive too fast. Some people also put one outside their property to protect them **(24)** ............ burglars. In fact, you'll find them everywhere: at sporting events to catch poor behaviour, in shops and in hospitals. Parents are even buying them to put in their baby's bedroom to **(25)** ............ they are OK. It's clear that from a very young age we need to get **(26)** ............ to appearing on camera for the rest of our lives and to remember we're being watched.

---

| 21 | **A** almost | **B** just | **C** quite | **D** about |
|----|----|----|----|----|
| 22 | **A** places | **B** roads | **C** centres | **D** streets |
| 23 | **A** encourage | **B** let | **C** try | **D** make |
| 24 | **A** of | **B** to | **C** with | **D** from |
| 25 | **A** wonder | **B** check | **C** find | **D** make |
| 26 | **A** comfortable | **B** happy | **C** around | **D** used |

## Part 6

### Questions 27–32

For each question, write the correct answer.
Write **one** word for each gap.

---

### The Polar Bear
*by Sally Nicholson*

We're doing a project at school on polar bears. Male polar bears can be as long as 2.5 metres and weigh up to 600 kg.  They are one of **(27)** ..................... biggest land-based meat-eaters in the world. Although a polar bear is a very strong swimmer, **(28)** ..................... spends most of its time on land. As a result it is in trouble because **(29)** ..................... global warming. The melting ice is reducing the land it lives on. The bear's diet consists mainly of seals. The polar bear has an incredibly strong sense of smell, and it can locate a seal from far away, **(30)** ..................... when it's underwater. They are known for their bright white fur but, **(31)** ..................... fact, their fur is clear and seems white because of the way it reacts to light. It may surprise you, but under this warm blanket of fur they have black skin, **(32)** ..................... helps them enjoy the heat from the sun.

---

# Test 4 WRITING

## Part 1

You **must** answer this question.
Write your answer in about **100 words** on the answer sheet.

___

### Question 1

Read this email from your English-speaking friend Mike and the notes you have made.

**EMAIL**

From: Mike

Subject: Thanks for the invitation!

Hi

I've just read your email. I'd love to come to your party. It's been ages since we saw each other and I'm really looking forward to it.

*Good!*

You didn't say where you're having the party. Is it at your house or have you hired somewhere?

*Tell Mike*

I know the party starts at 7.00 p.m. but I thought I could come a little earlier that day so we can have some time together. Would this be OK or are you busy?

*Say what you prefer*

Oh yes, before I forget, would you like me to bring any food?

Write back soon!

Mike

*Suggest something*

Write your **email** to Mike using **all the notes**.

# Part 2

Choose **one** of these questions.
Write your answer in about **100 words** on the answer sheet.

---

## Question 2

You see this notice in an English-language magazine.

> **Articles wanted!**
>
> **WHAT IS YOUR FAVOURITE PIECE OF TECHNOLOGY?**
>
> How long have you had it?
>
> What do you use it for?
>
> **Write an article answering these questions and we will put it in our magazine.**

Write your **article**.

## Question 3

Your English teacher has asked you to write a story.

Your story must begin with this sentence.

*I sat down and looked around me.*

Write your **story**.

# Test 4 LISTENING

## Part 1

### Questions 1–7

For each question, choose the correct answer.

---

**1** What did the girl do yesterday?

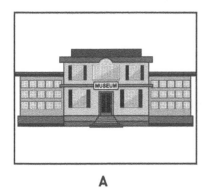

A

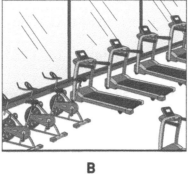

B

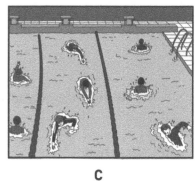

C

**2** What are people saying is causing a problem?

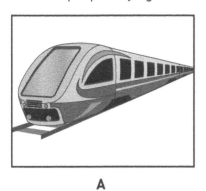

A

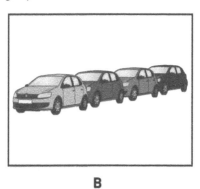

B

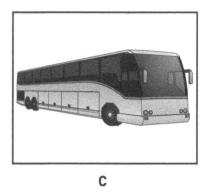

C

**3** Which building doesn't the girl like?

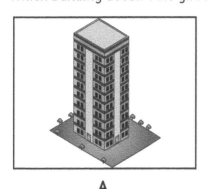

A

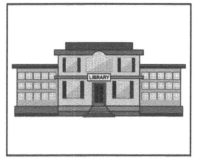

B

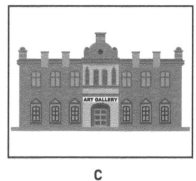

C

**4** How long has the boy had his mobile phone?

A                                    B                                    C

**5** What would be the best day for the girl to collect the book?

A                                    B                                    C

**6** Where will the boy be going on Saturday?

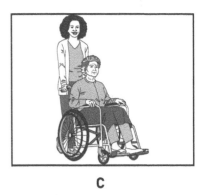

A                                    B                                    C

**7** Which item of food does the boy go out to buy?

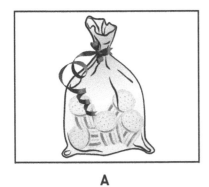
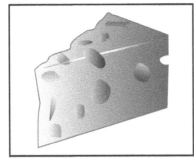
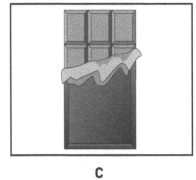

A                                    B                                    C

# Part 2

26

## Questions 8–13

For each question, choose the correct answer.

---

8   You will hear two friends talking about going shopping.
    The girl says

   **A**  the video game she wants is not available.

   **B**  she needs to book an English exam.

   **C**  she forgot to buy some French practice tests.


9   You will hear two friends talking about a website.
    What does the boy say about the company?

   **A**  You can save money if you buy from the website.

   **B**  It has been having problems.

   **C**  It should be easy to find it on the Internet.


10  You will hear a father and his daughter talking about buying a present.
    The girl tells her father

   **A**  he mustn't tell her mother what the present is.

   **B**  she wants to buy her mother more than one present.

   **C**  she's getting her mother the same perfume that she bought before.


11  You will hear a brother and sister talking about lunch.
    The girl says

   **A**  their parents need to buy some tins of soup.

   **B**  her brother takes too long washing up.

   **C**  there's no bread left.


12  You will hear two friends talking about how one of them is.
    What does the boy say about his accident?

   **A**  He was running quite slowly.

   **B**  He has to go to hospital.

   **C**  He's having problems walking.


13  You will hear two friends talking about starting guitar lessons.
    When do the boy's lessons begin?

   **A**  next week

   **B**  next month

   **C**  the next day

## Part 3

27

### Questions 14–19

For each question, write the correct answer in the gap. Write **one** or **two words** or a **number** or a **date** or a **time**.

---

You will hear an announcement about a school sports day.

## Sports Day

Sports Day takes place on **(14)** ………………..

You can enjoy some **(15)** ……………….…... in the hall while we get things ready.

The first-aid tent is near the school **(16)** …………….…….

Parents will find a copy of the timetable on the
**(17)** …………………….

You might receive a prize for **(18)** ……………….….. if you're not successful in an event.

Speak to Mrs Thomas if you want to play **(19)** ………………….…..

# Part 4

28

## Questions 20–25

For each question, choose the correct answer.

---

You will hear an interview with a woman called Jan Prince, who was a talented musician as a child.

**20** What does Jan say about her childhood?

**A** Her parents bought her a little piano.

**B** She used to play before she left for school.

**C** She didn't find playing the piano difficult.

**21** Jan explains that her parents

**A** didn't agree at first which school she should go to.

**B** both played musical instruments.

**C** found a music teacher to give Jan lessons.

**22** While Jan was at school

**A** she didn't like the other children.

**B** she didn't bother to practise much.

**C** she liked the same music as her friends.

**23** Jan explains that

**A** she decided not to follow her parent's advice.

**B** it was difficult finding a job.

**C** she had always been interested in gardening.

**24** What does Jan say about her customers?

**A** They always book another appointment with her.

**B** They sometimes make it difficult for her to leave.

**C** They ask her to teach them how to play.

**25** What does Jan say about her daughter?

**A** She wants to listen to her views when she goes to secondary school.

**B** She would like her to study something completely different to music.

**C** She thinks her father is pushing her too hard to learn the piano.

# Test 4 SPEAKING

1A

1B

Audio scripts and Model answers on pages 183–249.

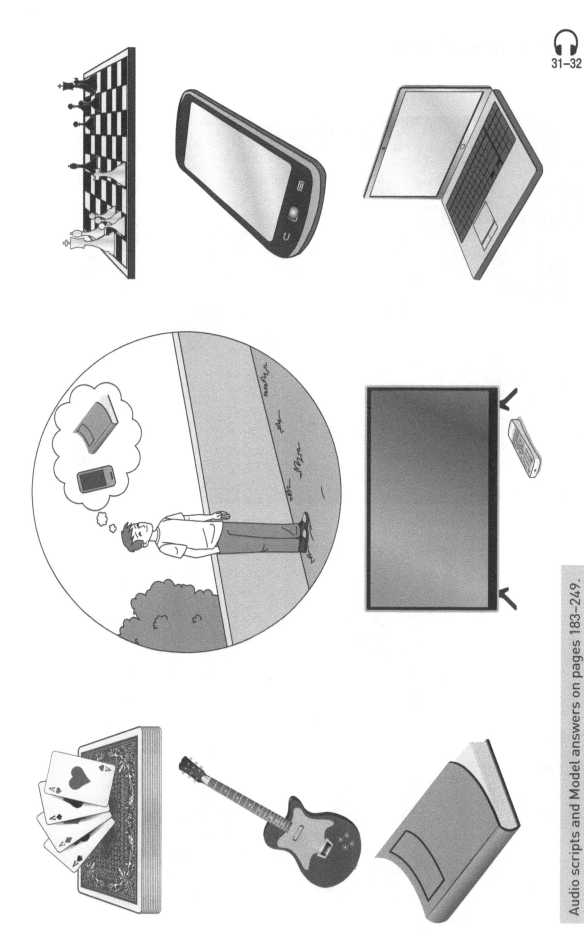

Some things a teenager could do if he had the day off school

Audio scripts and Model answers on pages 183–249.

# Test 5

# Test 5 READING

## Part 1

### Questions 1–5

For each question, choose the correct answer.

---

**1**

Hi Steve

Fancy coming round to my house after school to watch a film?

Tell your mum my dad can take you home and will get us something to eat for dinner.

Let me know.

John

**A** John's dad will collect them from school.

**B** Steve's mum needs to take him home.

**C** Steve can eat with John.

**2**

### FOR SALE

Football boots. Worn once but were too small - perfect condition! £35 or nearest offer. Phone 29974490 for details.

**A** The boots are almost new.

**B** The boots must sell for £35.

**C** The boots are size 'small'.

**3**

### School gym

The gym is not to be used without a teacher being present.

Please wait outside until the lesson starts.

**A** The gym is being used by teachers.

**B** The gym lesson is outside today.

**C** Do not enter the gym until a teacher arrives.

4

| To: Claire |
| --- |
| From: Sue |

Claire

I'm meeting Jemma at 6.00 p.m. at the bus stop. If you can't get there by then, call me and we'll see you later at the dance class.

Sue

A  Jemma and Sue are meeting before the dance class.

B  Claire can't go to the dance class.

C  Jemma should call Sue if she's meeting them at the bus stop.

5

These gardens are for the general public.
To avoid damage to plants and flowers, ball games are not allowed.

A  This is not a play area.

B  The public are not allowed in this area.

C  Please be careful when playing ball games.

## Part 2

## Questions 6–10

For each question, choose the correct answer.

---

The young people below all want to improve their English.
On the opposite page there are descriptions of eight English language schools.
Decide which English language school would be the most suitable for the people below.

**6**

Marcia hopes to work in business. She wants to develop her business English and practise giving presentations and taking part in meetings. She attends college full-time so needs a course later in the day.

**7**

Carlos is 15 and wants to spend a month in the UK studying English on a summer course. He wants to live with an English-speaking family, especially one with children of his own age.

**8**

Isabelle is preparing for her English exams and needs to practise her speaking skills. She is still at school and her parents have suggested she get a private teacher who can visit her at home.

**9**

Franco studies English at school and has his exams soon. He finds writing in English difficult and is looking for an online tutor who can mark his work and help him improve.

**10**

Koichi is going to continue studying English after he leaves school and wants to practise his English-speaking skills during the summer holidays. He is looking for an evening course with students at his own level.

# English Language Schools

**A Broadchurch English**

Part-time, full-time, evening and weekend courses for general and exam English. We run small group classes and we make sure we put you with people with similar abilities. Choose from general classes or practise individual skills such as speaking or writing.

**B Crowbridge Business School of English**

Try our new one-to-one Business courses. These lunchtime sessions will give you the chance to practise that presentation you have planned as well as offering general one-hour conversation lessons. Situated close to the city centre and the business district, we run our lunchtime courses from Monday to Friday from 12.00–2.00 p.m.

**C Manor Language School**

Join us on one of our popular four-week courses this summer. We run English classes from beginner up to advanced and offer a full social programme. Choose the family you will be staying with and share the experience of life with adults and their children over the summer.

**D Results School of English**

Results offers a range of courses at all levels for people working in the world of business. Our part-time, evening and full-time courses will help you develop the skills you need to give talks and take part in discussions and conversations at work.

**E Cartland Summer Schools**

We're pleased to announce our summer schools are open for enrolment for this year. Our two-, three- or four-week adult courses are aimed at those wanting to experience English culture. After morning lessons you'll join other students on one of our afternoon trips. We can provide accommodation with a local family or arrange private accommodation.

**F English Alive**

English Alive offers private language classes in cities across the country. Our conversation classes are designed for those who cannot attend lessons in a school. We provide tutors for online lessons, face-to-face at your place or in our cafe classes. Our teachers are all fully qualified and have experience in general English and exam preparation.

**G Online English School**

We all have busy lives and finding time to practise English is challenging. Our online classes are aimed at students of all ages and promise the very best tutors to help you achieve your goals. Whether it's a general course or a particular area of English such as speaking or writing, contact us now for further information.

**H Live English!**

We're excited to announce the start of our new summer 'Live English!' programme. We'll be meeting up with students in the cafe in Lime Street every lunchtime for real English-speaking practice. We'll provide you with a topic and a questionnaire and you'll go out on the streets and interview local people with another student for support.

## Part 3

### Questions 11–15

For each question, choose the correct answer.

# Why do some people like feeling frightened at fairs?

## Nicola Smith writes about scary rides

If there's one thing that divides me and my friends into two different groups, it's scary rides like the roller coaster. There are those, like my sister, who are willing to stand in a queue for hours waiting to get onto the latest ride. Then there are other people like me, who prefer to wait at the bottom and hold everyone's bags. I sometimes wonder what it is that makes us so different.

Some people think it's to do with the way children today are over-protected by their parents. Kids are rarely given the chance to do anything that might result in them getting hurt. Rides like the roller coaster allow people to feel fear, scream, shout, throw their arms in the air and enjoy themselves, knowing they are safe. My sister is like this and seems to be very scared but also having great fun.

But if that's the reason, why do I avoid going on these rides? My parents were just as concerned about my safety as my sister's. In fact, as I was the first to be born, they probably worried about me even more to begin with. So this doesn't explain the difference between us. Clearly there must be some other reason why some of us enjoy feeling frightened out of our lives and others prefer to have a quiet life.

But perhaps science has the answer. It might actually be because of our brains and particular chemicals in our body. There is one chemical called dopamine that is linked to our enjoyment of doing exciting things. People with more of this chemical are likely to enjoy activities like roller coasters. So, perhaps I don't simply have a lack of courage but of dopamine compared to my sister. Fortunately, as we get older, we are less likely to choose to take part in rides like the roller coaster. Perhaps older people are clever enough to realise that we should avoid such things and take it easy, though I'm not sure my sister will agree.

**11** Nicola says her sister

    **A**  is prepared to spend ages waiting to get on a ride.

    **B**  is similar to her.

    **C**  tries to get her to join her in the queue.

    **D**  doesn't understand people who dislike scary rides.

**12** What does Nicola say about some children?

    **A**  They complain about the way their parents over-protect them.

    **B**  Their parents worry about them not being safe.

    **C**  They aren't allowed to go on rides.

    **D**  The rides don't scare them.

**13** What does Nicola say about her parents?

    **A**  Their behaviour explains the difference between Nicola and her sister.

    **B**  They were more worried about her for a while.

    **C**  They worried more than other parents.

    **D**  They didn't worry much about her sister.

**14** Nicola says that

    **A**  we all enjoy doing exciting things.

    **B**  using biology as an explanation is too simple.

    **C**  she might have less dopamine than her sister.

    **D**  she doesn't have enough courage to go on rides.

**15** What would Nicola say about the future?

| **A** She is likely to join her sister on a ride. | **B** More people of her age will have the same opinion as her. |
|---|---|
| **C** Scary rides will be as popular with older as well as younger people. | **D** She'll be too old to go on a ride. |

## Part 4

### Questions 16–20

Five sentences have been removed from the text below.
For each question, choose the correct answer.
There are three extra sentences which you do not need to use.

# My dance classes

*by Stella Cullen, age 16*

Like most parents, mine spent a lot of time trying to persuade me to take part in activities outside school. **16** Then one day a friend at school told me about a local dance group she was thinking of joining and asked if I wanted to go with her. So after school we went to talk to the dance teacher. She explained everything to us and we both decided to sign up.

Mum and Dad were really pleased to hear I'd finally signed up for something. **17**

They think it's better if you develop an interest in doing something yourself. They think you're more likely to succeed if you're interested.

And the dance classes? Well, I've now been attending for three years and I really enjoy it. We are organised into age groups and at 16, I'm now in the oldest class. We practise street dance and I'm quite good, even if I say so myself. **18** I really enjoy working with them. It's fun helping them with their routines and they are always so enthusiastic.

We also take part in events like local and even national dance shows, and relatives turn up to see their children perform. **19** I know they're proud of me as they tell me all the time. But I feel a bit embarrassed when people I know are watching me and I perform better if they're not there.

I'm now almost at the age where I'll be too old to continue dancing with the group as the age limit is 17. **20** The dance school has become very successful and is opening new classes next year. The director has asked if I'd be willing to be a permanent leader for one of the groups and of course I said 'yes'!

**A** I also help out leading some of the younger children.

**B** However, I have already made plans to continue with them.

**C** On the other hand, some of the dances are really difficult.

**D** To be honest, I prefer it when my mum and dad don't come.

**E** I hadn't danced before then.

**F** And they were pleased it was dancing.

**G** However, they never insisted, and I never found anything I was interested in.

**H** But I hadn't always loved dancing.

# Part 5

## Questions 21–26

For each question, choose the correct answer.

---

### Honey

People have known about the **(21)** ............ of honey for thousands of years. It's even been called liquid gold, and the Romans actually used it to pay their taxes **(22)** ............ of gold!

A lot of work goes into making honey. The next time you're in the supermarket take a look at those jars on the shelves. Then consider that one honeybee will only be able to **(23)** ............ one-twelfth of a teaspoon of honey in its **(24)** ............ life! So bees have to collect the nectar from two million flowers to make half a kilo of honey. Honey is **(25)** ............ to be good for our health. In the past it was used to help deal with burns and cuts. And for sports people today, the **(26)** ............ sugars found in honey make it an ideal way to get a little extra energy when it's needed.

---

| 21 | **A** products | **B** interests | **C** benefits | **D** gifts |
|----|----|----|----|----|
| 22 | **A** instead | **B** place | **C** rather | **D** compared |
| 23 | **A** build | **B** set | **C** close | **D** produce |
| 24 | **A** complete | **B** whole | **C** all | **D** full |
| 25 | **A** known | **B** familiar | **C** famous | **D** clear |
| 26 | **A** real | **B** natural | **C** correct | **D** straight |

## Part 6

### Questions 27–32

For each question, write the correct answer.
Write **one** word for each gap.

---

### The Loch Ness Monster
#### by Susie Edwards

We've come to the end of our holiday in Loch Ness, Scotland, but sadly we haven't seen the monster! People have reported seeing something strange in Loch Ness for years. The tour guide told us that the first stories about it appeared **(27)** ..................... newspapers in the early 1930s. The reports said that people **(28)** ..................... seen 'Nessie' – that's what people call the monster. There was even a photo of the creature showing its head and neck coming out of **(29)** ..................... water.

The tour guide said that scientists think that if there is something down there, **(30)** ..................... could be a giant eel. Researchers haven't found anything in the loch that suggests there are very large creatures, but with **(31)** ..................... many eels living there, it's possible there might be a particularly large one **(32)** ..................... might look like a monster.

# Test 5 WRITING

## Part 1

You **must** answer this question.
Write your answer in about **100 words** on the answer sheet.

---

### Question 1

Read this email from your English-speaking friend Kate and the notes you have made.

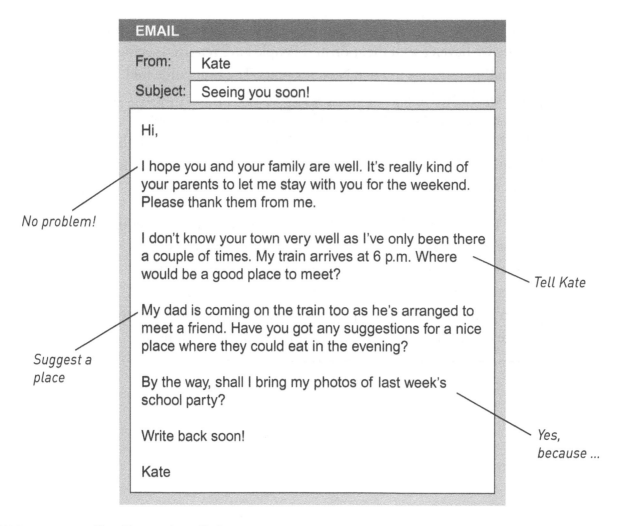

**EMAIL**

From: Kate

Subject: Seeing you soon!

Hi,

I hope you and your family are well. It's really kind of your parents to let me stay with you for the weekend. Please thank them from me.

*No problem!*

I don't know your town very well as I've only been there a couple of times. My train arrives at 6 p.m. Where would be a good place to meet?

*Tell Kate*

My dad is coming on the train too as he's arranged to meet a friend. Have you got any suggestions for a nice place where they could eat in the evening?

*Suggest a place*

By the way, shall I bring my photos of last week's school party?

Write back soon!

Kate

*Yes, because ...*

Write your **email** to Kate using **all the notes**.

## Part 2

Choose **one** of these questions.
Write your answer in about **100 words** on the answer sheet.

---

## Question 2

You see this notice in an English-language magazine.

| Articles wanted! |
|---|

**HAVE YOU GOT A FAVOURITE SHOP NEAR YOU?**

What kind of things does it sell?

What do you like about it?

**Write an article answering these questions and we will put it in our magazine.**

Write your **article**.

## Question 3

Your English teacher has asked you to write a story.

Your story must begin with this sentence.

*It was Monday morning and the start of a new year at school.*

Write your **story**.

# Test 5 LISTENING

## Part 1

### Questions 1–7

For each question, choose the correct answer.

---

**1**  Where was the boy when he had his accident?

A

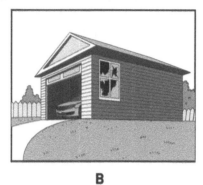

B

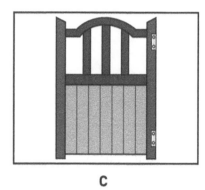

C

**2**  What has the mother already bought for her daughter's birthday?

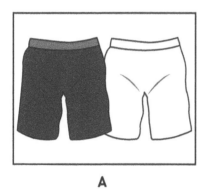

A

B

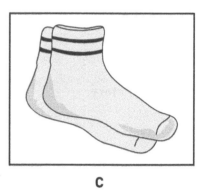

C

**3**  When is the picnic?

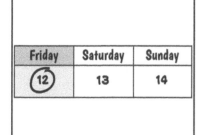

A

B

C

**4** What did the girl forget to buy for the party?

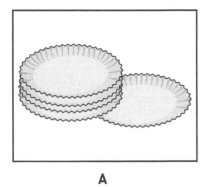

A

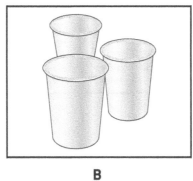

B

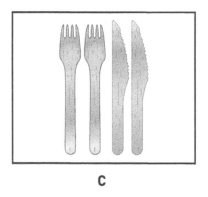

C

**5** What has the man lost today?

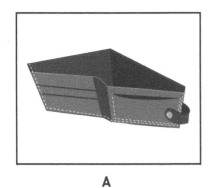

A

B

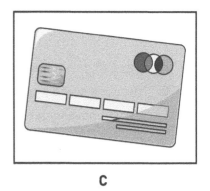

C

**6** Which country does the girl think will win the match?

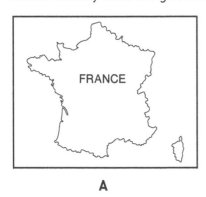

A

B

C

**7** Where should the girl go to get a drink?

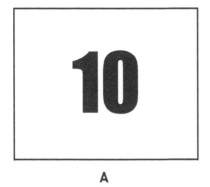

A

B

C

# Part 2

34

## Questions 8–13

For each question, choose the correct answer.

---

**8** You will hear two friends talking about a car.
The boy says

**A** his mum thinks it's smaller than she had expected.

**B** his mum will give him driving lessons when he's old enough.

**C** the car is second-hand.

**9** You will hear two friends talking about a school trip.
What does the girl say about the day of the trip?

**A** They can go shopping when they get back.

**B** There are some interesting activities arranged for them in the museum.

**C** She will have to get up earlier than usual.

**10** You will hear a mother and her son talking about exams.
What changes are there to the exam timetable?

**A** Maths is now on a different day.

**B** There are fewer exams on Friday.

**C** They are not doing exams on Friday.

**11** You will hear two friends talking about keeping animals in a zoo.
What do they agree about?

**A** Zoos help us protect some animals.

**B** They feel angry about the fact that animals are kept in zoos.

**C** They think the animals are badly treated.

**12** You will hear two friends talking about writing essays.
What does the girl say about using a computer?

**A** She doesn't like using one.

**B** She makes too many mistakes.

**C** Using a computer will affect her handwriting.

**13** You will hear two friends talking about a piece of furniture.
The girl says

**A** her sister needs a wardrobe for university.

**B** she's only had the bed a short while.

**C** the new desk she bought has fallen apart.

## Part 3

35

### Questions 14–19

For each question, write the correct answer in the gap. Write **one** or **two words** or a **number** or a **date** or a **time**.

You will hear a man talking about a college open evening.

---

### College Open Evening

Interested in studying in a more adult environment? Come along to our Open Evening on **(14)** ………………..

You will be shown round the college by our student **(15)** …………….…... .

We'll give you a timetable of events and a **(16)** …………….…… when you arrive.

There will be a dance performance at **(17)** …………………...

For further details of subjects, pick up our **(18)** ……………..….. from reception.

Please hand your **(19)** ……………..….. in to a teacher before you leave.

---

# Part 4

## Questions 20–25

For each question, choose the correct answer.

_____

You will hear an interview with a young woman called Jemma Bruce, who is an award-wining baker.

**20** Jemma explains that the baking competition
    **A** led to her being on TV.
    **B** was between students at her school.
    **C** was not easy to win.

**21** What does Jemma say about her grandmother?
    **A** Her grandmother used to take care of her when she was little.
    **B** Her grandmother didn't like going to the park.
    **C** Jemma always had to help her grandmother with painting.

**22** Jemma says her parents
    **A** don't bother to do the cooking every evening.
    **B** would be happy for Jemma to cook dinner sometimes.
    **C** take an interest in her baking skills.

**23** What does Jemma say about baking cakes?
    **A** It's sometimes difficult to find the ingredients she needs.
    **B** She sometimes forgets to do her schoolwork.
    **C** It gives her the chance to forget about things at school.

**24** How did Jemma feel about baking a cake for her grandmother's birthday?
    **A** She didn't like people watching her making it.
    **B** She knew people were looking forward to seeing it.
    **C** She was no more nervous than usual.

**25** In the future, Jemma
    **A** hopes she can bake when she goes to university.
    **B** wants to bake the perfect cake.
    **C** knows what she wants to study.

# Test 5 SPEAKING

1A

1B

Audio scripts and Model answers on pages 183–249.

## Some sports a teenager could do with her friends

Audio scripts and Model answers on pages 183–249.

# Test 6

# Test 6 READING

## Part 1

## Questions 1–5

For each question, choose the correct answer.

---

**1**

Hi Steve

I hope you had a great holiday with your family.

Let me know if you can play next Saturday so I can tell the team captain.

John

**A** John wants to know if Steve is enjoying his holiday.

**B** Steve needs to contact the captain.

**C** John wants to know if Steve can play this weekend.

**2**

**LAPTOP FOR SALE**

In very good condition and comes with laptop bag.
Needs a new battery but still works.

**A** The battery has a fault.

**B** The laptop has been used for work.

**C** The bag costs extra.

**3**

**Collecting a parcel?**

Please bring something to prove who you are when picking up parcels from the customer help desk.

**A** Please bring something to identify yourself.

**B** Bring your parcel to the help desk.

**C** Ask for help if you need to pick up parcels.

**4**

Hi Emma,

Are you still going shopping for Mum's present?

I forgot to get a card, so could you get one for me?

Helen

A Helen needs to get a present for her mum.

B Helen didn't remember to get a card.

C Helen wants to go shopping with Emma.

**5**

**Parents evening**
Please go to reception and collect our information sheet before meeting your child's teacher.

A Parents should give the information sheet to a teacher.

B Please meet your teacher at reception.

C Please go to reception first.

# Part 2

## Questions 6–10

For each question, choose the correct answer.

---

The young people below are all interested in doing an after-school activity.
On the opposite page there are descriptions of eight after-school activities.
Decide which activity would be the most suitable for the people below.

**6**  Federica gets quite stressed during exams and is interested in finding ways to relax. She has an exam soon and would like to find something that she can start on a Monday or Tuesday.

**7**  Tomoko wants to learn how to play a musical instrument. She would like to be able to practise at home as well as at school but can't afford to buy an instrument herself.

**8**  Miguel is interested in art and would like to study it at university. He has exams coming up soon and would like to have the chance to get help with his painting and drawing skills.

**9**  Robert has often dreamt of having his own business when he leaves school. He would like to learn more about how to use the Internet to develop a business idea.

**10**  Sinita enjoys working on computers and is keen to learn about web design. Her family has a small business and she would like to be able to create a website for it during the activity.

# After-school activities

## A Get Playing

Mr Evans is running his music group every Wednesday from 3.30 p.m. to 5.00 p.m. Don't forget to bring your musical instrument along, as we only have a small number ourselves and might not even have the one you play. We're hoping to form a school orchestra and to play at the end of the school year.

## E Exam Help

We're pleased to announce the start of our exam preparation classes for art students. Planning and timing is important if you're facing an exam, so come along on a Monday afternoon for tips from Mrs Simpson. If you have something you are working on at the moment, why not bring it along?

## B Build It!

Come along to the IT room on Tuesday after school and learn how to create attractive web pages. We'll look at some of the main things that make websites user-friendly and show you how to make one yourself. Come along with an idea of what you want your website for, and we'll help you build it.

## F Your Choice

Now's your chance to learn a new skill that will give you hours of enjoyment. Our music group meets every Thursday. Try a wide range of instruments until you find the one that suits you. Once you've discovered it, you'll get the chance to practise and can even borrow the instrument to play in your own time.

## C Gallery Visit

If you're looking for things to do after school, why not join us this week when we visit the art gallery? Each week we look at a different painter and examine his or her works. You'll be amazed by some of the stories we have to tell and will learn what inspired some of the world's best-known artists.

## G Don't Mention Exams

If you're bored with exams and would like something different to occupy your mind, why not come along to room 229 every Wednesday and join the 'talk club'? Each week we will discuss a topic that is very important today. You'll develop your discussion skills and have the chance to forget about exams for an hour or two.

## D Time for You

Join our small group of students for one hour of rest and relaxation. Feel lighter and happier as you practise breathing deeply and learn ways to help you clear your mind of stressful or unhappy thoughts. We run our group on Monday afternoon immediately after lessons, so you'll be able to practise as much as you need.

## H Selling in the 21st century

The world wide web has completely changed the way business is carried out. Join our group on Thursday at 3.30 p.m. to look at how marketing works in the 21st century. Learn how well-known businesses make use of the Internet to increase customer numbers and make sales. If you have a business idea this is an opportunity you can't afford to miss.

## Part 3

### Questions 11–15

For each question, choose the correct answer.

---

# Your Choice

*Elena Reynolds tells us what subjects her friends think should be taught at school*

It's not often you get the chance to decide which subjects you should be learning at school. So when our teacher asked us for our opinion we were quick to offer suggestions. The discussion proved to be so interesting that the school has told us they are thinking about how three of our ideas could be added to the curriculum. What do you think about our three suggestions?

Number one on our list was being able to offer help to someone who has had an accident or been taken ill. We are all used to sitting in the biology class learning about all the different parts of the human body, but we aren't taught what to do if something goes seriously wrong. One of us could have an accident at school, for example, and nobody would know what to do. We felt very strongly that having training in how to give first aid to someone in need, perhaps a brother, sister, friend or parent, could end up saving someone's life.

The next subject we felt was important was how to manage financial matters. We learn how to work out complicated problems in our maths classes, but nobody tells us how to work out how much we might owe if we borrow money. Learning maths is important, but it is just as important to learn how to manage our money – something that is never taught. We all agreed that this would help us later in life when we will have to make our money last, pay our bills and know how best to save.

Finally, the last subject on our list was learning what your rights are as a shopper. We all know somebody who had been cheated by a company or sold something that didn't work as it should. But how many of those people knew the best way to make a complaint or what the law says about issues like this? We felt that knowledge of things like this would put us in a much stronger position in the future when we have difficulties.

We all now hope that our suggestions will be considered by the school and perhaps we'll be given the chance to learn these important skills.

**11** What does Elena say about her school?

    **A** Students are never asked for their opinion.

    **B** The curriculum never changes.

    **C** The school has now changed the curriculum.

    **D** It has listened to the students' suggestions.

**12** What does Elena think is the problem with learning biology?

    **A** Things often go wrong in the lesson.

    **B** Students spend too long sitting at their desks.

    **C** It doesn't teach skills to use in an emergency.

    **D** Knowledge of it helps save someone's life.

**13** Elena says that learning about personal finance

    **A** is more important than doing maths.

    **B** is important for when students get older.

    **C** can be complicated.

    **D** will stop people borrowing money.

**14** Why does Elena think students need to learn about people's rights as shoppers?

    **A** All companies cheat their customers.

    **B** It will stop companies producing things that don't work properly.

    **C** It will give people more power when they have a problem.

    **D** She was once sold something that didn't work.

**15** What would Elena say about these skills?

| | |
|---|---|
| **A** They can help people when they face challenges in life. | **B** Schools will never teach subjects like these. |
| **C** They can only give people a basic understanding of issues. | **D** School isn't the best place to learn them. |

## Part 4

### Questions 16–20

Five sentences have been removed from the text below.
For each question, choose the correct answer.
There are three extra sentences which you do not need to use.

---

# Learning English Through Film

*Solange Figueira tells us about her school's English Film Club*

My friends and I have all been learning English at school for the last three years and I think we all enjoy it. However, some of us thought it could be made more fun sometimes if we could learn it in different ways than just sitting in the classroom. **16** That's when we had the idea of starting a film club where we could watch and discuss films in English. Not just films, but perhaps a TV series that is available at the time.

We spoke about the idea with our teacher and she agreed it was a great suggestion. **17** Because we had a busy timetable preparing for exams, we couldn't have the club during our lessons. So, in the end we decided to run it after school before we went home. We agreed to meet once a month and to allow enough time to watch the film or programme and then discuss it afterwards.

That was six months ago, and I can report that it has been a fantastic success. We have a room in the school where students can meet to relax. It has comfortable chairs, somewhere to make hot drinks and it doesn't really feel like being at school. We use this room for our film shows. **18** Some people sit in the armchairs, others lie around on the floor on soft cushions. We have a big TV screen at the front of the room which we use to show the films.

The school has been really helpful. **19** Each month before we end a session we ask for suggestions for the next meeting. We decide what it is we want to watch, and the teacher orders it ready for the next session. I enjoy watching the films but the discussions that follow are great. **20** I think because we've been listening to the language for an hour or two, it's easier to speak it afterwards.

---

**A** Our teacher rarely has to ask us to remember to speak in English.

**B** The problem was when to do it.

**C** Therefore we have to meet on different days.

**D** But some films aren't very good for listening practice.

**E** It has opened an account we use to buy films or series online.

**F** Practising grammar and vocabulary from books can sometimes get a little boring.

**G** Sometimes we find it difficult to agree what to watch.

**H** It's just like being at home really.

## Part 5

### Questions 21–26

For each question, choose the correct answer.

---

### Gràcia Festival

If you're visiting Barcelona in August, be sure not to miss one of its most well-known festivals, *La Fiesta Major de Gràcia* or Gràcia Festival. This festival **(21)** ........... for one week and is extremely popular. Each year streets in the Gràcia **(22)** ........... of the city have a competition to see which one can be the best decorated street of all. People **(23)** ........... on an idea for their street and then decorate it. The street can often become a tunnel of light and colour. Visitors can enjoy plays and **(24)** ........... music, which take place in the **(25)** ........... squares of Gràcia, and try some of the local food from street markets. The festival gets very busy and it can take ages to get from one **(26)** ........... of a street to the other, especially during the evening, when locals join the tourists to enjoy the festivities.

---

| 21 | **A** lasts | **B** goes | **C** holds | **D** rests |
|----|----|----|----|----|
| 22 | **A** route | **B** piece | **C** place | **D** area |
| 23 | **A** discuss | **B** choose | **C** decide | **D** make |
| 24 | **A** live | **B** alive | **C** living | **D** life |
| 25 | **A** head | **B** main | **C** first | **D** key |
| 26 | **A** edge | **B** line | **C** top | **D** end |

## Part 6

### Questions 27–32

For each question, write the correct answer.
Write **one** word for each gap.

---

# The Great Wall of China
## *by Freddie Chapman*

We've been learning about the Great Wall of China in school. I didn't know that it's actually a number of shorter walls rather **(27)** ..................... one long one. Different sections **(28)** ..................... built over many years, with work beginning over 2,000 years ago. Originally, China was made up of separate states and the wall began as a defence from invasions from the north by individual states.

The part from the Ming Dynasty (1368–1644) is an incredible 8,850 kilometres long and it's difficult **(29)** ..................... imagine that it was all built by hand. It must **(30)** ..................... been very dangerous work as lots of people are supposed to have died when it was built. A lot of the wall has been badly damaged over the years, but **(31)** ..................... of the best sections are around Beijing and it has become a very popular tourist destination. In fact, it became so popular **(32)** ..................... the Chinese government decided to limit the number of people who could visit it each day.

# Test 6 WRITING

## Part 1

You **must** answer this question.
Write your answer in about **100 words** on the answer sheet.

---

### Question 1

Read this email from your headteacher Mr Talbot and the notes you have made.

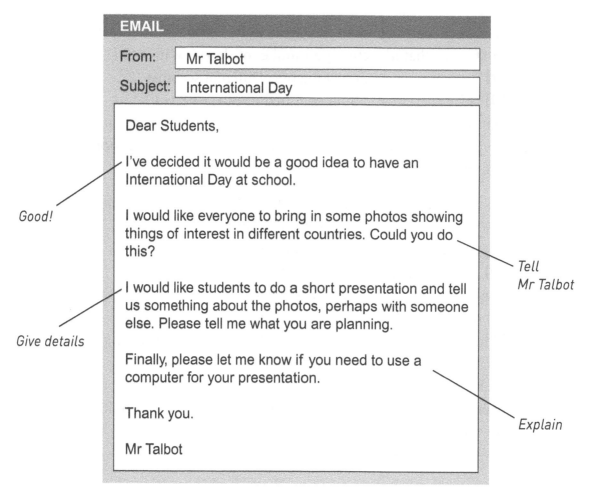

**EMAIL**

From: Mr Talbot

Subject: International Day

Dear Students,

I've decided it would be a good idea to have an International Day at school. — *Good!*

I would like everyone to bring in some photos showing things of interest in different countries. Could you do this? — *Tell Mr Talbot*

I would like students to do a short presentation and tell us something about the photos, perhaps with someone else. Please tell me what you are planning. — *Give details*

Finally, please let me know if you need to use a computer for your presentation. — *Explain*

Thank you.

Mr Talbot

Write your **email** to Mr Talbot using **all the notes**.

## Part 2

Choose **one** of these questions.
Write your answer in about **100 words** on the answer sheet.

---

## Question 2

You see this notice in an English-language magazine.

**Articles wanted!**

**WHAT KIND OF FOOD DO YOU LIKE TO EAT?**

Is it something you eat at home?

When do you usually eat it?

**Write an article answering these questions and we will put it in our magazine.**

Write your **article**.

## Question 3

Your English teacher has asked you to write a story.

Your story must begin with this sentence.

*It was 8.30 and I was late for school.*

Write your **story**.

# Test 6 LISTENING

## Part 1

### Questions 1–7

For each question, choose the correct answer.

---

**1** Where does the boy think his homework is?

A

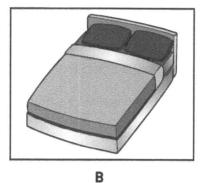

B

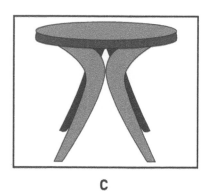

C

**2** What does the girl's father want her to buy?

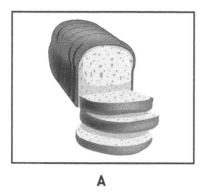

A

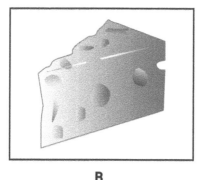

B

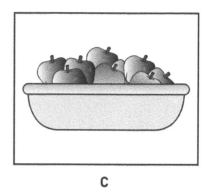

C

**3** What does the boy want to hire?

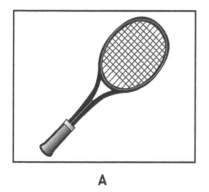

A

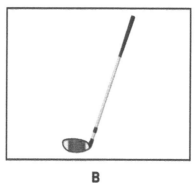

B

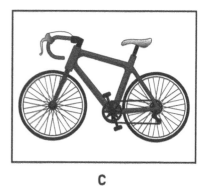

C

**4**   What has been damaged?

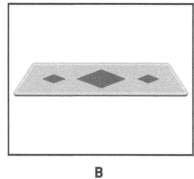

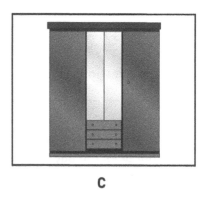

A                        B                        C

**5**   Why might the students be back late?

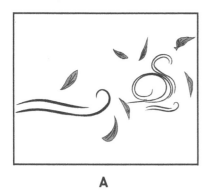

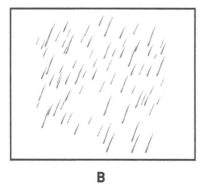

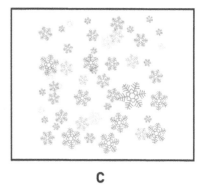

A                        B                        C

**6**   What is the girl not interested in?

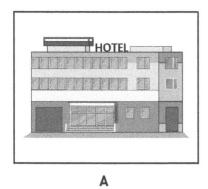

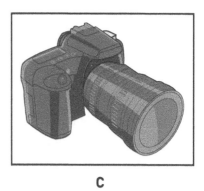

A                        B                        C

**7**   Which date is the girl's birthday?

A                        B                        C

# Part 2

42

## Questions 8–13

For each question, choose the correct answer.

---

**8** You will hear two friends talking about a book.
What does the boy say about it?

  **A**  He is enjoying it.

  **B**  He wouldn't read it if he had the choice.

  **C**  He knows how it ends.

**9** You will hear two friends talking about a bicycle.
The girl says

  **A**  she has to phone the shop to see if it's ready to collect.

  **B**  she is going to take her bike to school.

  **C**  she has been too busy to go to the shop.

**10** You will hear a father and his daughter talking about her brother Alan.
What do they decide to do?

  **A**  The daughter will cook the dinner.

  **B**  tell Alan he might have to heat his dinner up

  **C**  tell Alan to get something to eat while he's out

**11** You will hear two friends talking about travelling to a new school.
The girl thinks

  **A**  the bus will take too long.

  **B**  the train is too expensive.

  **C**  she could walk part of the way.

**12** You will hear two friends talking about feeling nervous before an exam.
What does the girl advise the boy to do?

  **A**  Be prepared to arrive early.

  **B**   Chat with friends before the exam.

  **C**  Revise the night before.

**13** You will hear two friends talking about a library they go to.
The boy says the staff

  **A**  are not very polite at times.

  **B**  are always telling him to be quiet.

  **C**  are slow to serve people.

## Part 3

### Questions 14–19

For each question, write the correct answer in the gap. Write **one** or **two words** or a **number** or a **date** or a **time**.

You will hear a man talking about a football training course.

---

## Football Training

Keen to **(14)** ..................... and learn new skills? Join our training programme.

The sessions will be led by a **(15)** ...................... trainer.

Find out if you're playing in the best **(16)** ..................... on the field.

You can join one of our **(17)** ........................ different groups, depending on your ability.

The course starts on **(18)** .....................

For further information, collect an application form from the **(19)** ...................... .

## Part 4

44

## Questions 20–25

For each question, choose the correct answer.

---

You will hear an interview with a boy called Jason Wright, who does skateboarding.

**20** What does Jason say about his first attempt at skateboarding?

   **A** He knew he would be good.

   **B** He found it difficult to stand on the skateboard.

   **C** He found it easier than he expected.

**21** Jason says that beginners

   **A** think everyone is better than them.

   **B** can learn from others.

   **C** shouldn't do certain tricks until they are advanced.

**22** What does Jason say about equipment?

   **A** You can often find a cheap helmet.

   **B** Don't use cycling equipment for skateboarding.

   **C** Be willing to spend more on good quality equipment.

**23** Jason says people taking up skateboarding

   **A** are likely to get injured.

   **B** must be serious about doing it.

   **C** should try other sports as well.

**24** When trying a new trick Jason says

   **A** he is sometimes nervous.

   **B** he always falls over.

   **C** he doesn't give up until he succeeds.

**25** What does Jason say is one advantage of skateboarding?

   **A** There are always skateparks nearby.

   **B** You can do it by yourself.

   **C** It's more fun than football.

# Test 6 SPEAKING

1A

1B

Audio scripts and Model answers on pages 183–249.

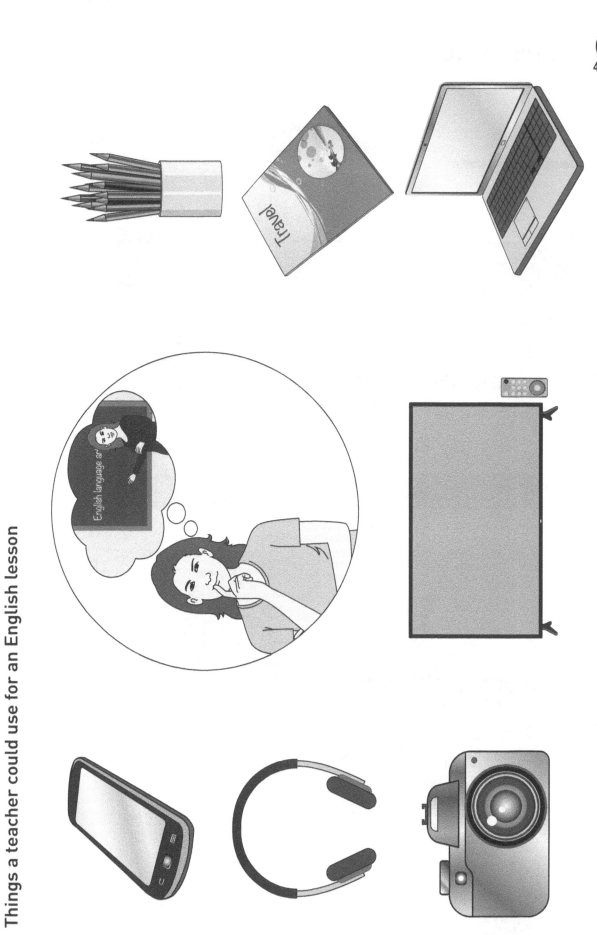

**Things a teacher could use for an English lesson**

Audio scripts and Model answers on pages 183–249.

47–48

# Test 7

# Test 7 READING

## Part 1

### Questions 1–5

For each question, choose the correct answer.

---

1

**PLAYGROUND FLOODS**

**Due to heavy rain the playground is closed until further notice.
Use the main hall for your break.**

**A** You will be informed when the playground is open again.

**B** Please see the notice in the playground.

**C** Heavy rain has damaged the hall.

2

Hi Ann

Thanks for the invite to your party but I'm visiting my grandmother that day. Can I give you your present this evening?

Call me so we can arrange to meet later.

Janet

**A** Janet's grandmother is visiting her.

**B** Janet is sorry for giving Ann her present late.

**C** Janet wants to see Ann today.

3

**EXAMS**

**Are you taking the English exam?
You can't enter unless exam fees have been paid before Friday.**

**A** Friday is the last day to pay for exams.

**B** Please pay fees by Thursday.

**C** Do not enter the exam room.

**4**

| To: Evie |
| From: Jenny |
| Hiya Evie |
| I phoned the dance class. It costs £9.50 but there's a student discount. |
| We can pay when we arrive but we must book to make sure there's a place for us. |
| Jenny |

A  They have to pay before the day of the lesson.

B  They need to reserve a place.

C  Students pay £9.50.

**5**

> ## School snacks
> All our sandwiches were made today.
> 50% off cold drinks.
> Open 12.00–4.00

A  Sandwiches are fresh today

B  Sandwiches need to be eaten today.

C  Everything half price between 12.00 and 4.00.

# Part 2

## Questions 6–10

For each question, choose the correct answer.

---

The young people below all want to go into town to buy something.
On the opposite page there are eight descriptions of eight shops.
Decide which shop would be the most suitable for the people below.

**6**

Debbie is looking for a dress for her end-of-year school party. Her mum and dad are paying but they have told her they don't want to spend too much.

**7**

William needs some football boots. He can only go on Thursday evening, so he is looking for somewhere that opens late. He must have the boots before Saturday as he is playing that day.

**8**

Michael wants a present for his mother's birthday. She has just taken an interest in baking and wants to start making cakes, but she doesn't have much equipment. He is going into town on Thursday evening.

**9**

Paul is going to his friend's party tonight and wants to buy a cake to take with him. He only has his pocket money to spend so he is looking for a bargain.

**10**

Donna has just had her bedroom decorated and wants something to put on the wall. She would love to have a few photos of her favourite singers or pop groups to look at.

# Shops in town

## A Suzie's

Don't miss our closing down sale! Come along to Suzie's while you still can! Everything must go before we close our doors for the last time on Saturday. We have posters of your favourite artists, CDs, music magazines and much more. Everything is 'buy one and get one free'. Open late all week.

## E Belle

Coming soon! We're pleased to announce that Belle will be opening on Saturday 11 August. We have high-quality clothing for the fashion-conscious older woman. We believe that age is just a number and our dresses, skirts, blouses and more will have you looking like a thousand dollars.

## B Salford City FC Shop

Looking for a present for that football fan friend? The Salford City FC Shop is situated just around the corner from the ground and has a range of souvenirs. Buy the club shirt or scarf, check out our ties in club colours or pick a photo or poster of one of your favourite players.

## F Michelle's

Come in and look around Michelle's and enjoy the latest in fashion for young people. We are a well-known store offering customer satisfaction with items at reasonable prices. We offer a fantastic range of clothes and accessories – that stylish dress for a special occasion or something casual to wear around the house.

## C HG Sports

Don't miss our half term offers. Make the most of your school holiday and come along to HG Sports for our special prices on sports clothes. We stock all the top names in sportswear for all major sports. And don't forget we are open for late night shopping every Tuesday and Thursday until 9.00 p.m.

## G Prices Books

The well-known award-winning baker and author Tania Wilkes will be coming into the shop on Saturday. Tania will be talking about her latest book, which is full of delicious recipes for cakes, bread and sweets. You'll have the chance to ask Tania any questions and purchase a signed copy of her book.

## D Emma's Cakes

Looking for a cake for a special occasion or something to enjoy after dinner? We guarantee we'll have something that will put a smile on your face or the face of the lucky person you're buying for. All our cakes are made the same day, and don't forget we reduce prices on everything after 5.00 p.m. so nothing gets wasted.

## H Lakefields

We offer a great selection of products, often at reduced prices. You'll find everything for the kitchen, bedroom, bathroom or living room. This week we have a special offer on everything for the cook and baker, with up to 50% off some of our kitchen products. Be quick as things are selling fast.

## Part 3

### Questions 11–15

For each question, choose the correct answer.

---

# The Joy of Language

*Friedrich Conti, aged 15, talks about speaking more than one language*

I was born in Berlin. My mother is German and my dad is Italian. They both speak each other's language quite well, so I grew up hearing and slowly learning both. But it didn't stop there. When I was three years old we moved to the UK, and we've been here ever since. I found myself surrounded by people speaking something completely different and started to discover English too. And the result is that I can speak three languages.

My friends find it hard to imagine how I didn't get very confused, hearing all these different languages around me as I grew up. But it wasn't a problem at all. On some days my parents spoke Italian, on another day it was German. It wasn't something they 'taught' me. I just got used to understanding and slowly speaking each one. When we moved and I went to school the same thing happened; I found myself learning English just by being around English people.

Perhaps because I haven't had to work at this I have a very positive attitude about learning languages. It has certainly been helpful at school. I'm studying French and, compared to some of my friends, I don't find it very difficult. And the German teacher often invites me into her conversation classes to help out, which I really enjoy. I don't know what I want to do when I finish school but I certainly like the idea of studying languages at university – which ones, I don't yet know.

I do know I'm very lucky to be in this position and I try to encourage my friends to learn another language, even though I can see it must be hard for some of them. Compared to some school subjects, you can get so much pleasure from learning another language. If you visit the country where people speak the language you're learning, you have a great chance to practise. There's something special about reading novels in the original language and even watching foreign films. And I know that having a second or third language is really useful when you start looking for a job.

---

**11** When Friedrich was a child

   **A**  he lived in Italy for a while.

   **B**  he was always surrounded by lots of people at home.

   **C**  his parents spoke to him in English.

   **D**  he heard his parents speak German and Italian.

**12** What does Friedrich say about growing up?

   **A**  His friends were confused when he spoke a different language.

   **B**  People had a problem understanding him.

   **C**  He learnt the languages in a natural way.

   **D**  His parents spoke to him slowly.

**13** At school Friedrich

   **A**  finds French easier to learn than some of his friends.

   **B**  gets help from his German teacher.

   **C**  doesn't work very hard.

   **D**  has learnt that positive thinking helps when learning a language.

**14** What does Friedrich say about learning another language?

   **A**  Schools should encourage students to do it.

   **B**  You can read different novels.

   **C**  It has advantages that some other subjects don't offer.

   **D**  It's harder than other subjects.

**15** What would be a good opening sentence to this article?

**A**
| Learning languages was much more fun before I went to school. |
| --- |

**B**
| My family background has been such a help for my studies. |
| --- |

**C**
| Managing three languages was quite a challenge before I started school. |
| --- |

**D**
| My parents often told me the importance of learning another language. |
| --- |

# Part 4

## Questions 16–20

Five sentences have been removed from the text below.
For each question, choose the correct answer.
There are three extra sentences which you do not need to use.

---

# Environmental Concerns

*Amy Fisher is angry at the way we are polluting our world*

Young people today are becoming more and more concerned about the environment and how slowly we seem to be dealing with the problems we face. A recent event where I live made me and my friends particularly angry. Not long ago a local company in my town was fined for pouring dangerous chemicals in a river that runs near our school. It used to be somewhere my friends went in the summer to fish or swim. **16**

It's true that we are all responsible for the problem. The amount of stuff we waste and just throw away with no thought for the environment is shocking. A lot of the rubbish we put in the dustbin gets buried under the ground. **17** Some of it ends up in the sea and, of course, the oceans around the world are becoming polluted with plastics, putting the lives of some of our most loved creatures in danger.

We can all reduce the amount of rubbish we throw out by simply recycling, or by thinking how we can reuse items better. This would help reduce the amount of our rubbish that ends up getting buried in the ground. But I think companies are also responsible. **18** Surely it would be possible to sell these in materials that are easier to recycle, like paper or cardboard?

I think the government should be much better at encouraging companies to be more friendly to the environment. **19** This would help avoid the growing amount of waste that is difficult to recycle. I think companies that do act in a responsible way should be given an award for being a good example to other businesses.

And those companies like the one that polluted our local river should be punished much more. It's illegal to throw rubbish away like this in my country. **20** I think the government should have much stronger punishments for companies that act in such a selfish way.

---

**A** But nobody listened to us.

**B** Why are they wrapping food and other goods in plastic?

**C** However, they will continue to do it.

**D** It should try to persuade businesses to change the way they wrap goods.

**E** Now people are not allowed to go near it.

**F** But where does all this plastic come from?

**G** Yet some companies are still prepared to do it.

**H** As a result, the land gets polluted by dangerous materials.

# Part 5

## Questions 21–26

For each question, choose the correct answer.

---

### Chocolate

The Spanish explorer Hernán Cortés was the first European to see the Aztec Indians **(21)** ............ a warm drink made of chocolate. He brought it back to Spain, where sugar was added to the drink and it quickly **(22)** ............ very popular. However, since it was expensive to produce, it was only **(23)** ............ members of Spanish society who could enjoy it. Spain then decided to grow the cacao tree itself, but **(24)** ............ though the way of making it remained secret for many years, other countries eventually started to produce their own. It continued to be a luxury drink for the rich until machines **(25)** ............ along and made it cheaper to produce. But we have Daniel Peter of Vevey, Switzerland, to thank for the milk chocolate bar. In 1876 he invented a way of making milk chocolate to eat and later went on to **(26)** ............ the Nestlé company with Henri Nestlé.

---

| | | | | | | | |
|---|---|---|---|---|---|---|---|
| **21** | **A** doing | **B** preparing | **C** building | **D** working |
| **22** | **A** became | **B** turned | **C** reached | **D** fell |
| **23** | **A** expensive | **B** rich | **C** high | **D** full |
| **24** | **A** just | **B** same | **C** equal | **D** even |
| **25** | **A** made | **B** set | **C** came | **D** ran |
| **26** | **A** start | **B** set | **C** switch | **D** do |

## Part 6

### Questions 27–32

For each question, write the correct answer.
Write **one** word for each gap.

---

## Taking a Year Off
*by Lucy Andrews*

Our careers tutor was talking today about what's called a gap year. She started **(27)** ..................... explaining that taking a year out between school and university can be a sensible decision rather **(28)** ..................... going straight back into studying. Getting a job means you can save some money, which would be helpful when you go to university. You will also gain useful skills, which will be just **(29)** ..................... important when you go to job interviews after university. Many people spend the year travelling. This doesn't **(30)** ..................... to be expensive as there are also job opportunities in other countries that would help you pay for your time away from home. **(31)** ..................... is usually possible to find work in hotels or restaurants. The main point though is to plan this well or it can become a wasted year when you sit around doing nothing **(32)** ..................... university starts.

# Test 7 WRITING

## Part 1

You **must** answer this question.
Write your answer in about **100 words** on the answer sheet.

___

### Question 1

Read this email from your English-speaking friend Chris and the notes you have made.

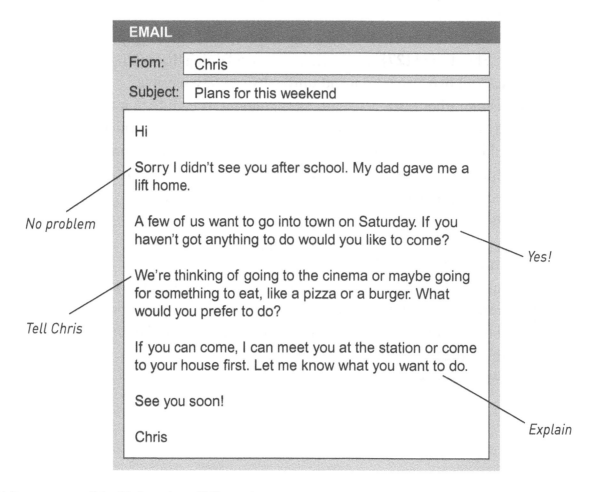

**EMAIL**

From: Chris

Subject: Plans for this weekend

Hi

Sorry I didn't see you after school. My dad gave me a lift home. — *No problem*

A few of us want to go into town on Saturday. If you haven't got anything to do would you like to come? — *Yes!*

We're thinking of going to the cinema or maybe going for something to eat, like a pizza or a burger. What would you prefer to do? — *Tell Chris*

If you can come, I can meet you at the station or come to your house first. Let me know what you want to do. — *Explain*

See you soon!

Chris

Write your **email** to Chris using **all the notes**.

## Part 2

Choose **one** of these questions.
Write your answer in about **100 words** on the answer sheet.

---

## Question 2

You see this notice in an English-language magazine.

**Articles wanted!**

**IS THERE A SPORT YOU LIKE?**

Do you play it or watch it?

What do you like about it?

**Write an article answering these questions and we will put it in our magazine.**

Write your **article**.

## Question 3

Your English teacher has asked you to write a story.

Your story must begin with this sentence.

*I checked every pocket but my keys weren't there.*

Write your **story**.

# Test 7 LISTENING

## Part 1

### Questions 1–7

For each question, choose the correct answer.

---

**1**   When is the concert?

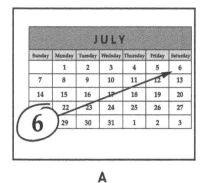

A                                      B                                      C

**2**   What did the boy's mother enjoy doing at the party?

A

B                                                                          C

**3**   What was the weather like on the journey to the football match?

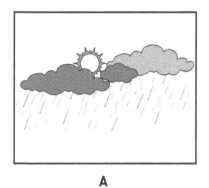

A

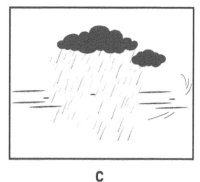

B                                                                          C

**4** What time does the exam start?

A        B        C

**5** What is the girl's mother doing?

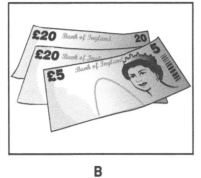
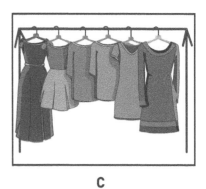

A        B        C

**6** What size of shirt does the boy need?

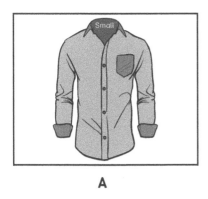
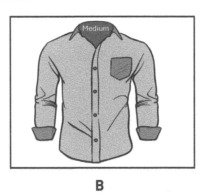
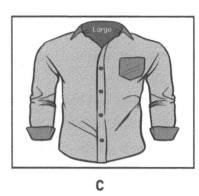

A        B        C

**7** What did the father do that was wrong?

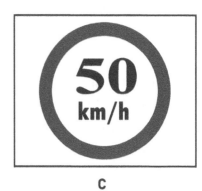

A        B        C

# Part 2

50

## Questions 8–13

For each question, choose the correct answer.

---

**8** You will hear two friends talking about school dinners.
The boys says

   **A** the queue is too long.

   **B** he's trying to eat healthy food.

   **C** there are some days he doesn't like the food on offer.

**9** You will hear two friends talking about their plans for the weekend.
Why is the girl staying at home?

   **A** Some of their friends can't come out.

   **B** The shopping centre will be busy.

   **C** She has people visiting.

**10** You will hear a brother and sister talking about where they want to sit in their mother's car.
What do they agree to do?

   **A** They will sit in different seats on the way there and on the way back.

   **B** They will both sit in the back.

   **C** They will ask their mother to decide.

**11** You will hear two friends talking about a school party.
The boy says

   **A** there will be lots of food.

   **B** it will be better than last year's party.

   **C** he finds the teachers funny.

**12** You will hear two friends talking about a laptop.
What does the girl say about it?

   **A** It's sometimes quite slow to start.

   **B** She likes it better than her previous one.

   **C** She needs to buy some programs for it.

**13** You will hear two friends talking about the weather.
What does the boy say they should do?

   **A** be prepared to change their plans

   **B** stay at home

   **C** go to the cinema

## Part 3

### Questions 14–19

For each question, write the correct answer in the gap. Write **one** or **two words** or a **number** or a **date** or a **time**.

You will hear a girl called Sarah talking about one of her interests.

> ## My Interests
>
> Sarah has helped out at the leisure centre for
> **(14)** ……………….. months.
>
> She discovered she liked it after serving at a
> **(15)** …………….…... for older people.
>
> Now, she is helping teenagers with an **(16)** ………………...
>
> She helps out at the centre for about **(17)** …………………...
> hours per month.
>
> Sarah feels more **(18)** ………………….. since she became a
> volunteer.
>
> When she has **(19)** ……………….…. for jobs her record of being
> a volunteer will be very useful.

# Part 4

52

## Questions 20–25

For each question, choose the correct answer.

---

You will hear an interview with a boy called John Edwards, who is talking about camping.

**20** What does John say about school?

   **A**  He often thinks about other things than studying.

   **B**  He enjoys lessons that take place outside.

   **C**  He doesn't really like it.

**21** John says

   **A**  he misses not having central heating when he's camping.

   **B**  camping makes him feel good.

   **C**  you have to get up earlier when you're camping.

**22** What does John say about his friends?

   **A**  He has given up trying to get some of them to go camping.

   **B**  They don't all agree that camping is enjoyable.

   **C**  They have all been camping at least once.

**23** John says putting up a tent

   **A**  is more enjoyable if you do it with other people.

   **B**  should be avoided in bad weather.

   **C**  takes longer to do in bad weather.

**24** Why does John say camping is better than staying in a hotel?

   **A**  He doesn't like hotel food.

   **B**  You don't have to check in.

   **C**  He enjoys the food more.

**25** Who will John be going camping on holiday with this year?

   **A**  His friends.

   **B**  His parents.

   **C**  He doesn't know yet.

# Test 7 SPEAKING

53–54

1A

1B

Audio scripts spend Model answers on pages 183–249.

55–56

A pet for a family with young children

Audio scripts and Model answers on pages 183–249.

# Test 8

# Test 8 READING

## Part 1

### Questions 1–5

For each question, choose the correct answer.

---

1

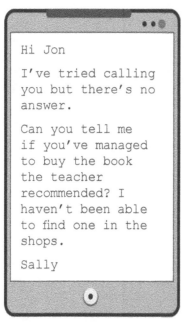

Hi Jon

I've tried calling you but there's no answer.

Can you tell me if you've managed to buy the book the teacher recommended? I haven't been able to find one in the shops.

Sally

**A** The shops don't have the book.

**B** Sally has lost her book.

**C** Sally wants to know the name of the book the teacher recommended.

---

2

**FOR SALE**

Skateboard, including lots of safety equipment. As good as new.
£15 or near offer.

**A** The skateboard is in perfect condition.

**B** Safety equipment costs extra.

**C** It will cost at least £15.

---

3

**Table Tennis Competition**

Free entry for members of the centre.
There is a small charge for non-members.
No registration on competition day.

**A** Sign up on the day of the competition.

**B** There is no charge for members.

**C** Only members can join the competition.

**4**

| To: David |
| --- |
| **Subject**: Your phone |
| Hi!<br><br>You left your mobile phone at my house when you came round this evening.<br><br>My dad says he'll put it through your letterbox in the morning before school.<br><br>Jamie |

A  Remember to collect your mobile phone before school tomorrow.

B  Come round this evening to get your phone.

C  My dad will drop your phone through your door tomorrow morning.

**5**

### Notice

This room is booked for exams.
Please go to Room 204 and the secretary will advise you.

A  The class will take place in Room 204.

B  No books allowed in exam room.

C  Speak to the secretary for help.

## Part 2

### Questions 6–10

For each question, choose the correct answer.

---

The young people below all want to download an app.
On the opposite page there are descriptions of eight apps.
Decide which app would be the most suitable for the people below.

**6**  Carlos likes playing games on his phone. His favourites are those that allow him to play against his friends. He is very careful about staying safe online and wants to decide who he plays against.

**7**  Federico is mad about sport and wants an app that will allow him to keep up with all the latest news. He's particularly interested in French, German and UK football and loves talking about football.

**8**  Elaine is looking for an app that will help her order food online. She wants one that offers information about lots of different restaurants in her area that can deliver to her house.

**9**  Jan loves going to music concerts and wants an app that could tell her which singers and bands are playing in her area. If she could buy tickets through the app that would be perfect.

**10**  Leonora is keen on keeping fit and is looking for an app she can use to measure her fitness level. Her favourite sports are running and cycling. She also is careful with her diet.

# Recommended apps

## A Snazzer

Snazzer is the number one app for those interested in making sure they don't miss their favourite acts. Sign up, tell us who your favourite band and singers are and we'll email you a weekly list of performances within your area. If you find one listed you can book your place online.

## B BitRelease

Download BitRelease for the best songs and playlists available. Weekly interviews with your favourite singers or bands, reviews of the latest performances and the chance to join well-known artists and ask them questions in our weekly online discussion groups. You can even buy your favourite tracks from our online store.

## C Results Xtra

If you can't make a game or your favourite team plays miles away and you need minute-by-minute news of all the action, Results Xtra is for you. We have reports of European soccer matches, live as they happen. Join our competitions to find goal of the week, chat with other fans online to discuss results and much more.

## D Tracker

The next time you go out jogging or get on your bike, take Tracker with you. You'll get a map of your route, the distance, time taken and your heart rate throughout the activity. And we all know what you eat can affect your energy levels, so use our daily food planner too.

## E PlayMe

No need to get bored while you wait for a bus to school. Forget that long journey when you next go on holiday. On PlayMe you can join others from around the world to play some of our popular games. Make international friends while you compete against each other. You choose the game and we'll provide a competitor.

## F The Reporter

Once you've downloaded The Reporter, you'll wonder how you ever managed without it. Keep up to date with what's going on around you, get the latest news, football reports from across the UK, weather forecasts and travel updates. And don't miss our daily recipe from top chefs for last minute ideas for dinner.

## G Challenge Me!

How many baskets can you get? How far can you jump? How fast can you run 100 metres? Challenge Me gives you the chance to practise these and other sports in online games against other people. You're in control. You decide whether to play with people around the world or just with your friends.

## H Simply Order

We all know that feeling. It's Friday evening, your friends are round and you all want something special to eat. Simply Order lists all the restaurants and fast food shops in your area, their menus and any special offers they may have. Pass the phone round, choose your meals and sit back and wait for dinner to arrive.

## Part 3

### Questions 11–15

For each question, choose the correct answer.

---

# Reading for Pleasure

*Andrew Kilburn talks about his love of reading. But books or e-books?*

I love reading. While my friends are sitting around with their headphones listening to their favourite songs or talking about the latest football match, I'll be sitting quietly reading. It's not that I don't like these other activities, but reading has a special place in my heart. My friends know this and one of the things that surprises them is that they rarely see me reading an electronic book, or e-book as they're called. More likely, I'll be holding a traditional, paper book and enjoying reading it.

I suppose this is surprising. According to some people, the book is dead and sooner rather than later everything we read will be in electronic form. And so something that has been around for hundreds of years will no longer exist. As everybody spends most of their time looking at screens, whether that's their laptop or mobile phone, this would seem a sensible conclusion to come to. But I'm not so sure. I think the book will be around for a lot longer still.

I'll admit there are many advantages to an e-book. It's cheaper for publishers to produce an e-book compared to a paper one, and because of this we don't have to pay so much for them. Also, with the advantages of technology, we can search through books like an electronic dictionary much more quickly. And it's easier to get an e-book – no need to go to a bookshop or library. All I have to do is get my phone or laptop out, pay and download it. I can be reading the book in seconds.

But my love of reading is about more than the words on the page or the screen. It's about sitting in the armchair and reaching out for my latest novel on the table. It's to do with appreciating the artwork on the cover, enjoying the feel and the smell of the paper, and knowing where I've reached in the book. And then when it's finished I can fill a space in the bookcase, putting it next to the others I've read and taking pleasure in seeing them all. This is much more satisfying than looking at links on an electronic reader. Give me a paperback any day!

---

**11** What does Andrew say about his friends?

    **A** They think he acts in a way they don't expect.

    **B** Their hobbies and interests don't appeal to him.

    **C** They don't read books.

    **D** They think he's too quiet at times.

**12** Andrew believes that

    **A** the traditional book is in danger of not being used anymore.

    **B** people spend too much time looking at screens.

    **C** what people are predicting might not happen.

    **D** it is surprising that electronic books are popular.

**13** What does Andrew say about electronic books?

    **A** We shouldn't have to pay so much for them.

    **B** You can read one quickly.

    **C** They are less expensive than a traditional book.

    **D** Searching for one online is easy.

**14** Andrew argues that

    **A** you can get more words on a page than on a screen.

    **B** there are various reasons why he enjoys reading a book.

    **C** traditional books can take up too much space.

    **D** traditional books are easier to hold.

**15** What would Andrew say about the future?

| | |
|---|---|
| **A** Lovers of traditional books don't need to fear new technology. | **B** Despite their advantages, electronic books aren't worth the money. |
| **C** We need to protect the traditional book. | **D** We need to accept change and stop looking back to the past. |

## Part 4

### Questions 16–20

Five sentences have been removed from the text below.
For each question, choose the correct answer.
There are three extra sentences which you do not need to use.

# A working visit to Stratford-upon-Avon

*Tomas Kaminski tells us about an interesting way he practised his English*

I'm studying English at a school in the UK at the moment and having a wonderful time, meeting new friends and getting to know the country. We have the chance to go on lots of trips and recently we visited the famous town of Stratford-upon-Avon, the birthplace of William Shakespeare. **16** [ ] Our English teacher wanted us to do more than that.

Before we went, we prepared for the trip. **17** [ ] Some students did one on the environment, while another group wrote some questions about hobbies and interests. There were five groups altogether. I'm really interested in business studies and my group had questions to ask local businesspeople and shopkeepers.

We were there for the whole day and we all thought it would be best to do the research in the morning. **18** [ ] When we arrived in Stratford, each group went off around the town to ask local people their questions. It was really good fun. We had the chance to practise our English and the local people were very friendly and helpful. In fact, they told our teacher how polite they thought we all were.

Stratford is a lovely town and we spent the afternoon enjoying the sights. After lunch we looked round Holy Trinity Church, and of course we visited the house where the world's most famous playwright was born and grew up. **19** [ ] I got home feeling exhausted but I had had a fantastic day out.

Apart from being fun it was a great way to practise our English, and not only because we were able to speak to local people. **20** [ ] We took it in turns to stand up and explain to the other groups what our questions were about and the things we found out. We all enjoyed it so much we're hoping to repeat it later in the year in a new location.

**A**   We could then relax in the afternoon and go sightseeing.

**B**   However, many of the shops were closed.

**C**   We worked in teams and created some questionnaires on different subjects.

**D**   In class the next day we presented the results of our questionnaires.

**E**   That was followed by some fun boating on the river before we left.

**F**   On the other hand, the weather was better than we had expected.

**G**   But we didn't just walk around the town taking photographs.

**H**   As a result, we managed to get a tour for free.

## Part 5

### Questions 21–26

For each question, choose the correct answer.

---

# parkrun

In October 2004, Paul Sinton-Hewitt decided to organise a run with a
**(21)** ............ of his friends. They met at a park in London and set out
on a five-kilometre run. At the end of the run **(22)** ............ of them
was given a piece of paper with the time they'd **(23)** ............ to finish.
Then they all walked off for a coffee and a chat.
The friends didn't know it at the time, but that meeting was the
**(24)** ............ of what became a worldwide Saturday morning run.
'parkrun', spelled with a small 'p', is a weekly run held in local
parks, where people of all ages and abilities can run a timed 5k. The
**(25)** ............ are free, are run by volunteers and take place in 2,000
locations around the world, with over 350,000 people taking part
each week and over 5 million people having **(26)** ............ a parkrun.

---

| 21 | **A** club | **B** lot | **C** set | **D** group |
|----|-----------|-----------|-----------|-------------|
| 22 | **A** each | **B** every | **C** either | **D** part |
| 23 | **A** done | **B** taken | **C** made | **D** lasted |
| 24 | **A** basic | **B** introduction | **C** one | **D** first |
| 25 | **A** acts | **B** actions | **C** events | **D** roles |
| 26 | **A** served | **B** closed | **C** completed | **D** ended |

## Part 6

### Questions 27–32

For each question, write the correct answer.
Write **one** word for each gap.

---

# Cream Teas
### *by Lucas Novak*

One thing I'll remember from our holiday in England is 'cream teas'. No, this isn't tea with cream added to **(27)** ..................... instead of milk. A cream tea is something special you can order. It's a pot of tea and a small, round cake called a scone, **(28)** .................... is cut in half and has thick cream and jam placed on each piece. Although you can get them in cafes all over the country, the main places **(29)** ..................... eat them are Devon and Cornwall in the south-west of England. Each has a different opinion about how these should **(30)** ..................... served. In Devon, the view is the cream should be placed on the scone **(31)** ..................... then the jam on top of the cream. However, in Cornwall, they insist it's the other way round. I tried both ways and it was equally wonderful. They could be **(32)** .................... most delicious thing I've ever eaten!

# Test 8 WRITING

## Part 1

You **must** answer this question.
Write your answer in about **100 words** on the answer sheet.

___

### Question 1

Read this email from your English teacher Miss Evans and the notes you have made.

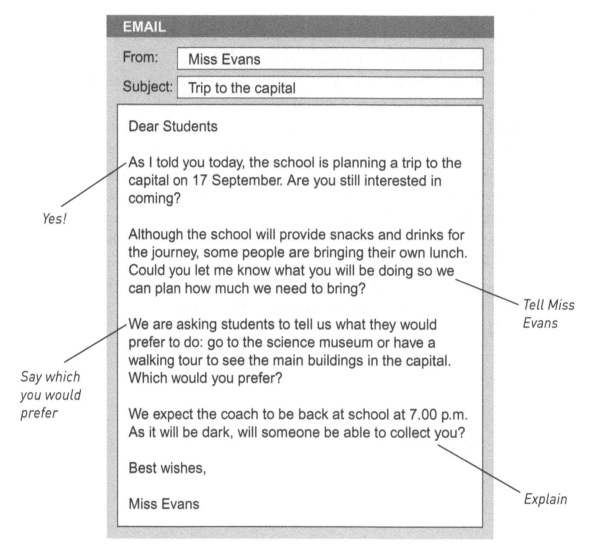

EMAIL

From: Miss Evans

Subject: Trip to the capital

Dear Students

As I told you today, the school is planning a trip to the capital on 17 September. Are you still interested in coming?

*Yes!*

Although the school will provide snacks and drinks for the journey, some people are bringing their own lunch. Could you let me know what you will be doing so we can plan how much we need to bring?

*Tell Miss Evans*

We are asking students to tell us what they would prefer to do: go to the science museum or have a walking tour to see the main buildings in the capital. Which would you prefer?

*Say which you would prefer*

We expect the coach to be back at school at 7.00 p.m. As it will be dark, will someone be able to collect you?

Best wishes,

Miss Evans

*Explain*

Write your **email** to Miss Evans using **all the notes**.

## Part 2

Choose **one** of these questions.
Write your answer in about **100 words** on the answer sheet.

---

## Question 2

You see this notice in an English-language magazine.

---

**Articles wanted!**

**WHAT IS YOUR FAVOURITE SUBJECT AT SCHOOL?**

How long have you studied this subject?

What do you like about it?

**Write an article answering these questions and we will put it in our magazine.**

---

Write your **article**.

## Question 3

Your English teacher has asked you to write a story.

Your story must begin with this sentence.

*It was late and I felt really tired.*

Write your **story**.

# Test 8 LISTENING

## Part 1

57

### Questions 1–7

For each question, choose the correct answer.

---

**1**  What does the girl want to eat?

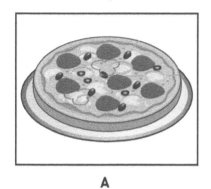

A

B

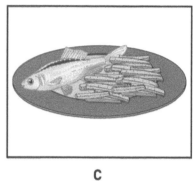

C

**2**  Why doesn't the boy want to go to the cinema?

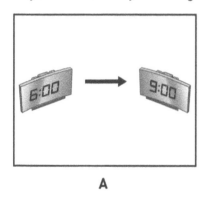

A

B

C

**3**  What time does the boy want his mum to collect him?

A

B

C

**4**  How much is the school trip?

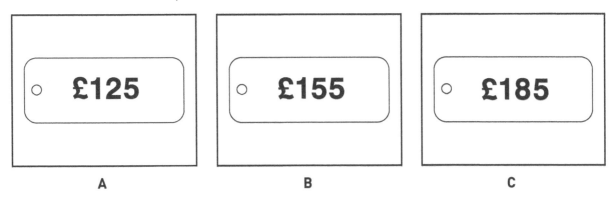

**5**  Which TV programme is on at the moment?

**6**  Which day has the most exams?

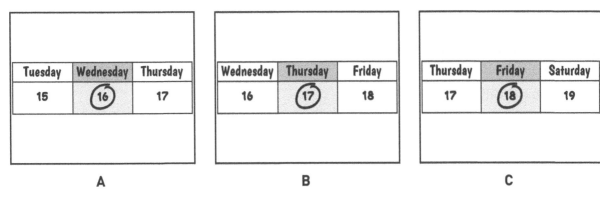

**7**  Which item of food or drink does the girl want now?

## Part 2

58

### Questions 8–13

For each question, choose the correct answer.

---

8   You will hear a brother and sister talking about a quiz show on TV.
    Why doesn't the girl want to watch it?

    **A**   The questions are too easy.

    **B**   There's another programme she wants to watch.

    **C**   She doesn't find quiz shows interesting.


9   You will hear two friends talking about opening a bank account.
    The boy says

    **A**   his parents will have to share his account.

    **B**   he usually finds it difficult to save money.

    **C**   he finds the app a bit difficult to understand.


10  You will two friends talking about the girl's birthday.
    The girl

    **A**   would like her present to be a surprise.

    **B**   doesn't want a present.

    **C**   would like to go out for a meal.


11  You will hear two friends talking about doing a presentation at school.
    What do they agree to do?

    **A**   The girl will do the talking.

    **B**   The boy will write the presentation.

    **C**   The girl will give out the questionnaires.


12  You will hear two friends talking about a concert.
    The girl says

    **A**   the tickets were too expensive.

    **B**   she wishes the band had played more well-known songs.

    **C**   she found it difficult to see the stage.


13  You will hear two friends discussing what to do in the afternoon.
    What do they decide to do?

    **A**   wait to see what their friends are doing

    **B**   go to the boy's house

    **C**   go out for dinner

## Part 3

59

### Questions 14–19

For each question, write the correct answer in the gap. Write **one** or **two words** or a **number** or a **date** or a **time**.

---

You will hear a boy called Tom Ducker giving a presentation at school about a research project.

## Research Project

The first part of the questionnaire contained ten
**(14)** ……………….. questions.

Tom's group went to a **(15)** ……………….. to do the research.

They interviewed people below 21 and people older than
**(16)** ………………..

Older people like to shop online for items for their
**(17)** ………………..

Older people think shopping centres are too noisy and
**(18)** ………………..

A lot of older people shop online each week for
**(19)** ………………..

# Part 4

60

## Questions 20–25

For each question, choose the correct answer.

---

You will hear an interview with a girl called Tina Steel, who went abroad to study Spanish.

20 Tina explains that

    **A** she's going to university when she gets back from Spain.

    **B** she couldn't find a language school in the UK.

    **C** she has to take an exam at school.

21 Why did Tina choose Madrid?

    **A** She knew a family there.

    **B** She had been there before.

    **C** Her parents thought it was safer than other cities.

22 Tina said the other students on the course

    **A** used English instead of Spanish.

    **B** got to know each other very well.

    **C** kept talking in class.

23 What does Tina say about the language school?

    **A** She found the course quite hard.

    **B** The course wasn't worth the money.

    **C** It was in a nice location.

24 Tina said the family she lived with

    **A** introduced her to their friends.

    **B** were very relaxed.

    **C** could not have been better.

25 If Tina goes again

    **A** she would stay with the same family.

    **B** she would choose a different school.

    **C** she would spend less time in Spain.

# Test 8 SPEAKING

1A

1B

Audio scripts spend Model answers on pages 183–249.

63–64

## Some things that parents could give their daughter when she goes away to university

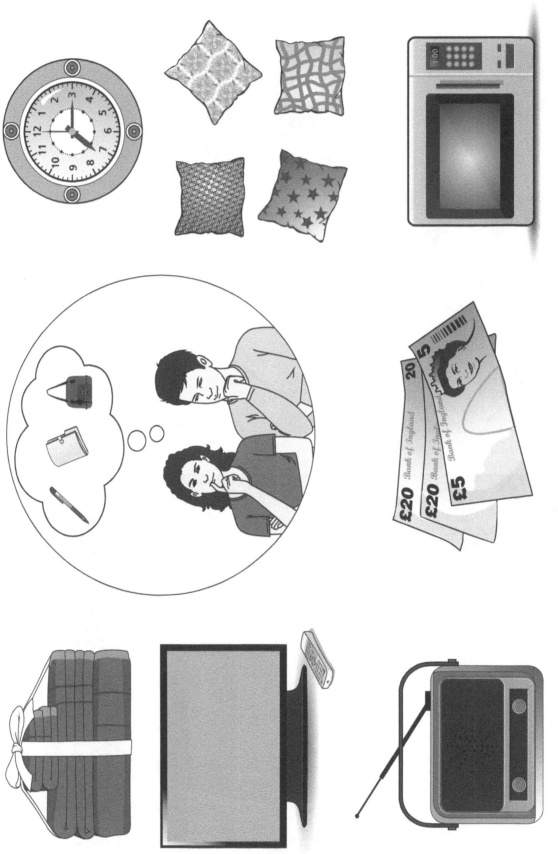

Audio scripts and Model answers on pages 183–249.

# Mini-dictionary

 Here are some of the more difficult words from the practice tests. Definitions and examples are from *Collins COBUILD Dictionaries.*

## TEST 1

**elsewhere** /els'weə/ ADVERB in other places or to another place • *If you are not happy, then go elsewhere.*

**inventor** /ɪn'ventə/ (**inventors**) NOUN the first person to think of something or to make it • *Who was the inventor of the telephone?*

**leggings** /'legɪŋz/ PLURAL NOUN tight trousers, usually made out of cloth which can stretch • *She is wearing tight, black leggings.*

**plug in** /plʌg 'ɪn/ (**plugs in, plugging in, plugged in**) PHRASAL VERB If you **plug** a piece of electrical equipment **in**, you connect it to the electricity supply. • *I had a TV, but there was no place to plug it in.*

**researcher** /rɪ'sɜː'tʃə/ (**researchers**) NOUN someone who tries to find out facts about something • *He chose to join the company as a market researcher.*

## TEST 2

**acacia** /ə'keɪʃə/ (**acacias**) NOUN a tree which grows in warm countries and which usually has small yellow or white flowers • *The children fell asleep on the sand under an acacia tree.*

**animal kingdom** /ænɪməl 'kɪŋdəm/ NOUN All the animals, birds and insects in the world are known as the **animal kingdom**. • *These birds are unusual in the animal kingdom.*

**root** /ruːt/ (**roots**) NOUN the part of a plant that grows under the ground • *She dug a hole near the roots of an apple tree.*

**safari park** /sə'fɑːri pɑːk/ (**safari parks**) NOUN A **safari park** is a large park where wild animals, such as lions and elephants, live freely. People can pay to drive through the park and look at the animals. • *These animals can be seen in most zoos and safari parks.*

**tooth fairy** /'tuːθ feəri/ (**tooth fairies**) NOUN The **tooth fairy** is an imaginary creature, who exists in some cultures and who takes away children's teeth when they fall out and gives them money instead. • *Look under your pillow because the tooth fairy might have called!*

**wild** /waɪld/ NOUN Animals that live **in the wild** live freely and are not looked after by people. • *Only around a thousand giant pandas still live in the wild.*

## TEST 3

**bison** /ˈbaɪsən/ **(bison)** NOUN a large hairy animal with a big head that mainly lives in North America • *A small herd of bison has been living there.*

**commercial** /kəˈmɜːʃəl/ ADJECTIVE used when talking about the buying and selling of things • *New York is a centre of commercial activity.*

**homemade** /ˈhəʊmmeɪd/ ADJECTIVE made in someone's home, rather than in a shop or factory • *I miss my mother's homemade bread.*

**litter** /ˈlɪtə/ NOUN paper or rubbish that people leave lying on the ground in public places • *I hate it when I see people dropping litter.*

**litter picker** /ˈlɪtə pɪkə/ **(litter pickers)** A tool that is used for picking litter up off the ground. • *I bought a litter picker online for a couple of pounds.*

**plogging** /ˈplɒgɪŋ/ NOUN An activity in which people jog and pick up litter at the same time. • *I went plogging with a friend this morning.*

**prehistoric** /priːhɪˈstɒrɪk/ ADJECTIVE **Prehistoric** people and things were around at a time before information was written down. • *We saw some famous prehistoric cave paintings on holiday.*

**volunteer** /vɒlənˈtɪə/ **(volunteers)** NOUN someone who does work without being paid for it, because they want to do it • *Mike was a member of the local volunteer fire brigade.*

## TEST 4

**auction house** /ˈɔːkʃən haʊs/ **(auction houses)** NOUN An **auction house** is a place where things are sold to the person who offers the highest price. • *The letters were sold by the auction house on Wednesday.*

**blanket** /ˈblæŋkɪt/ **(blankets)** NOUN A **blanket** of something is a layer which is on top of something else . • *Everything is covered with a green blanket of ferns and trees.*

**evidence** /ˈevɪdəns/ NOUN an object or a piece of information that makes you believe that something is true or has really happened • *There is no evidence that he stole the money.*

**live** /lɪv/ **(lives, living, lived)** VERB You say **live and let live** as a way of saying that you should let other people behave in the way that they want to. • *I'm a big believer in live and let live.*

**melt** /melt/ **(melts, melting, melted)** VERB Something that **is melting** is changing from a solid to a liquid because of heat. • *The floods have been caused by high rainfall and melting snow.*

**polar bear** /ˈpəʊlə beə/ **(polar bears)** NOUN a large white bear which is found near the North Pole • *Today, only seals and polar bears live there.*

**record** /rɪˈkɔːd/ **(records, recording, recorded)** VERB to store something that someone says or does in a computer file or on a disk so that it can be heard or seen again later • *Viewers can record the films.*

**seal** /siːl/ **(seals)** NOUN a large animal with a rounded body and short fur that eats fish and lives near the sea • *The hungry seals dive into the water to look for food.*

**shredder** /ˈʃredə/ **(shredders)** NOUN a machine for cutting things such as documents into very small pieces • *The office didn't have a document shredder.*

**surveillance camera** /səˈveɪləns ˈkæmrə/ **(surveillance cameras)** NOUN A **surveillance camera** is a camera that watches an area carefully and records what is going on. • *Their faces were caught on surveillance cameras.*

**voluntary** /ˈvɒləntri/ ADJECTIVE Something that is **voluntary** is done because someone wants to do it, and not because they have to do it. • *Taking part is completely voluntary.*

**volunteer** /vɒlənˈtɪə/ **(volunteers)** NOUN someone who does work without being paid, because they want to do it • *My dad helps in a local school as a volunteer.*

## TEST 5

**chemical** /ˈkemɪkəl/ **(chemicals)** NOUN a substance resulting from a reaction involving changes to atoms or molecules • *The programme was about the use of chemicals in farming.*

**dopamine** /ˈdɒpəmɪn/ NOUN a chemical in the brain that is to do with how people feel pleasure • *This part of the brain controls the release of dopamine.*

**eel** /iːl/ **(eels)** NOUN a long, thin fish that looks like a snake • *He explained that eels have really bad eyesight.*

**loch** /lɒx/ **(lochs)** NOUN a large area of water in Scotland that has land all around it • *They lived twenty miles north of Loch Ness.*

**nectar** /ˈnektə/ NOUN a sweet liquid in flowers, which bees and other insects collect • *The bees gather nectar from different flowers.*

**result** /rɪˈzʌlt/ **(results, resulting, resulted)** VERB If something **results in** a situation or event, it makes that situation or event happen.
• *Fifty per cent of road accidents result in head injuries.*

**ride** /ˈraɪd/ **(rides)** NOUN a trip on a horse or a bicycle, or on a roller coaster • *We went on several roller coaster rides .*

**roller coaster** /ˈrəʊləˈkəʊstə/ **(roller coasters)** NOUN a small railway at a fair that goes up and down steep slopes fast and that people go on for fun • *I've been on the roller coaster five times.*

## TEST 6

**defence** /dɪˈfens/ NOUN action to protect someone or something against attack • *The land was flat, which made defence difficult.*

**first aid** /fɜːst ˈeɪd/ NOUN simple medical treatment that you give to an ill or injured person • *Each group leader had to do a course in basic first aid.*

**invasion** /ɪnˈveɪʒən/ **(invasions)** NOUN an occasion when an army enters a country and attacks it • *Cyprus has been divided since an invasion in 1974.*

**marketing** /ˈmɑːˈkɪtɪŋ/ NOUN **Marketing** is the organisation of the sale of a product, for example, deciding on its price and how it should be advertised. • *He works for the marketing department.*

**shopper** /ˈʃɒpə/ **(shoppers)** NOUN a person who goes to shops and buys things • *All we could see were crowds of Christmas shoppers.*

## TEST 7

**award** /əˈwɔːd/ **(awards)** NOUN a prize that a person or company is given for doing something well • *He won an award for his new book.*

**cardboard** /ˈkɑːdbɔːd/ NOUN thick, stiff paper that is used for making boxes • *All my things are in a cardboard box.*

**chemical** /ˈkemɪkəl/ **(chemicals)** NOUN a substance resulting from a reaction involving changes to atoms or molecules • *The programme was about the use of chemicals in farming.*

**fashion-conscious** /ˈfæʃənkɒnʃəs/ ADJECTIVE If someone is **fashion-conscious**, they think a lot about their clothes and appearance.
• *In her twenties, my mother was very fashion-conscious.*

**fine** /faɪn/ **(fines, fining, fined)** VERB If someone **is fined**, they have to pay money because they have done something wrong • *She was fined £300 for driving dangerously.*

**gap year** /ˈgæp jɪə/ **(gap years)** NOUN If a student has a **gap year**, they take a break from studying after they have finished school. • *My brother went around the world in his gap year.*

**guarantee** /gærənˈtiː/ **(guarantees, guaranteeing, guaranteed)** VERB to promise that something will happen • *I guarantee that you will enjoy this film.*

**reuse** /riːˈjuːz/ **(reuses, resuing, reused)** VERB When you **reuse** something, you use it again instead of throwing it away. • *Try where possible to reuse paper.*

## TEST 8

**appreciate** /əˈpriːʃieɪt/ **(appreciates, appreciating, appreciated)** VERB to like something • *Everyone can appreciate this kind of art.*

**artwork** /ˈɑːtwɜːk/ NOUN drawings and photographs that are included in something such as a book or advertisement • *The band have finished the artwork for their new album.*

**paperback** /ˈpeɪpəbæk/ NOUN a book with a thin cardboard or paper cover • *I'll buy the book when it comes out in paperback.*

**planner** /ˈplænə/ **(planners)** NOUN a chart for writing down things such as meetings, tasks and goals • *You should make a note to yourself on your daily planner so you don't forget.*

**publisher** /ˈpʌblɪʃə/ **(publishers)** NOUN a person or a company that publishes books, newspapers or magazines • *The publishers planned to produce the magazine every week.*

**safety** /ˈseɪfti/ ADJECTIVE intended to make something less dangerous • *There are child safety locks on all the gates.*

**scone** /skɒn/ **(scones)** NOUN a small cake made from flour and fat, usually eaten with butter • *We chatted over tea and scones.*

**turn** /tɜːn/ **(turns)** NOUN If two or more people **take it in turns** to do something, they do it one after the other several times. • *It's a long way to Washington, so our parents took it in turns to drive.*

**worldwide** /wɜːldˈwaɪd/ ADJECTIVE throughout the world • *The TV presenter has a worldwide reputation.*

# Audio scripts

These are the audio scripts for the Listening and Speaking parts of the tests. Listen to the audio online at:
**www.collins.co.uk/eltresources**

## TEST 1 LISTENING

## Part 1

## Track 01

*Preliminary English Test for Schools, Listening.*
*There are four parts to the test. You will hear each piece twice.*
*We will now stop for a moment.*
*Please ask any questions now, because you must not speak during the test.*
*Now look at the instructions for Part 1.*
*For each question, choose the correct answer.*

*Look at Question 1.*

**1** *What date is the school closed?*

| | |
|---|---|
| Boy: | Have you been told your exam date yet? |
| Girl: | No, not yet. We're having a practice test on the 15th, so maybe they'll tell us then. |
| Boy: | I don't like not knowing. I need to plan my studies. |
| Girl: | I thought it was on the 16th, but the teacher reminded us that was a holiday and the school won't be open. |
| Boy: | Well, I just hope it's not the 13th. I don't want an exam on my birthday. |

*Now listen again.*

**2** *Where is Sam meeting his friends?*

| | |
|---|---|
| Sam: | Hello Mum. I'm in town at the moment. I'm just getting something to eat in the museum café. I'm seeing some mates at the football stadium later. We're getting tickets for Saturday's match. After that I've got nothing to do so I wondered if we could meet after you finish work. What about seeing that film you were talking about? We could meet outside the cinema. Call me back if you can. |

*Now listen again.*

**3** *What has stopped working?*

| | |
|---|---|
| Dad: | Susie? If you're not busy could you put the kettle on? I've been working in the garden and my hands are dirty. |
| Susie: | OK. Are you hungry? I was going to put something in the microwave if you're stopping for lunch. |
| Dad: | That's kind of you but no thanks. I'm going to clean up and go into the shops. |
| Susie: | OK. Don't forget Mum asked you to get a new iron. The one that's upstairs hardly gets hot. |

*Now listen again.*

**4** *How much is the school trip?*

| | |
|---|---|
| Woman: | Now some of you have been asking about the cost of the school trip next month. Mrs Taylor has been speaking to a new coach company to see if their price was lower. The previous company we used told us the coach would cost £50 per student, which we thought was far too expensive. However, the new company is much cheaper and they will only charge £30 each. If you are going, we will need a £10 deposit by the end of the week. |

*Now listen again.*

**5** *When does the art class normally start?*

| | |
|---|---|
| Man: | Hello. This is Clevedale Leisure Centre. We are closed for the weekend but will be open again on Monday. If you'd like to speak to someone about the activities we offer our reception desk will be open at 8.30. There is one change to our Monday timetable. If you're planning on coming along to the weekly art class, the session will be starting at 9.30 for next week only, not the usual time of 9.00. |

*Now listen again.*

**6** *When is the dance performance?*

| | |
|---|---|
| Boy: | Did you get the email about the dance performance? |
| Girl: | Yes, I got it this morning. I'm really glad we're not doing it in May like they said at first. I don't think I'm ready yet. I think we all need a bit more time to practise. |
| Boy: | I know. We haven't really had much time at all. |
| Girl: | We've got the school holidays in July. I wish it could have been then, but I suppose June isn't too bad. |

*Now listen again.*

**7** *Where is the boy going to buy his dad a shirt?*

| | |
|---|---|
| Girl: | Have you decided what you're getting dad for his birthday? |
| Boy: | Yes, I think I'm going to get him a shirt. I was looking online but I can't see anything he'd want. |
| Girl: | It might be cheaper online. |
| Boy: | True, but I saw him looking at one he liked in that shop we went in last weekend. You know, the one just around the corner from the market. I think I'll get that one for him. |

*Now listen again.*

*That is the end of Part 1.*

## Part 2

## Track 02

*Now look at Part 2.*
*For each question, choose the correct answer.*

**8** *You will hear two friends talking about doing homework.*

Boy: I was thinking about going to the library to do my homework. Do you want to come too?

Girl: I'm not sure. It's been getting quite busy in there lately. I prefer studying somewhere quiet.

Boy: Has it? I'll work from home then.

Girl: I can come to your place if you like so we can do it together. We can listen to that new album I was telling you about after we finish our homework. Not while we're studying though because I find it hard to focus.

*Now listen again.*

**9** *You will hear two friends talking about doing an after-school activity.*

Boy: The school has sent my mum a letter about getting me to do an after-school activity.

Girl: Have they? Well, that's good, isn't it? I really enjoy the activity I do after school. I go to the gym. I'd have to pay for it if I did it somewhere else.

Boy: I know but by the time I finish my lessons I'm tired and I just want to go home and relax.

Girl: Well, I saw some of your friends at school asking teachers about after-school activities. Why don't you have a chat with them and find out if there's anything you can do together?

*Now listen again.*

**10** *You will hear two friends talking about a holiday.*

Girl: Are you going anywhere exciting for your holiday?

Boy: I don't know yet. My mum and dad are still trying to decide where to go. I've told them I want to go to Spain but they said they want to go somewhere here.

Girl: Well, there are lots of nice places to go in the UK.

Boy: I know but I want to go somewhere warm and sunny. We stayed in the UK last year and it rained the whole week. It was lucky we were in a hotel as the campsite we were planning to go to was flooded.

*Now listen again.*

**11** *You will hear two friends talking about a video game.*

Boy: Have you heard about that new video game Robot Wars?

Girl: Yes, the game is supposed to be really good although the graphics aren't as good as they could be.

Boy: Do you think you'll get it? I'd love to play it to see what it's like.

Girl: I'd like to but I don't think I have enough to buy it. I'm saving up for a new pair of trainers at the moment. I was thinking I could ask my mum to get it for my birthday as it's only a few weeks away.

*Now listen again.*

**12** *You will hear a girl and her father talking about her plans for the weekend.*

Father: You're going to a party on Saturday, aren't you?

Girl: Yes, it's Carol's birthday party. It should be good. A lot of my friends are going and I'm getting a lift back from Carol's mum, so I don't have to worry about getting home.

Father: Well, have a good time but don't get back too late, will you? You've got a busy week next week.

Girl: I know, and I've got some homework to finish on Sunday. I just hope I can find a nice dress to wear for the party when I go shopping on Saturday morning.

*Now listen again.*

**13** *You will hear two friends talking about one of their teachers.*

Girl: Do you have Mr Jennings for English? I think we've got him next year.

Boy: Yes, he's been our teacher for the past two years. He's quite strict, but he keeps the noisy students quiet, so it's easy to concentrate in his class. I like him.

Girl: Does he give a lot of homework?

Boy: Actually, he probably gives us less than other teachers. He always tells us that as long as we read the novels we have to study for the exam, we'll have lots to talk about in the lesson.

*Now listen again.*

*That is the end of Part 2.*

## Part 3

## Track 03

*Now look at Part 3.*
*For each question, write the correct answer in the gap.*
*Write one or two words or a number or a date or a time.*
*Look at Questions 14 to 19 now. You have 20 seconds.*
*You will hear a teacher talking about an end-of-year party.*

Teacher: OK everyone, I'm sure you're all looking forward to celebrating your final year at school. I'd just like to give you some information about the party. Please make sure you arrive a few minutes before the start at 7.00 in order to listen to the headteacher's talk.

The party is due to end at 11.30. In previous years we've had complaints from neighbours about the way some parents have parked their cars. Could you tell the person who will be driving you home to park in the school car park and not on the main road.

We've arranged a school bus service to take home students who don't have anyone to collect them. If you're using this service, please meet Mr Adams in the gym. He will escort you to the coach pick-up point.

I'm sure you're all looking forward to the meal. We've arranged the menu with an outside company. There are two options for the main meal and we need to inform them about who wants what. In order to help us and them get this right, could you let the school secretary know what you'd like before Friday.

As you all know, Miss Atkinson has volunteered to be our DJ for the evening, and you've all been busy telling her what music you want her to play. Please remember that the school band will also be playing for 30 minutes during the evening and we hope everyone can give them a lot of support.

Finally, we don't want anyone leaving the school on their own when it's all over. If you're being collected by someone, make sure you stay in the hall until someone calls you to go to the main exit.

*Now listen again.*

*That is the end of Part 3.*

## Part 4

## Track 04

*Now look at Part 4.*
*For each question, choose the correct answer.*
*Look at Questions 20 to 25 now.*
*You have 45 seconds.*
*You will hear an interview with a woman called Sylvia Evans, who helps students with their career choices.*

| | |
|---|---|
| Man: | This morning I'm speaking to Sylvia Evans about choosing a career in hairdressing. |
| Sylvia: | Thanks. Yes, it's an exciting, creative profession and I think one where we don't have to worry too much about technology taking away jobs. If you're often asked by friends how you managed to style your hair in a particular way, or what shampoo you use, it may well |

be that you have what it takes to start a career in this industry.

| | |
|---|---|
| Man: | What makes it so exciting, Sylvia? |
| Sylvia: | Well, hairdressers are really important for people who use them. When someone enters the shop they're putting their trust in you to make them look and feel fantastic. A great style can have an enormous impact on how the customers feel about themselves. You want them to leave the shop with a smile on their face. |
| Man: | And what about pay? |
| Sylvia: | Salaries will be different from one hairdresser's to the next but you can expect to earn a pretty good salary. Of course, this will depend on your level of experience. However, how much you earn can also be due to how popular you become with the customers. A hairdresser who attracts people to the shop will be a favourite with the boss and will be in a strong position to ask for a pay rise. |
| Man: | I suppose young people need qualifications? |
| Sylvia: | Actually, it's possible to enter the profession without any qualifications, but it will be an advantage to do a course at college. You can choose to focus on hairdressing or take a course in other areas of the industry as well. This is an excellent idea as the more skills you have the more popular you will be for an employer. |
| Man: | Are there any other things to consider? |
| Sylvia: | Apart from qualifications, you'll need to show you're good at communicating. You must be able to listen to your customers' requests, offer good advice and be someone they might want to share a problem with. You should also be the kind of person who can see what jobs need doing when things are quiet and get them done. |
| Man: | And what about your career? |
| Sylvia: | It depends. Some people continue working in hairdressing, but often move from one shop to the next. Some go on to work in the theatre or the film industry, though there's a lot of competition for these jobs. There are also enormous opportunities for people who want to start their own business. |

*Now listen again.*

*That is the end of Part 4.*

*You now have six minutes to write your answers on the answer sheet.*

*That is the end of the test.*

**TEST 1 SPEAKING**

**Part 1**

# Track 05

| | |
|---|---|
| Examiner: | Good afternoon. |
| | Can I have your mark sheets, please? |
| | I'm Simon Rickard and this is Cathy Irving. |
| | What's your name, Candidate A? How old are you? |
| Candidate A: | My name's Joshua Kulig and I'm 13 years old. |
| Examiner: | And what's your name, Candidate B? How old are you? |
| [PAUSE FOR YOU TO ANSWER] | |
| Examiner: | Candidate B, where do you live? |
| [PAUSE FOR YOU TO ANSWER] | |
| Examiner: | And Candidate A, where do you live? |
| Candidate A: | I live in Switzerland. I live with my family in an apartment in a small village near the mountains. |
| Examiner: | Candidate A, have you got any hobbies or interests? |
| Candidate A: | I'm learning to play the piano. I go to classes after school and I also practise at home. |
| Examiner: | Candidate B, what do you do to relax? |
| [PAUSE FOR YOU TO ANSWER] | |
| Examiner: | Candidate A, tell me about your family. |
| Candidate A: | My mother works as a teacher in a big school and my father is a police officer. I haven't got any brothers or sisters but my cousins live in the same village. |
| Examiner: | Candidate B, tell me about your favourite subject at school. |
| [PAUSE FOR YOU TO ANSWER] | |
| Examiner: | Thank you. |

**Part 2**

# Track 06

| | |
|---|---|
| Examiner: | Now I'd like each of you to talk on your own about something. I'm going to give each of you a photograph and I'd like you to talk about it. |
| | Candidate A. Here is your photograph. It shows people out shopping. |
| | Please tell us what you can see in the photograph. |
| | Candidate B, you just listen. |
| Candidate A: | This photograph shows a family out shopping. There are four people in the family – mum, dad and their two children, a boy who looks about five years old and a |

girl who's a little bit older. I think they're paying for their shopping in a supermarket. They're standing at the checkout and on the left of the photo you can see a man's arm. He works at the checkout and he's taking something from the little boy. There's some fruit – bananas and apples and a small orange – by the checkout. I think the man has said something funny because the family are all laughing, It's a very happy photograph.

| | |
|---|---|
| Examiner: | Thank you. |
| | Candidate B. Here is your photograph. It shows some young people in a classroom. |
| | Please tell us what you can see in the photograph. |
| | Candidate A, you just listen. |
| [PAUSE FOR YOU TO ANSWER] | |
| Examiner: | Thank you. |

**Part 3**

# Track 07

| | |
|---|---|
| Examiner: | Now, in this part of the test you are going to talk about something together for about two minutes. I'm going to describe a situation to you. |
| | A girl is going on holiday with her parents. She wants to buy something to eat on the journey. Here are some things she could buy to eat on the journey. |
| | Talk together about the different things she could get and say which one would be best. |
| | All right? Now, talk together. |
| Candidate A: | So, we need to choose something that she can eat on the journey to her holiday. All of these things are OK apart from the ice-cream. That wouldn't last very long. What do you think? |
| [PAUSE FOR YOU TO ANSWER] | |
| Candidate A: | Yes, that's true even though they're my favourite things. I think the chips are like the ice cream. They need to be eaten quickly. Cold pizza isn't really very nice either, is it? |
| [PAUSE FOR YOU TO ANSWER] | |
| Candidate A: | Yes, I agree. The family can stop somewhere to get something to eat if they want, can't they. Especially if it's a long journey. But yes, let's say the sandwich is the best thing to buy, shall we? |
| [PAUSE FOR YOU TO ANSWER] | |
| Examiner: | Thank you. |

## Speaking Part 4

# Track 08

| | |
|---|---|
| Examiner: | Candidate A, do you like going on long journeys? |
| Candidate A: | Sometimes, yes. I like travelling in my mum's car because we listen to music and sing some songs. It's always a lot of fun. |
| Examiner: | And what about you, Candidate B? |
| [PAUSE FOR YOU TO ANSWER] | |
| Examiner: | Candidate B, what do you like to take with you on a journey? |
| [PAUSE FOR YOU TO ANSWER] | |
| Examiner: | And how about you, Candidate A? |
| Candidate A: | I like to read as well, maybe not a book but a magazine. Of course, I also like to take my phone. I can message my friends, listen to music, watch videos, that kind of thing. |
| Examiner: | Candidate B, is it better to travel during the day or late at night? |
| [PAUSE FOR YOU TO ANSWER] | |
| Examiner: | And what about you, Candidate A? |
| Candidate A: | I think it's better to travel at night as the roads are quieter. But maybe it's more difficult for the driver if it's dark. Also, the driver might feel more tired if it's later in the day. |
| Examiner: | Thank you. That is the end of the test. |

## TEST 2    LISTENING

## Part 1

# Track 09

*Preliminary English Test for Schools, Listening.*
*There are four parts to the test. You will hear each piece twice.*
*We will now stop for a moment.*
*Please ask any questions now, because you must not speak during the test.*
*Now look at the instructions for Part 1.*
*For each question, choose the correct answer.*
*Look at Question 1.*

**1**   *What time did the girl's mum make the appointment at the dentist?*

| | |
|---|---|
| Girl: | Mum, what time did you say I've got to go to the dentist tomorrow? |
| Mum: | I booked it for 1.30 because you only have half a day at school tomorrow, don't you? I can meet you at the dentist as I finish work at 12.30. |
| Girl: | Sorry but I can't go that early. The teacher told us we have a revision class for an hour after lunch, so I won't be able to get there on time. Can you try and change it to about 3.30? |

*Now listen again.*

**2**   *How has the boy's father been going to work this week?*

| | |
|---|---|
| Girl: | I saw your dad on his motorbike on Saturday. I thought you said he'd stopped using it? |
| Boy: | No, he still uses it, but not for work anymore. After that accident he had he decided he's only going to keep it for weekends. |
| Girl: | Oh, I see. Yes, they're a bit dangerous, aren't they? |
| Boy: | Mum's told him to use the car for work as it's safer, but he's going by train this week because there's a problem with the car. |

*Now listen again.*

**3**   *Which event is cancelled?*

| | |
|---|---|
| Girl: | Are you going to the football match on Saturday? |
| Boy: | I'm not sure. The weather is going to be terrible and I don't feel like getting freezing cold standing out in the rain. |
| Girl: | I know. I'm the same. |
| Boy: | I was thinking of going to the basketball match but that's been postponed for some reason so I might watch some swimming. Do you fancy coming? We can see who's the fastest! |
| Girl: | OK, let's do that. |

*Now listen again.*

**4**   *What does the woman say will be very busy at the weekend?*

| | |
|---|---|
| Woman: | This is Jenny from the youth centre. I'm calling about the camping trip this weekend. I'm afraid we're going to have to change our plans for getting there. You've probably heard about the strike at the airport, which means there'll be no flights. We're only a small group and rather than cancel the holiday, two of the volunteers have kindly offered to drive. But as it's a holiday weekend and there'll be traffic jams on the motorway, we've decided to go by train instead. I'll be in touch with more details. |

*Now listen again.*

**5**   *How many cakes does the girl want to order?*

| | |
|---|---|
| Man: | Hello. Can I help you? |
| Girl: | Yes, it's my sister's birthday party in a few weeks and I'd like to order some cakes. |
| Man: | OK, any particular ones? |
| Girl: | Well, lots of different ones would be nice. You have so many nice ones. There are thirty people altogether, so one each. |
| Man: | OK. We can get them done for you by then. We normally ask for seven days |

to make large orders. Is it a special birthday?

Girl: She'll be 18, so quite special yes.

*Now listen again.*

**6** *What has the mother stopped drinking recently?*

Boy: Where's Mum? I haven't seen her this morning.

Girl: She's still in bed. I think she got back late from her meeting last night.

Boy: I've got an idea. Let's make her breakfast in bed, shall we? You make her some toast and I'll do her a coffee – OK?

Girl: I think you'd better make that a tea. She hasn't been making coffee lately.

Boy: OK. I'll take her up a glass of water as well.

*Now listen again.*

**7** *When does the teacher say he can meet the parents?*

Man: Hello. I'm just phoning about the meeting we arranged at school. I'm really looking forward to seeing you and talking about your child's progress. I understand my secretary arranged it for the 11th August. However, unfortunately I'm away that day and won't be back till late. I'd certainly like to meet you before school starts again on the 1st September, so I was wondering if you were free at any time on the 18th August. If you could call back and speak to my secretary, we'll arrange the date.

*Now listen again.*

*That is the end of Part 1.*

## Part 2

## Track 10

*Now look at Part 2.*
*For each question, choose the correct answer.*

**8** *You will hear two friends talking about a new shop.*

Boy: I was thinking about going to that new clothes shop. Would you like to come?

Girl: Yes, I was planning on going there anyway. My friend was telling me about it. I think it's their first day of business today and they have a celebrity opening the shop.

Boy: I need to get some new trainers. What about you?

Girl: I don't need anything, but I've still got my birthday money to spend so I just want to see if there's anything on special offer. If not, I'll save my money.

*Now listen again.*

**9** *You will hear two friends talking about a football match.*

Girl: I'm looking forward to seeing the game tonight. It's on TV at 7.30.

Boy: Why don't you come to my house? My mum and dad said I can invite some friends round to watch the match, as long as we don't make too much noise. Dad has to be up for work early tomorrow and needs to sleep.

Girl: OK, that sounds like a lot of fun. What time?

Boy: About 7.00? My mum said she'd make some sandwiches for us and we can buy some snacks on the way home from school.

*Now listen again.*

**10** *You will hear two friends talking about the school holiday.*

Boy: Do you know what day we break up for the holiday?

Girl: Well, term ends on Friday 19th but we haven't got to go to school that day because there's a teacher training day on the Friday. So our last day is Thursday.

Boy: Great, so that means we've got ten days free altogether including the weekends.

Girl: I hope the weather's nice. If it is, we should try to do something interesting. I don't fancy sitting around at home every day getting bored. Let's get some mates round to plan a few things to do.

*Now listen again.*

**11** *You will hear a boy and his mother talking about the evening meal.*

Boy: What's for dinner tonight, Mum?

Mother: I'm not sure yet. I was going to cook curry, but we don't have all the ingredients. I'm not sure I'll have time to go shopping today because I'm working late.

Boy: Well, I could go to the supermarket on the way home from school. What do you need?

Mother: OK, I think we've got all the spices I need but we don't have any rice so could you get a bag of that? We don't need chicken. There's some in the freezer.

*Now listen again.*

**12** *You will hear two friends talking about a mobile phone.*

Boy: I haven't seen you using your phone today. Did you forget to bring it?

Girl: No, it's in the shop being mended. When I switched it on yesterday it was fine for a while and then it switched itself off. I tried again and had enough time to check my emails and go on the Internet but then the same thing happened. It's got a brand new battery but it only lasts a few minutes. If there's something wrong with it, I'm hoping they'll replace it for a new one.

*Now listen again.*

**13** *You will hear two friends talking about a fast-food restaurant.*

Girl: What did you think of that burger yesterday? I thought it was delicious.

Boy: I know. It was lovely. I heard about the restaurant from one of my mates. I had a look at the online reviews and they weren't bad either. That's why I suggested it.

Girl: The service was quick as well. It only took a few minutes.

Boy: I'll definitely go there again. It's not too far from school and it's not too expensive, so maybe we can go there once a week on the way home.

*Now listen again.*

*That is the end of Part 2.*

## Part 3

## Track 11

*Now look at Part 3.*
*For each question, write the correct answer in the gap.*
*Write one or two words or a number or a date or a time.*
*Look at Questions 14 to 19 now. You have 20 seconds.*
*You will hear a man talking about activities at a youth centre.*

Man: Thanks for phoning Kilbury Youth Centre. I'm afraid we are now closed for the day and will open again tomorrow at 10.00. If you're phoning about activities this coming weekend we have a full timetable of events. On Saturday those going to the indoor skiing trip will be meeting at 9.00 outside the centre. Please bring your own sandwiches as food is not provided at the ski centre. If you aren't going and are looking for things to do, the club will have lots to interest you. Tom will be running another workshop on playing the guitar for those of you interested in music. This starts at 10.00 and will be held in the studio at the back of the building. On Saturday afternoon our regular art group will meet at 1.00. We provide all the materials you'll need but please remember to tidy the room when you've finished as people have to use the room after you for other activities. If you're free on Saturday evening don't forget our quiz night. If you have your own team, bring them along. Remember no more than six people per team. If

you're on your own, we can find a team for you. The quiz starts at 7.00. We're closed on Sunday morning but will be open at 1.00. If the weather stays fine, we're hoping to run our monthly barbecue and we're looking for club members to help with it. If you're free, can you call Elizabeth on 0161 773 1212. Finally, we want to see more and more young people using the club and we need your help. If you have time next week, why not help us deliver the club newspaper to local people? If you can join us next Wednesday evening at 7.00 we'd be really grateful.

*Now listen again.*

*That is the end of Part 3.*

## Part 4

## Track 12

*Now look at Part 4.*
*For each question, choose the correct answer.*
*Look at Questions 20 to 25 now.*
*You have 45 seconds.*
*You will hear an interview with a woman called Moira O'Neil, who helps students studying in the UK find a family to live with.*

Man: I'm speaking to Moira O'Neil about helping students find a family to live with when they stay in the UK.

Moira: Thanks. For younger people they'll never forget the family they live with. It may be the first time they've been away from home on their own. They need to feel safe, welcomed and part of the family, and the family needs to be happy with the arrangement too.

Man: What types of family do this?

Moira: Some of them will be young couples with children, though we don't have too many of these at the moment. Most of our families are older or retired, or families with older children – people who have time to spend with the student. We also have a few single people.

Man: And what do students usually request?

Moira: When students apply to the college and request a family, they'll be asked whether they want to live in a house with young children or not, and if they're happy with pets in the house. Some students will be vegetarians and we find most of them will prefer to live with people who avoid eating meat.

Man: What about the needs of the family?

Moira: It's the same for the families who sign up. They will also tell us about things they want or don't want. For example, they may ask for a student who speaks a particular language, perhaps their child is learning the language at school. Some families might just want to cook meals and provide a room, though we always prefer a family to do more than this.

Man: What do you mean by that?

Moira: It's important the student feels part of the family during their stay. They should certainly be invited to eat dinner together with the family and not be expected to take food to their room. It's also nice if the family takes them out occasionally to explore the local area. It's not unusual for families to invite the student to family parties sometimes.

Man: What kind of things should a host family try to provide?

Moira: Well, when a family applies to offer the service, someone from the college will often visit them. Obviously, we'd want to see that the house is kept clean and tidy and the room the student will be sleeping in needs to be OK. There are certain things the room must have, such as a desk and of course internet access to study. If everything seems OK, we sign them up.

*Now listen again.*

*That is the end of Part 4.*

*You now have six minutes to write your answers on the answer sheet.*

*That is the end of the test.*

## TEST 2 SPEAKING

## Part 1

## Track 13

Examiner: Good morning.

Can I have your mark sheets, please?

I'm Sarah Hunt and this is Donald Edmondson.

What's your name, Candidate A? How old are you?

Candidate A: My name's Anniek Tindermann and I'm 15 years old.

Examiner: And what's your name, Candidate B? How old are you?

[PAUSE FOR YOU TO ANSWER]

Examiner: Candidate B, where do you live?

[PAUSE FOR YOU TO ANSWER]

Examiner: And who do you live with, Candidate B?

[PAUSE FOR YOU TO ANSWER]

Examiner: Candidate A, where do you live?

Candidate A: I come from the Netherlands. I live in Amsterdam.

Examiner: And who do you live with, Candidate A?

Candidate A: I live with my mum, dad and brother.

Examiner: Candidate A, do you like studying English?

Candidate A: Yes, I do. I find it very hard sometimes, especially grammar, but I'm looking forward to being able to speak English well.

Examiner: Candidate B, what about you?

[PAUSE FOR YOU TO ANSWER]

Examiner: Candidate A, tell us about a teacher you like.

Candidate A: I like several of the teachers at my school but I think my favourite is my art teacher. She's good at helping us learn how to draw and paint and our lessons are always fun.

Examiner: Candidate B, how do you get to school every day?

[PAUSE FOR YOU TO ANSWER]

Examiner: Thank you.

## Part 2

## Track 14

Examiner: Now I'd like each of you to talk on your own about something. I'm going to give each of you a photograph and I'd like you to talk about it.

Candidate A. Here is your photograph. It shows people eating dinner.

Please tell us what you can see in the photograph.

Candidate B, you just listen.

Candidate A: This photograph has been taken in a family kitchen. It's a beautiful room, with nice white furniture. There are five people sitting around a table. I think it might be a mother, father and three girls although the oldest daughter looks almost the same age as the mother. They're all laughing and looking at the youngest daughter. We can't see her face, but it looks like she's about ten years old. They're all having dinner, but I can't see what it is they're eating. They all have a plate in front of them and there are two dishes in the centre of the table with more food.

Examiner: Thank you.

Candidate B. Here is your photograph. It shows someone with a laptop.

Please tell us what you can see in the photograph.

Candidate A, you just listen.

[PAUSE FOR YOU TO ANSWER]

Examiner: Thank you.

## Part 3

## Track 15

Examiner: Now, in this part of the test you're going to talk about something together for about two minutes. I'm going to describe a situation to you. A girl is going on a walking trip with her school. She is trying to decide what to take with her. Here are some things she could take.
Talk together about the different things she could take and say which one would be best.
All right? Now talk together.

Candidate A: So, the girl is going on a trip with her school. What do you think she should take? I'm not sure a map is necessary. Won't the teachers know where to go?

[PAUSE FOR YOU TO ANSWER]

Candidate A: Yes, and if it's just one day, she won't need one, will she? The walking boots might be useful as they're going walking. I think they're important.

[PAUSE FOR YOU TO ANSWER]

Candidate A: Yes, I agree. So, that leaves the mobile phone and the umbrella. I don't think it's useful to have an umbrella on a walking trip, do you? And I think it would be good to leave her mobile phone at home so she can relax and not be checking for messages.

[PAUSE FOR YOU TO ANSWER]

Candidate A: Yes, I agree. Let's say the walking boots.

Examiner: Thank you.

## Part 4

## Track 16

Examiner: Candidate A, have you been on a school trip recently?

Candidate A: No, not for quite a long time. We went to a museum last year. I enjoyed it but it was only a morning trip and we had to go back to school in the afternoon.

Examiner: And what about you, Candidate B?

[PAUSE FOR YOU TO ANSWER]

Examiner: Candidate B, is there anywhere you want your school to take the students?

[PAUSE FOR YOU TO ANSWER]

Examiner: And how about you, Candidate A?

Candidate A: I'd like to go to another country. Maybe for a whole week. I know some of the older students in our school do trips like that in the summer.

Examiner: Candidate B, do you often take photos when you go on a trip with your friends?

[PAUSE FOR YOU TO ANSWER]

Examiner: And what about you, Candidate A?

Candidate A: I take lots of photos and videos on my phone. I love to show them to everyone when we get back. I delete the ones I don't want and keep the others on my laptop.

Examiner: Thank you. That is the end of the test.

## TEST 3    LISTENING

## Part 1

## Track 17

*Preliminary English Test for Schools, Listening.*
*There are four parts to the test. You will hear each piece twice.*
*We will now stop for a moment.*
*Please ask any questions now, because you must not speak during the test.*
*Now look at the instructions for Part 1.*
*For each question, choose the correct answer.*
*Look at Question 1.*

**1**  *Which day is the school play taking place this year?*

Boy: I'm excited about taking part in the play, aren't you?

Girl: Yes, it'll be fun. It's a shame they had to change the date. My brother was coming but he has to work on the 7th July, so he'll miss it.

Boy: Oh, that's a pity. I don't know why they decided not to do it on the 30th June. Do you?

Girl: No idea. Anyway, I'm looking forward to it. And with school finishing the day after it, on the 8th, it will be a lovely end to the week.

*Now listen again.*

**2**  *Where was the cat found?*

Man: Finally, a story about a cat that didn't want to move home. Mr and Mrs Rogers had sold their house and were enjoying their new home 15 miles away in Creighton. However, after a few days their cat disappeared. They spent days looking for it in the streets where they lived, and they knocked on neighbours' doors to see if they'd seen it. Finally, they had a phone call from the people who had moved into their old house. They'd just seen the cat waiting at the door to come in!

*Now listen again.*

**3**   *What did the boy do on holiday?*

Girl:     Welcome back! Did you enjoy your holiday?

Boy:      We had a great time, thanks. As usual my mum, dad and sister spent most of the time lying on the beach, but you know how bored I get doing that, don't you?

Girl:     I know, you don't like taking things easy, do you?

Boy:      I was planning on hiring a bike to go cycling but the roads were quite busy and I eventually decided to go water-skiing for the first time. It was great!

*Now listen again.*

**4**   *Which book does the woman think was too long?*

Woman:    So that's my review of three excellent books for teenagers. To sum up, *Electric Dreams* is perfect for anyone looking for some romantic fiction, though I think it could have been a little shorter. *The Final Day* is a fantastic thriller that will keep you entertained from start to finish. You'll be thinking about the ending long after you've put it down. And *The Lost World*? Well, it's a long time since I read any science fiction, but I really enjoyed it.

*Now listen again.*

**5**   *Which item did the mother forget to buy?*

Boy:      Where have you been all morning?

Girl:     I went shopping with mum. She took ages as usual. She decided to look for a dress. I'd forgotten how long it takes for mum to buy herself clothes. Then it was off to the supermarket to get some flowers. That took forever as the place was really busy and we had to queue for a long time. Then, as we were walking home, she remembered she needed some frozen food. So we had to go all the way back again!

*Now listen again.*

**6**   *When does the film begin?*

Boy:      Are we all still going to the cinema tomorrow?

Girl:     Yes, we said we'd go after school. The film starts at 4.00, although there's a later one if we miss it. I'll be getting the train into town. I think it leaves at 3.00 and I told everyone we can meet at the cinema at 3.15. That will give us time to get something to eat. Why don't you get the train with me?

Boy:      OK, that's a good idea.

*Now listen again.*

**7**   *Where will Mr Taylor be if anyone needs him?*

Mr Taylor:    Hello. This is Mr Taylor from the college office. About the plans for the weekend trip to London – the coach to the train station leaves at 8.45 from college. I'm not joining you on the trip, but I'll be by the coach, organising the luggage. Remember, just one bag. We've been able to book the train tickets in advance, so there's no need to go to the ticket office when you arrive. Mrs Jacobs will be going with you and she tells me the train leaves from platform 4 at 9.30.

*Now listen again.*

*That is the end of Part 1.*

## Part 2

## Track 18

*Now look at Part 2.*
*For each question, choose the correct answer.*

**8**   *You will hear two friends talking about seeing a doctor.*

Boy:      Do you fancy coming to the park later for a game of football?

Girl:     I can't. I've got an appointment at the doctor's. I hurt my foot in the gymnastics class the other day and my mum thinks someone should look at it.

Boy:      That's a shame. What happened at gymnastics then?

Girl:     Nothing exciting. I didn't fall doing a difficult move or anything like that. We were getting the equipment out at the beginning of the lesson and I kicked my foot against the door, right on my little toe. It really hurt!

*Now listen again.*

**9**   *You will hear a boy talking to his mother about travelling to school.*

Boy:      Mum, it's started to rain. Can I have a lift to school?

Mum:      Not this morning I'm afraid. It's not raining very heavily and the walk will do you good. Anyway, you might meet one of your friends on the way and you can have a chat.

Boy:      But I don't want to sit around in school in a wet uniform.

Mum:      Then go upstairs and get the coat I bought for you last year. You could have taken an umbrella, but you forgot to bring the last one home, didn't you?

*Now listen again.*

**10**   *You will hear two friends talking about going to the cinema.*

Girl:     So what film would you like to see this evening?

| Boy: | I'm not sure. That one we saw advertised on TV looked good. It's called 'Long Shot' I think. |
|---|---|
| Girl: | OK. Let's see that. I'll get the tickets this time as you bought them last time we went. |
| Boy: | There's another one that looks interesting – 'Shark Attack' – although that might be a bit too scary. And 'The Banker' is a really good film but I've already seen it. No, on second thoughts, let's go with my first choice. Let's meet at the cinema later. |

*Now listen again.*

**11** *You will hear a girl talking to her father about decorating her bedroom.*

| Dad: | Have you decided how you want to decorate your bedroom yet? I'm going to the shop soon and I can get the paint if you want. |
|---|---|
| Girl: | I'm not sure what colour to paint the walls. My friend Lisa's room is all white and it looks fantastic. |
| Dad: | Why don't I just buy some white paint then and we can try that? |
| Girl: | I'll come with you. There's no point wasting money. I'll decide what to do when we've had a look at what they've got. |

*Now listen again.*

**12** *You will hear two friends talking about meeting someone at the station.*

| Girl: | Sam texted me to say he's arriving tomorrow morning at 11.00. He wanted to know how to get to your house. |
|---|---|
| Boy: | He texted me too. I said I'd meet him at the station. My dad was going to give me a lift but he's got to go into work now, so I'm going by myself. My mum's given me some money for a taxi to get back from the station as he'll probably have a lot of luggage to carry. |
| Girl: | Say hello from me when you see him. |

*Now listen again.*

**13** *You will hear two friends talking about a TV show.*

| Boy: | I decided to watch that music show you were talking about. Did you see it? |
|---|---|
| Girl: | I did, yes. It was OK but a lot of the songs were really for my mum and dad's generation. They like that kind of show. |
| Boy: | I enjoyed it. I like a lot of the songs, actually. |
| Girl: | It was OK, and I'd heard of most of the groups on the show, but I don't think I'll watch it next week. I'm usually in bed by the time it comes on anyway. |

*Now listen again.*

*That is the end of Part 2.*

## Part 3

## Track 19

*Now look at Part 3.*
*For each question, write the correct answer in the gap.*
*Write one or two words or a number or a date or a time.*
*Look at Questions 14 to 19 now. You have 20 seconds.*
*You will hear an announcement about a school trip.*

| Woman: | I just want to spend a few minutes making sure you all know what the plans are for the trip to the capital on Saturday. |
|---|---|
| | Please meet in the school playground at 6.30. The coach leaves at 6.45 and won't be able to wait for anybody who's late. The journey takes about two hours and we want to get there before the roads get busy. |
| | We're planning to have a fish and chip lunch, which you've already paid for. The school will also be giving everyone a cold drink for the journey, but if you need anything else you'll need to supply this yourself. |
| | Mr Porter and Mrs Evans will be taking you on a tour of the main sights when we arrive. We'll be doing this in two groups to make it easier to control numbers. We'll explain how this will work on the coach. |
| | We'll have lunch in the park. If the weather's nice we can sit outside on the grass but there's a café there if it rains. Your teachers will be ordering the lunch so please let them know if you don't like fish and chips. |
| | We're giving you the chance to spend some time on your own with friends in the afternoon. There's lots to do in the park but you may also want to go shopping. We'll be meeting to go home at 3.30 so please make sure you get to the park at least 15 minutes before we leave. |
| | And one last thing. There are still a number of students who haven't paid for the trip. We need your £15 by Friday at the latest or we may not be able to find space on the coach. If you have difficulties paying, please speak to Mrs Evans before Friday. |

*Now listen again.*

*That is the end of Part 3.*

## Part 4

## Track 20

*Now look at Part 4.*
*For each question, choose the correct answer.*
*Look at Questions 20 to 25 now.*

*You will hear an interview with a man called Tony Owen, who is a school's exam officer.*

| | |
|---|---|
| Woman: | This morning I'm speaking to Tony Owen about exams and how to make them a positive experience. |
| Tony: | Yes, thanks for inviting me on. Positive is the important word here. We all feel nervous before a big exam day and that's only to be expected. But being nervous can actually be a good thing and help us perform at our best. But there are certain things you can do to help yourself on the big day. |
| Woman: | So what's your first tip? |
| Tony: | Well, I'm afraid there's no magic answer to passing exams. You need to know the subject so it's important to prepare. Don't rely on luck to guess every answer correctly. You'll need to know the subject. So, spend time before the exam revising, on your own or with friends if that's better. |
| Woman: | Have you got any advice for students who feel very nervous? |
| Tony: | Some students suffer badly with this. Start by making sure you don't have any last-minute problems. Before you leave the house, check that you're taking everything you need. Make sure you know where the test centre is and plan to get there earlier rather than later to avoid any annoying traffic jams or if your train is cancelled. |
| Woman: | And once you're in the exam? |
| Tony: | Yes, follow the instructions. Listen carefully to what the examiner says and read the instructions on the exam paper twice or even three times to be sure you understand what to do. Try to make sure your mind is calm before you start. Deep breathing always helps, and allow negative thoughts to pass. |
| Woman: | And what about tips during the exam? |
| Tony: | You don't want to walk away from the exam thinking you didn't answer the questions properly, so don't work quickly and try to be the first to leave. If you have more than one question to answer, do the easy ones first. This will help you become more confident instead of taking ages over difficult questions to begin with. |
| Woman: | And what about when the exam is over? |
| Tony: | It's difficult to avoid sharing your thoughts with other students after the exam. I suppose some of us love to hear that others haven't done as well as us. But there'll always be one student who tells everyone they did really well or that |

you didn't answer a question correctly. Avoid people like this and go home!

*Now listen again.*

*That is the end of Part 4.*

*You now have six minutes to write your answers on the answer sheet.*

*That is the end of the test.*

## TEST 3    SPEAKING

### Part 1

# Track 21

| | |
|---|---|
| Examiner: | Good evening.<br>Can I have your mark sheets, please?<br>I'm Richard Burns and this is Christine Morton. |
| Examiner: | What's your name, Candidate A? How old are you? |
| Candidate A: | My name's David Dominguez and I'm 14 years old. |
| Examiner: | And what's your name, Candidate B? How old are you? |
| [PAUSE FOR YOU TO ANSWER] | |
| Examiner: | Candidate B, where do you live? |
| [PAUSE FOR YOU TO ANSWER] | |
| Examiner: | And Candidate A, where do you live? |
| Candidate A: | I come from Portugal. I live with my family in Coimbra. |
| Examiner: | Candidate A, what do you like to do at weekends? |
| Candidate A: | I like to meet my friends in the town centre. We go to the park to play football or walk around the shops. |
| Examiner: | Candidate B, what about you? |
| [PAUSE FOR YOU TO ANSWER] | |
| Examiner: | Candidate A, tell us about your favourite time of the year. |
| Candidate A: | I like the summer best. I like the weather in the summer and of course I like being on holiday! I often go and stay with my cousins, who live near the sea. We swim every day and we have a lot of fun together. |
| Examiner: | Candidate B, tell us what you use your mobile phone for most. |
| [PAUSE FOR YOU TO ANSWER] | |
| Examiner: | Thank you. |

### Part 2

# Track 22

| | |
|---|---|
| Examiner: | Now I'd like each of you to talk on your own about something. I'm going to give each of you a photograph and I'd like you to talk about it. |

Candidate A. Here is your photograph. It shows people taking part in sport.
Please tell us what you can see in the photograph.
Candidate B, you just listen.

Candidate A: In this photograph there are some boys playing football. I think it's football, although you can't see the ball as it's not in the picture. There are four boys altogether. Two of them are wearing white shirts. One of these boys is in the centre of the photo and has the number 5 on his shirt. The other two have dark shirts with the numbers 35 and 9 on the front. They all look about 14 or 15 years old. They're playing outside, probably in a park, and you can see the goal in the background. It looks like a lovely sunny day and the boys are enjoying themselves.

Examiner: Thank you.
Candidate B. Here is your photograph. It shows people making a film.
Please tell us what you can see in the photograph.
Candidate A, you just listen.
[PAUSE FOR YOU TO ANSWER]
Examiner: Thank you.

## Part 3

## Track 23

Examiner: Now, in this part of the test you're going to talk about something together for about two minutes.
I'm going to describe a situation to you.
An aunt is trying to decide what to get her eight-year-old nephew for his birthday.
Here are some things she could give him.
Talk together about the different things she could give him and say which one would be best.
All right? Now talk together.
Candidate A: Would you like to start?
[PAUSE FOR YOU TO ANSWER]
Candidate A: Yes, that's a good point. So no cake. I don't think sweets are a good idea either. His mum or dad might not want him to eat lots of sweet things. What about the toy car? He might like that.
[PAUSE FOR YOU TO ANSWER]

Candidate A: Yes, they do. So, that just leaves the camera and the money. Are these a good present?
[PAUSE FOR YOU TO ANSWER]
Candidate A: No, I agree. So, do you think the toy car or the colouring pencils?
[PAUSE FOR YOU TO ANSWER]
Candidate A: Yes, let's say the toy car.
Examiner: Thank you.

## Part 4

## Track 24

Examiner: Candidate A, have you bought anyone a present recently?
Candidate A: Yes. It was my brother's birthday a few weeks ago and I bought him a video game. We went shopping together and he chose it.
Examiner: And what about you, Candidate B?
[PAUSE FOR YOU TO ANSWER]
Examiner: Candidate B, what's the best present you've ever received?
[PAUSE FOR YOU TO ANSWER]
Examiner: And how about you, Candidate A?
Candidate A: When I was 13 my dad took me to my first football match. It was a big game and the atmosphere was fantastic. I'll never forget it because our team won.
Examiner: Candidate B, what do you prefer, giving or receiving presents?
[PAUSE FOR YOU TO ANSWER]
Examiner: And what about you, Candidate A?
Candidate A: I'm the same. I enjoy going shopping for presents for my mum and dad or my friends, but I get very excited when they buy me presents. So, I think I like giving and receiving them.
Examiner: Thank you. That is the end of the test.

## TEST 4    LISTENING

## Part 1

## Track 25

*Preliminary English Test for Schools, Listening.*
*There are four parts to the test. You will hear each piece twice.*
*We will now stop for a moment.*
*Please ask any questions now, because you must not speak during the test.*
*Now look at the instructions for Part 1.*
*For each question, choose the correct answer.*
*Look at Question 1.*

**1**  *What did the girl do yesterday?*

Boy: Sorry I couldn't meet up with you yesterday. Did you have a good time at the gym?

Girl: That's OK. My uncle was visiting us in the morning, so I didn't bother to go in the end and stayed at home in the morning. He was going into town in the afternoon and asked me if I wanted to go with him. He wanted to look around the museum, but I didn't fancy that, so I went swimming instead.

*Now listen again.*

**2** *What are people saying is causing a problem?*

Man: So, once again, many thanks for attending this parents evening. Before I finish, I'd just like to make a request. We've recently had problems with parents parking outside the school gates at home time. This is causing serious traffic jams and we've been getting complaints from angry people who have missed their train at the station or had to wait hours for their bus. If you do have to use your car to collect your child, could you please park away from the school.

*Now listen again.*

**3** *Which building doesn't the girl like?*

Boy: I hear you're moving to a new house.
Girl: Yes, that's right. My dad wants to move nearer where he works.
Boy: So, have you found somewhere?
Girl: Yes, it's an apartment not far from the centre of town, just round the corner from the art gallery. It's OK, but there's a big block of flats on the other side of the road, which isn't very nice to look at. But it's useful having the library close by, I suppose.

*Now listen again.*

**4** *How long has the boy had his mobile phone?*

Girl: I'm going shopping later - do you want to come?
Boy: Yes, I'll come with you. I need to see if I can get my phone looked at. It won't switch on.
Girl: You've had that phone for ages. Didn't you get it for your birthday last year?
Boy: No, this is a different one. I only bought it about three months ago so it shouldn't be going wrong already. I saved up for about six months to buy it so I'm a bit disappointed.

*Now listen again.*

**5** *What would be the best day for the girl to collect the book?*

Girl: Hi, Mary. Sue here. I'm just phoning to see if I can come round to collect that book I lent you as I need it for school. Are you around this week? I must have it for Wednesday, so I was wondering if you'll be in on Monday or Tuesday. I can

come either day though I'm a bit busy on Monday so the day after would be great. We can talk about the homework for Wednesday as well if you have time. Let me know if you're free.

*Now listen again.*

**6** *Where will the boy be going on Saturday?*

Girl: Got anything planned for Saturday, Rob?
Boy: Well, I was supposed to be seeing my grandmother. My mum wanted me to go out with them and give her the birthday present I bought her, but I didn't really want to go so my mum's going to give it to her. Anyway, I got a better offer.
Girl: What was that?
Boy: My dad and my uncle offered to take me to the football match. I'm meeting them for a coffee first.

*Now listen again.*

**7** *Which item of food does the boy go out to buy?*

Boy: I'm just going out to the shops. Do you need anything, Mum?
Mum: What are you going to get?
Boy: I just fancied some biscuits. I thought I'd go to the supermarket.
Mum: There's no need. I bought some earlier. They're in a bag in the kitchen. There's some chocolate too. But you could get some cheese for lunch if you don't mind going out.
Boy: OK, I'll go and get some.

*Now listen again.*

*That is the end of Part 1.*

**Part 2**

# Track 26

*Now look at Part 2.*
*For each question, choose the correct answer.*
**8** *You will hear two friends talking about going shopping.*

Boy: Are we still meeting after school to go into town?
Girl: Yes, if you want to. I was planning on buying a video game, but I phoned them and they don't have the one I want in the shop.
Boy: Well, we can still have a look around, can't we?
Girl: OK. We can go to the bookstore while we're there and see if they have the practice tests we need. I've been looking for a book for the English exam. I'll forget the French practice tests until we know which ones to get.

*Now listen again.*

**9** *You will hear two friends talking about a website.*

Girl: We said we'd find a place where the youth club could get some posters printed, didn't we?

Boy: It's OK, I haven't forgotten. I've been trying to find somewhere online. They're usually cheaper than going to a shop. There is one place that does what we need but I didn't save the website.

Girl: Do you think you can find it again?

Boy: Yes, no problem. The company was called Bright Print, so it should be simple to search for. Anyway, if I can't, my dad told me about one we could use as well.

*Now listen again.*

**10** *You will hear a father and his daughter talking about buying a present.*

Dad: It's Mum's birthday next week. Have you decided what to get her?

Girl: I've already bought her a present, but it's something both of you can use so I'm not telling you what it is.

Dad: That sounds interesting. I wonder what it could be!

Girl: Well, you'll have to wait and see. I want to get her something else as well. She was saying how much she liked that perfume I got her last year. I don't really want to get her the same thing again though.

*Now listen again.*

**11** *You will hear a brother and sister talking about lunch.*

Girl: If you're doing lunch for yourself could you make me something too?

Boy: Sure. I was going to make a cheese sandwich. Is that OK for you?

Girl: Sorry. I had the last slice of bread this morning. Is there anything else?

Boy: There's never any food in this house. Mum and Dad need to go shopping.

Girl: There are some tins of soup in the cupboard. I think I'll have one of them. I'll get the lunch organised as long as you wash the dishes afterwards. How does that sound?

*Now listen again.*

**12** *You will hear two friends talking about how one of them is.*

Girl: You weren't in school yesterday, were you? Are you OK?

Boy: Not really. I was out running on Sunday. I almost got to the end of the run and then I fell over. I wasn't going very quickly but I still hurt myself quite badly.

Girl: Oh, poor you! How are you today?

Boy: Very sore. I'm not having any problems walking around but lying in bed is very painful as I fell on my side and it really hurts when I lie down. I've been to the hospital and they said that nothing is broken.

*Now listen again.*

**13** *You will hear two friends talking about starting guitar lessons.*

Boy: Do you remember I was telling you about wanting to take guitar lessons? Well, I've found a tutor at last.

Girl: That's great. Have you been having lessons?

Boy: I went to see the woman soon after I spoke to you just to meet her. I get started next month. My mum knows her from when she was at university and she arranged for me to see her. I was hoping to have the first lesson next week but she's going away on holiday. But I'm sure the time will go quickly. I can't wait to get started.

*Now listen again.*

*That is the end of Part 2.*

## Part 3

## Track 27

*Now look at Part 3.*
*For each question, write the correct answer in the gap. Write one or two words or a number or a date or a time. Look at Questions 14 to 19 now. You have 20 seconds. You will hear an announcement about a school sports day.*

Man: Sports Day will take place on 19th July. We're starting first thing in the morning at 9.00 so that parents who bring you into school can stay until it begins. Just tell them to wait in the playground until we start.

We'll need the help of teachers to get everything ready for the activities, so we'll be asking you to stay in the hall while we do this. We'll be showing some music videos on the big screen to keep you entertained.

We don't expect to have any accidents, but we do have a first-aid person available for anybody who needs help. She'll be in a tent near the entrance to the school if you or a friend need her. If you can't move, she'll come to you!

As you can imagine, this takes a lot of organisation. We will have three or four activities taking place at the same time and it could get quite busy. Can you make sure you have a copy of the timetable with you, so you know when and where your events take place. The timetable will also be placed on the school gate to help parents find you.

Mrs Thomas will be giving out prizes for each event when the activities have finished. This will be a great opportunity for parents to take photos. It doesn't matter if you haven't come first, second or third in anything. We'll be giving out prizes for schoolwork too!

If you haven't signed up for all the events you want to take part in, speak to Mrs Thomas as soon as you can. She's asked me to tell you that we still have places available for the table tennis competition, so if this is your sport, get in touch with her quickly.

*Now listen again.*

*That is the end of Part 3.*

## Part 4

# Track 28

*Now look at Part 4.*
*For each question, choose the correct answer.*
*Look at Questions 20 to 25 now.*
*You have 45 seconds.*
*You will hear an interview with a woman called Jan Prince, who was a talented musician as a child.*

Man: This morning I'm speaking with Jan Prince about a talent she had as a child.

Jan: Thanks, yes. My talent was playing the piano. Mum and Dad had one in the house from when I was little, so I got used to playing it at a very early age, long before I started school. I seemed to be able to learn easily and everyone used to tell me how good I was.

Man: Were your parents musical?

Jan: My mum loved singing but couldn't play any instruments. It was my dad who encouraged me more. He was a music teacher and used to give me lessons. When I was 11 he persuaded my mum, who to start with wanted me to go to an ordinary school, that I should go to a school that was good at teaching music.

Man: Was school a happy time for you?

Jan: Yes, very much so. I know I wasn't like a lot of other children of my age. While they were buying and listening to popular music, I was practising Beethoven and Mozart. But at my school we all had similar tastes and I made some lovely friends.

Man: But you didn't follow a career in music?

Jan: No. My parents told me I should go to university and continue my music studies, but at 17 I decided I wanted to leave school and find a job. For some unknown reason I started to develop an interest in gardening and took that up as a career.

Man: So, do you still play?

Jan: Of course. I have my own piano at home, which gets used a lot. Also, many of my customers have pianos and they always ask me to play something for them when I go there to do the gardening. I sometimes have to insist on leaving as I have another appointment to go to.

Man: And what about your own children?

Jan: I have a ten-year-old daughter. She's learning to play the piano too but it's not something I push her to do. I'm not saying my dad did this to me, but I would like to give her more chance to tell us what she wants when she goes to secondary school, so I'll let her decide whether that's music or something completely different.

*Now listen again.*

*That is the end of Part 4.*

*You now have six minutes to write your answers on the answer sheet.*

*That is the end of the test.*

## TEST 4    SPEAKING

## Part 1

# Track 29

Examiner: Good morning.
Can I have your mark sheets, please?
I'm Angela Spencer and this is David Williams.

Examiner: What's your name, Candidate A? How old are you?

Candidate A: My name's Tania Mestres and I'm 14 years old.

Examiner: What's your name, Candidate B? How old are you?

[PAUSE FOR YOU TO ANSWER]

Examiner: Candidate B, where do you live?

[PAUSE FOR YOU TO ANSWER]

Examiner: And who do you live with, Candidate B?

[PAUSE FOR YOU TO ANSWER]

Examiner: And Candidate A, where do you live?

Candidate A: I come from Brazil. I live in an apartment in São Paulo.

Examiner: And who do you live with, Candidate A?

Candidate A: I live with my parents and my twin sister.

Examiner: Candidate A, what do you enjoy doing in your free time?

Candidate A: I play the guitar and I love to practise when I don't have anything else to do. I also like reading and listening to music.

Examiner: And Candidate B, what about you?

[PAUSE FOR YOU TO ANSWER]

| Examiner: | Candidate A, tell us what you did last weekend. |
|---|---|
| Candidate A: | Yes, I had a great time last weekend. My cousins came to our house and we had a big party with them on Saturday night. |
| Examiner: | Candidate B, tell us about your last holiday. |
| [PAUSE FOR YOU TO ANSWER] | |
| Examiner: | Thank you. |

## Part 2

## Track 30

| Examiner: | Now I'd like each of you to talk on your own about something. I'm going to give each of you a photograph and I'd like you to talk about it.<br>Candidate A. Here is your photograph. It shows two people sitting together.<br>Please tell us what you can see in the photograph.<br>Candidate B, you just listen. |
|---|---|
| Candidate A: | In this photograph there are two people. I think it's a father and his daughter or it could be her grandfather. They are both sitting at a table and laughing about something. I imagine the man is helping the girl with her homework because they are both holding a book or some sheets of paper. There's also a cup on the table with one or two pens or pencils in it, so I definitely think they are working. The man's wearing a light-coloured jumper and glasses. The girl has lovely curly hair and has a jumper on. They look very happy to be together. |
| Examiner: | Thank you.<br>Candidate B. Here is your photograph. It shows three people sitting together.<br>Please tell us what you can see in the photograph.<br>Candidate A, you just listen. |
| [PAUSE FOR YOU TO ANSWER] | |
| Examiner: | Thank you. |

## Part 3

## Track 31

| Examiner: | Now, in this part of the test you are going to talk about something together for about two minutes. I'm going to describe a situation to you.<br>A teenager has the day off school and he's trying to decide what to do.<br>Here are some things he could do. |
|---|---|

| | Talk together about the different things he could do and say which one would be best.<br>All right? Now talk together. |
|---|---|
| Candidate A: | OK, all of these things are good fun, what do you think? |
| [PAUSE FOR YOU TO ANSWER] | |
| Candidate A: | Yes, that's true. He can do all the other things on his own. I think the TV is the worst idea. If he wants, he can watch TV programmes on the laptop. |
| [PAUSE FOR YOU TO ANSWER] | |
| Candidate A: | Yes, the mobile phone or the laptop. But if he plays the guitar, I think that's one of the best things he can do. What do you think? |
| [PAUSE FOR YOU TO ANSWER] | |
| Candidate A: | I think the guitar. That's my choice. |
| [PAUSE FOR YOU TO ANSWER] | |
| Examiner: | Thank you. |

## Part 4

## Track 32

| Examiner: | Candidate A, what do you like to do if you're bored? |
|---|---|
| Candidate A: | I'm afraid I just watch videos or text my friends on my phone. If there's something good on TV I watch that. |
| Examiner: | And what about you, Candidate B? |
| [PAUSE FOR YOU TO ANSWER] | |
| Examiner: | Candidate B, do you watch much TV? |
| [PAUSE FOR YOU TO ANSWER] | |
| Examiner: | And how about you, Candidate A? |
| Candidate A: | Yes, I watch a lot of TV. My sister and I have our favourite programmes and we sometimes sit together to watch them. |
| Examiner: | Candidate B, do you prefer to relax or be active when you don't have anything to do? |
| [PAUSE FOR YOU TO ANSWER] | |
| Examiner: | And what about you, Candidate A? |
| Candidate A: | I'm not a very active person. I enjoy playing the guitar but most of the time I just go on my phone or watch TV. That's how I relax. |
| Examiner: | Thank you. That is the end of the test. |

## TEST 5    LISTENING

## Part 1

## Track 33

*Preliminary English Test for Schools, Listening. There are four parts to the test. You will hear each piece twice.*

*We will now stop for a moment.*
*Please ask any questions now, because you must not speak during the test.*
*Now look at the instructions for Part 1.*
*For each question, choose the correct answer.*
*Look at Question 1.*

**1**  *Where was the boy when he had his accident?*

Boy:    Hi Mum, it's me, Charlie. Nothing to worry about but I've had a little accident. I was playing football in the garden and the ball got stuck up that big tree. I tried climbing up to get it and then fell down. Nothing broken – there were a couple of people talking at the gate who came over to help. Anyway, I'm fine. Don't blame me for the garage window though. That was broken already, wasn't it? I'll see you when you get home.

*Now listen again.*

**2**  *What has the mother already bought for her daughter's birthday?*

Dad:    What shall we get Lizzie for her birthday? I haven't talked to her about it – have you?

Mum:   No, I haven't, but I think she'd like something to do with running. I saw a nice pair of shorts when I was in town, but I don't know if she'd like the style.

Dad:    What about a new pair of trainers?

Mum:   That's a great idea but it's always important to try them on first. I bought her a pair of running socks last week so that's a start.

*Now listen again.*

**3**  *When is the picnic?*

Woman:  Hello. You are through to CocoMac Arts Centre with information about this weekend's picnic. When we were planning the event the weather forecast looked very good for Saturday so we decided to have it then. It now seems we're likely to get some heavy rain, so we're moving it to Sunday. We apologise for having to make the change. If you've paid and aren't able to attend, you can get a refund for the picnic from tomorrow, that's Friday, or at any time over the weekend.

*Now listen again.*

**4**  *What did the girl forget to buy for the party?*

Boy:    So, I think we've got everything for Steve's party, haven't we?

Girl:   Yes, it was a good idea to get paper plates and cups. I forgot how many people were coming. I hope we've got enough cups.

Boy:    I'm sure we'll have plenty. And they can all be put in the recycle bin too. No washing up.

Girl:   Yes. I didn't remember to get wooden knives and forks. Plastic ones aren't very good for the environment, are they? I'm surprised the shops still sell them.

*Now listen again.*

**5**  *What has the man lost today?*

Father:  Hi. It's Dad here. I've just arrived at work and I can't find my wallet. I really hope I haven't lost it. It's not the one with my credit card in so I'm not too worried about that but there was some money in it. Can you have a look to see if I've left it at home? I don't know what's wrong with me lately. I lost my mobile phone last week, well, at least I thought I had until I found it in my desk.

*Now listen again.*

**6**  *Which country does the girl think will win the match?*

Boy:    I can't wait for the match this afternoon. Are you going to watch it?

Girl:   Of course. I've really enjoyed the competition so far. Italy played brilliantly in the last game I saw, and really deserved their win.

Boy:    I know. What about France and Poland today?

Girl:   Well, I love France and it would be great to see them win, though I don't think they will. Poland have been fantastic so far, haven't they!

*Now listen again.*

**7**  *Where should the girl go to get a drink?*

Man:    Hello, can I help you?

Girl:   Yes, I'd like a single to the city centre, please.

Man:    Here you are. That's £3.00 for a single. The next train leaves at 7.20 from Platform 11.

Girl:   Thanks a lot. Is there anywhere I can get a cold drink near here?

Man:    There's nothing on 11 I'm afraid, but there's a snack bar on Platform 10. That may be closed though, so try the self-service machine on Platform 14.

*Now listen again.*

*That is the end of Part 1.*

## Part 2

## Track 34

*Now look at Part 2.*
*For each question, choose the correct answer.*

**8**  *You will hear two friends talking about a car.*

Boy:    My mum's just bought another car. It's lovely.

| Girl: | What is it? |
|---|---|
| Boy: | I don't know the model but it's a Ford. She wanted a smaller one but after she took it on a test drive, she fell in love with it. |
| Girl: | So, is it brand new? |
| Boy: | No, I don't think we could afford a new car. I told her to keep the old one for me for when I'm old enough to take driving lessons but she said that was too long to wait. |

*Now listen again.*

**9** *You will hear two friends talking about a school trip.*

| Boy: | Are you going on the school trip to the museum next week or staying in school? |
|---|---|
| Girl: | No, I'm going on the trip. They've arranged activities for those who aren't going but I'm sure the trip will be more interesting. I thought we were meeting at 8.00 but it's 7.00, isn't it? That's a pity. I'm usually still in bed then. |
| Boy: | But it will be nice to get away from school for the day, won't it? |
| Girl: | True. And we might be able to look around the shops before we come back. |

*Now listen again.*

**10** *You will hear a mother and her son talking about exams.*

| Boy: | So, do you know what exams I've got next week? |
|---|---|
| Mother: | Yes, I've been looking at the timetable. It says you have maths on Thursday but the teacher told us Wednesday. |
| Boy: | No, you're thinking of English. We've got English on Wednesday. I'm looking forward to that one. I think I'll do well. |
| Mother: | And Friday looks like your busy day. You've got three exams according to the timetable. |
| Boy: | We're not doing one of those now. We've got one in the morning and one in the afternoon. |

*Now listen again.*

**11** *You will hear two friends talking about keeping animals in a zoo.*

| Girl: | We were having a discussion in class today about zoos and whether it's good to keep wild animals. I couldn't make my mind up. |
|---|---|
| Boy: | Well, there are some animals that wouldn't exist anymore if they weren't kept in a zoo. |
| Girl: | I know. That's what I said in the lesson. |
| Boy: | Plus. I think when visitors see them it makes them realise how fantastic some of these creatures are. It might make people angrier about the way they're treated. |

| Girl: | I'm not sure that's true. I think they just see it as a fun day out. |
|---|---|

*Now listen again.*

**12** *You will hear two friends talking about writing essays.*

| Boy: | Do you prefer writing your essays on a computer or with a pen and paper? |
|---|---|
| Girl: | Well, everyone tells me I've got lovely handwriting and I like to use a pen or a pencil so that it doesn't get worse. |
| Boy: | My handwriting has got so bad since I started using a computer for my essays. |
| Girl: | But also, if you make a mistake with a pen you have to start all over again, don't you? It's not like that on a computer. Anyway, our teacher won't accept work unless it's done on a computer. He says we should be using it to help us improve our writing skills. |

*Now listen again.*

**13** *You will hear two friends talking about a piece of furniture.*

| Girl: | It's my birthday soon and my mum and dad have offered to treat me to some new furniture for my bedroom. |
|---|---|
| Boy: | Oooh, lucky you! |
| Girl: | I'm getting a new desk to replace the one I have. That's falling apart. I'm keeping the bed. I only got that recently. I asked for a new wardrobe but I'm getting my sister's one as she's moving out to go to university. Oh, and they're also getting me a rug I saw in a shop. It'll be perfect for my bedroom. |

*Now listen again.*

*That is the end of Part 2.*

## Part 3

## Track 35

*Now look at Part 3.*
*For each question, write the correct answer in the gap. Write one or two words or a number or a date or a time.*
*Look at Questions 14 to 19 now. You have 20 seconds. You will hear a man talking about a college open evening.*

| Man: | Thanks for calling Trenstone College Information desk. Our open evening will take place on 12th June from 6.30 until 8.30 in the evening. This day is for 15- and 16-year-olds who are thinking of leaving school to study in a more adult environment. |
|---|---|
| | The evening will begin with a talk by the College Head. Following her welcome message you'll be shown round the college by our volunteers, all of them students at the college. They'll be able |

to answer any of your questions about life at the college and perhaps help you with any questions you may have about your studies.

However, we've also arranged sessions with all the tutors to give you a clear idea of the subjects you can do with us. On arrival we'll give you a timetable of events and a map of the building to help you find the rooms where each of the activities are taking place.

Our drama students have recently done very well in a national competition and they'll be performing in the gym. Whether you're interested in a career in dance or acting or just feel like being entertained, come along to see them at 7.30.

If you like what you see when you've had a look round, remember to take away our information sheet from reception. This will give you more details about the subjects on offer and explain what you need to do to apply.

Finally, we hope you have a wonderful evening at the college. We always aim to provide the best possible introduction to Trenstone and we're always interested in the opinions of parents and students. Please take a few minutes to fill in the questionnaire before you leave, and hand it in to a teacher.

*Now listen again.*

*That is the end of Part 3.*

## Part 4

## Track 36

*Now look at Part 4.*
*For each question, choose the correct answer.*
*Look at Questions 20 to 25 now.*
*You have 45 seconds.*
*You will hear an interview with a young woman called Jemma Bruce, who is an award-winning baker.*

Man:     Today I'm talking to Jemma Bruce, an award-winning baker who is only 16. Tell us about the award, Jemma.

Jemma:   Thanks, it was something that the local schools organised. We'd seen these programmes on TV where people compete against each other to be the best baker, so the schools decided to organise something similar for the students. I was so proud to represent my school and also to come first, as the students from the other schools were very good.

Man:     Where did you learn to bake?

Jemma:   I have my grandmother to thank for that. I used to stay with her for one or two days a week before I started going to

school and she needed to find activities to do with me. She didn't mind doing the normal things like painting and going to the park, but she always looked forward to baking with me.

Man:     Do you do any other kind of cooking?

Jemma:   To be honest, I'm not very keen on cooking generally. I think my mum and dad would like me to take an interest in it as it would save them the bother of having to cook dinner every evening. Maybe that's something I'll develop an interest in when I'm older.

Man:     What do you like about baking cakes?

Jemma:   Well, everyone likes eating cakes, don't they? My friends and family enjoy the things I make, which is nice to see. I also find it very relaxing and a nice way of forgetting about schoolwork. It can take quite a while to prepare all the ingredients and I find I'm able to forget about my studies for a while.

Man:     Do you cook for special occasions?

Jemma:   Yes, I'm always asked to bake something for family birthdays. The last one I made was actually for my grandmother, who was celebrating her 80th birthday. Mum and dad organised a big party and invited about 50 people. I knew they'd all be watching out for the cake, so I was a little more nervous than usual, but it all turned out OK.

Man:     And do you think you will take it up as a career?

Jemma:   I don't think that's likely. I want to carry on baking, but as a hobby because I enjoy it so much. I'm studying hard at school and want to go to university. I'm not sure what I want to study yet, but something creative would be perfect. I just hope I have an oven in my student accommodation!

*Now listen again.*

*That is the end of Part 4.*

*You now have six minutes to write your answers on the answer sheet.*

*That is the end of the test.*

## TEST 5     SPEAKING

## Part 1

## Track 37

Examiner:     Good morning.
              Can I have your mark sheets, please?
              I'm William Castle and this is Ros Walker.

Examiner:     What's your name, Candidate A? How old are you?

| Candidate A: | My name's Boris Volovik and I'm 13 years old. |
| Examiner: | And what's your name, Candidate B? How old are you? |

[PAUSE FOR YOU TO ANSWER]

| Examiner: | Candidate B, where do you live? |

[PAUSE FOR YOU TO ANSWER]

| Examiner: | And who do you live with, Candidate B? |

[PAUSE FOR YOU TO ANSWER]

| Examiner: | And Candidate A, what about you? Where do you live? |
| Candidate A: | I live in St Petersburg, in Russia. I live in an apartment not very far from the river. |
| Examiner: | And who do you live with, Candidate A? |
| Candidate A: | I live with my mother, my father and my two sisters. |
| Examiner: | Candidate A, what food do you like to eat? |
| Candidate A: | I like anything really. I enjoy pasta, pizza and also fast food like burgers. |
| Examiner: | And Candidate B, what about you? |

[PAUSE FOR YOU TO ANSWER]

| Examiner: | Candidate A, do you prefer being in the city or the countryside? |
| Candidate A: | I prefer being in the city. I like walking around the shops and having different things to do. |
| Examiner: | What about you, Candidate B? |

[PAUSE FOR YOU TO ANSWER]

| Examiner: | Candidate A, tell us about your favourite day of the week. |
| Candidate A: | I like Saturdays best. We don't have to go to school and so I often meet my friends and we do things together. Sometimes we play football, sometimes we watch a film together – we try to have fun! |
| Examiner: | Candidate B, tell us what your favourite meal of the day is. |

[PAUSE FOR YOU TO ANSWER]

| Examiner: | Thank you. |

## Part 2

## Track 38

| Examiner: | Now, I'd like each of you to talk on your own about something. I'm going to give each of you a photograph and I'd like you to talk about it. Candidate A. Here is your photograph. It shows people doing something together. Please tell us what you can see in the photograph. Candidate B, you just listen. |
| Candidate A: | In this photograph I can see a man and a teenage boy. They're |

probably father and son. The boy is wearing a T-shirt and the man has a light-coloured shirt on. They're both looking at a model ship. It looks like one of those ships that you make yourself by sticking small pieces together. They've finished making it and now it looks like they're painting it. The boy is holding a paintbrush and there are some paints on the table in front of him. Perhaps they're talking about what colour the ship should be.

| Examiner: | Thank you. Candidate B. Here is your photograph. It shows some young people outside. Please tell us what you can see in the photograph. Candidate A, you just listen. |

[PAUSE FOR YOU TO ANSWER]

| Examiner: | Thank you. |

## Part 3

## Track 39

| Examiner: | Now, in this part of the test you are going to talk about something together for about two minutes. I'm going to describe a situation to you. A teenager wants to do some sport with her friends. Here are some sports she could do with her friends. Talk together about the different sports she could do with her friends and say which one they would enjoy most. All right? Now talk together. |
| Candidate A: | OK, would you like to start? |

[PAUSE FOR YOU TO ANSWER]

| Candidate A: | Yes, I agree. I don't think they want to go running either. That seems a bit too serious and isn't really fun. What do you think? |

[PAUSE FOR YOU TO ANSWER]

| Candidate A: | Yes, cycling's a good idea. And so is football. You don't need any equipment for that, only a ball and somewhere to play. I don't think dancing is a good idea. I don't like dancing anyway. |

[PAUSE FOR YOU TO ANSWER]

| Candidate A: | Yes, I agree. So what do we think? |

[PAUSE FOR YOU TO ANSWER]

| Candidate A: | I like cycling too, so yes, let's say cycling. |
| Examiner: | Thank you. |

## Part 4

## Track 40

| | |
|---|---|
| Examiner: | Candidate A, do you like playing sports? |
| Candidate A: | Sometimes, yes. I like playing football with my friends after school and we play basketball as well sometimes. |
| Examiner: | And what about you, Candidate B? |
| [PAUSE FOR YOU TO ANSWER] | |
| Examiner: | Candidate B, do you do any sports at school? |
| [PAUSE FOR YOU TO ANSWER] | |
| Examiner: | And how about you, Candidate A? |
| Candidate A: | Yes, it's the same in our school. My school also has a very good basketball team and some of us practise that in lessons. |
| Examiner: | Candidate B, do you prefer doing a sport on your own or with other people? |
| [PAUSE FOR YOU TO ANSWER] | |
| Examiner: | And what about you, Candidate A? |
| Candidate A: | I agree. I prefer team sports. I try harder when I know my friends need me to play well. |
| Examiner: | Thank you. That is the end of the test. |

## TEST 6     LISTENING

## Part 1

## Track 41

*Preliminary English Test for Schools, Listening.*
*There are four parts to the test. You will hear each piece twice.*
*We will now stop for a moment.*
*Please ask any questions now, because you must not speak during the test.*
*Now look at the instructions for Part 1.*
*For each question, choose the correct answer.*
*Look at Question 1.*

**1**    *Where does the boy think his homework is?*

| | |
|---|---|
| Boy: | Mum, it's me. Can you do me a favour? I've just got into school and I've forgotten my homework. Could you bring it to the school reception for me? I was working at the kitchen table last night, but I tidied that up when I'd finished. And I remember that I made my bed before I left so I don't think it'll be on there. Try the chair in the kitchen. I think I put it on the seat when I was clearing the table. |

*Now listen again.*

**2**    *What does the girl's father want her to buy?*

| | |
|---|---|
| Father: | Are you going out to the supermarket? |
| Daughter: | Yes, Mum's just asked me to go. Do you need anything from there? |

| | |
|---|---|
| Father: | Yes, I fancy a sandwich for lunch. There's plenty of bread left, but I think your sister finished the cheese this morning. |
| Daughter: | OK, I'll get some for you. Mum wants me to get some apples and grapes, so I'll get them too while I'm out. |

*Now listen again.*

**3**    *What does the boy want to hire?*

| | |
|---|---|
| Boy: | I'm just phoning to find out about hiring equipment from the centre. |
| Woman: | Yes, how can I help you? |
| Boy: | My father plays golf at your club and I know he was able to hire things for that, so I wondered if you have any tennis rackets. My friend and I want to play. |
| Woman: | Yes, that's not a problem. |
| Boy: | Great. We'll come along now. Is there somewhere safe we can leave our bikes? |
| Woman: | Yes, you can bring them into the centre. |

*Now listen again.*

**4**    *What has been damaged?*

| | |
|---|---|
| Girl: | Hello, Mum. You know I said I wanted to help you with the decorating and do some painting? Well, I've had a little accident. I put the tin of paint on the cupboard and was standing on the back of the sofa to get up high, when suddenly the sofa fell forwards. I jumped off and knocked the paint off the cupboard. I'm afraid some of it has gone on the rug. I've tried getting it off, but I just seem to be making it worse. |

*Now listen again.*

**5**    *Why might the students be back late?*

| | |
|---|---|
| Teacher: | Hello. I'm just calling about the school trip tomorrow. We've been checking the weather forecast and it's not looking very good. We're likely to get a lot of rain, but that's not a problem as we'll be inside most of the day. But there's a possibility of snow, which could mean we're delayed on the way back. But at least the strong winds they predicted won't be as bad as they thought. Please check the school website for the latest news. |

*Now listen again.*

**6**    *What is the girl not interested in?*

| | |
|---|---|
| Brother: | Mum and Dad were talking about booking a holiday earlier. |
| Sister: | I know. Dad wants to go somewhere he can take lots of photos, but that usually means we have to walk round lots of old buildings. I don't like the sound of that. |

| | |
|---|---|
| Brother: | I hope they choose a good hotel. I know mum said she wanted one with a nice swimming pool. |
| Sister: | Yes, that would be great. I just want to relax by the pool and read a good book. |

*Now listen again.*

**7** *Which date is the girl's birthday?*

| | |
|---|---|
| Boy: | Are you looking forward to your birthday party? |
| Girl: | Yes, it's only going to be my family coming but it's always lovely to have them around the house. Actually, I'm having the party on the 27th, a week after my birthday. |
| Boy: | So not on the 20th? That's a shame. It's always nice to celebrate on the day, isn't it? |
| Girl: | I know. We were going to have it on the 13th, the week before, but some people couldn't come then. |

*Now listen again.*

*That is the end of Part 1.*

## Part 2

## Track 42

*Now look at Part 2.*
*For each question, choose the correct answer.*
**8** *You will hear two friends talking about a book.*

| | |
|---|---|
| Boy: | Have you finished that book the teacher told us to read? |
| Girl: | Yes. I read it all in one day. What about you? |
| Boy: | I've read about half of it. It's not really the kind of story I enjoy, to be honest. I prefer science fiction. I'm only reading it because I have to. |
| Girl: | You've got to finish it before the lesson on Friday. We're having a discussion about it in class. |
| Boy: | I know. I'll try and get it finished tonight. If not, maybe you can tell me how it ends? |

*Now listen again.*

**9** *You will hear two friends talking about a bicycle.*

| | |
|---|---|
| Boy: | When are you going to get your bike repaired? I've got nobody to go out cycling with. |
| Girl: | I took it in to the shop three days ago. They phoned yesterday morning and said they'd finished the work. I just haven't had time to go and collect it. |
| Boy: | Let's go after school this afternoon. It's on the way home, isn't it? |
| Girl: | OK, that's a good idea. As you've already got your bike at school, we can go out for a ride together after I've collected it. |
| Boy. | Great! I'll meet you at the school gates. |

*Now listen again.*

**10** *You will hear a father and his daughter talking about her brother Alan.*

| | |
|---|---|
| Father: | What time is Alan getting home? I need to get dinner ready. |
| Daughter: | He's just texted me. He says his train's been cancelled and he doesn't know when the next one is. |
| Father: | Can you text him back and tell him I'm starting dinner because I'm going out later this evening. He can always warm it up in the microwave if he's late. |
| Daughter: | OK. Don't bother cooking for me. I'm seeing my friends later and we'll get something while we're out. |
| Father: | There'll be some left over so you can have it when you get in if you're hungry. |

*Now listen again.*

**11** *You will hear two friends talking about travelling to a new school.*

| | |
|---|---|
| Boy: | Have you decided how you're going to get to the new school next year? |
| Girl: | Not yet. I was going to get the bus, but they no longer run the service. |
| Boy: | Why did they change it? It used to go right to the school gates. That just leaves the train. Unless we go by bike? |
| Girl: | It's too far to cycle. The train isn't too expensive, and the school is quite close to the station, so I could do the last bit on foot. Do you want to travel to the new school with me? |
| Boy: | I'll think about it. |

*Now listen again.*

**12** *You will hear two friends talking about feeling nervous before an exam.*

| | |
|---|---|
| Boy: | How are you feeling about the exam next week? I'm getting a bit nervous. |
| Girl: | You'll be OK. You've worked hard so there's not much more you can do. |
| Boy: | That's true. I'm sure I know the subject well enough. |
| Girl: | If I were you, I'd relax the night before. One more night's revision isn't going to make any difference. But make sure you give yourself plenty of time to get to the exam centre, even if you get there early. And don't spend time chatting with people before the exam. That will only make you more nervous. |

*Now listen again.*

**13** *You will hear two friends talking about a library they go to.*

| | |
|---|---|
| Girl: | Fancy coming to the library in town after school? |
| Boy: | Yes, OK. I was telling my friends how quiet it is there compared to the school library. |
| Girl: | I know. And there are lots of tables so it's easy to find somewhere to work. |

Boy: Some of the people who work there are a bit rude though. I asked one of them to help me find a book and she said she didn't have time to help me. But they have a computer system for when you borrow books so at least you don't have to wait for them to serve you.

*Now listen again.*

*That is the end of Part 2.*

## Part 3

## Track 43

*Now look at Part 3.*
*For each question, write the correct answer in the gap.*
*Write one or two words or a number or a date or a time.*
*Look at Questions 14 to 19 now. You have 20 seconds.*
*You will hear a man talking about a football training course.*

Man: Many thanks for coming along to the sports centre today. I just want to spend a minute or two telling you about the new training programme for those interested in playing football at a higher level. So, what's the course about? Well, it's all about helping you to keep fit and develop your footballing skills.

We're very lucky to have an excellent trainer to guide you through the course. Kevin McNamara, a professional trainer with many years' experience, will be running the course. He has worked with top players from local football teams, knows the game very well and will be able to share his experience with you.

Kevin will watch your progress during the course and help you learn what your strengths are as well as identifying whether you might be better defending rather than attacking or the other way around. By the end of the course, you'll have a better idea what your best position is on the field.

Of course, all of you will want to get the chance to play the game and you'll have plenty of opportunities to do just that. It's a mixed ability course so we'll divide you up into three groups and you'll play at the level that best suits your ability. However, there'll always be a chance to move up or down if necessary.

These courses are extremely popular, so make sure you sign up soon or you may be turned away. The next course will begin on 13th August, so you only have a few weeks to make up your mind. If you're interested and decide this is for you, pick up an application form from the reception desk and I look forward to seeing you all in August.

*Now listen again.*

*That is the end of Part 3.*

## Part 4

## Track 44

*Now look at Part 4.*
*For each question, choose the correct answer.*
*Look at Questions 20 to 25 now.*
*You have 45 seconds.*
*You will hear an interview with a boy called Jason Wright, who does skateboarding.*

Woman: How did you get started with skateboarding?

Jason: There were some kids who used to hang out near where I lived. I spent evenings watching them practise. They got talking to me and then one day one of them let me try his skateboard. I'd never even stood on one before and I didn't expect to be any good, but I managed not to fall over and surprised myself by how quickly I learnt to do it.

Woman: So what did you do after that introduction?

Jason: Well, luckily there are a few skateboarding parks near where I live so I started to use them. There are always people around who are better than you or who can do a particular trick better than you, so there's always something new to learn, whether you're a complete beginner like I was then or more advanced like I am now.

Woman: What equipment do you need for skateboarding?

Jason: Well, apart from the skateboard, you must wear things to protect you from getting injured. So, you'll need a good quality helmet. Don't buy a cheap one as it may not give you the protection you need – that's important. A good cycling helmet is OK. You need to protect other parts of the body as well, especially your elbows and knees, and a good pair of trainers is also important.

Woman: Have you ever been injured?

Jason: Yes, I've broken a couple of bones and hurt my arm. I think if you're serious about taking it up as a hobby you need to accept that you will get injured, hopefully nothing too serious though. It's more dangerous than some other sports. But you can injure yourself doing any sport really, can't you?

Woman: Do you ever worry about hurting yourself when you're learning new tricks?

Jason: Definitely, if you're trying something new it can easily result in you falling over. This is a good reason for using the right equipment. But part of the fun of skateboarding is facing your fears and trying something new. You will fall over sometimes but if you finally succeed with the move, it's a great feeling.

| Woman: | What do you like about skateboarding? |
|---|---|
| Jason: | Lots of things really. I've made some great friends and I love hanging out with them at skateparks. But the great thing about skateboarding is you can do it on your own as well if you want. If your friends aren't around and you want to play a game of football, you're out of luck. But with skateboarding you can just pick up your board and off you go. |

*Now listen again.*

*That is the end of Part 4.*

*You now have six minutes to write your answers on the answer sheet.*

*That is the end of the test.*

## TEST 6    SPEAKING

### Part 1

## Track 45

| Examiner: | Good morning. Can I have your mark sheets, please? I'm Catherine Huntingford and this is Mark Davies. |
|---|---|
| Examiner: | What's your name, Candidate A? How old are you? |
| Candidate A: | My name's Esther Lenherr and I'm 13 years old. |
| Examiner: | And what's your name, Candidate B? How old are you? |
| [PAUSE FOR YOU TO ANSWER] | |
| Examiner: | Candidate B, where do you live? |
| [PAUSE FOR YOU TO ANSWER] | |
| Examiner: | And who do you live with, Candidate B? |
| [PAUSE FOR YOU TO ANSWER] | |
| Examiner: | And Candidate A, where do you live? |
| Candidate A: | I come from Zurich in Switzerland but at the moment I'm living in Manchester in the UK. |
| Examiner: | And Candidate A, who do you live with? |
| Candidate A: | I live with my parents and my brother and sister. |
| Examiner: | Candidate A, what's your favourite way of travelling? |
| Candidate A: | I really like cars and they are my favourite way of travelling. I like sitting in the front seat next to my dad and looking out of the window. |
| Examiner: | Candidate B, what about you? |
| [PAUSE FOR YOU TO ANSWER] | |
| Examiner: | Candidate B, tell me how often you eat in a restaurant. |
| [PAUSE FOR YOU TO ANSWER] | |
| Examiner: | And Candidate A, what about you? |
| Candidate A: | We have lots of restaurants near my house in Zurich but they're |

quite expensive, so we don't go there very often, but we sometimes go out in Manchester.

| Examiner: | Thank you. |
|---|---|

### Part 2

## Track 46

| Examiner: | Now I'd like each of you to talk on your own about something. I'm going to give each of you a photograph and I'd like you to talk about it. Candidate A. Here is your photograph. It shows people sitting on a sofa. Please tell us what you can see in the photograph. Candidate B, you just listen. |
|---|---|
| Candidate A: | In this photograph I can see a man and a woman. I think they're at home, sitting on the sofa and watching TV in the living room. There's a football match on and the man is enjoying it. I can't see his face because he's looking at the TV and we can only see the back of his head, but I imagine he's interested in the game. The woman has turned away from the TV and is looking in our direction. She looks very bored and probably doesn't like football. I think she'd like to do something else or watch a different programme. |
| Examiner: | Thank you. Candidate B. Here is your photograph. It shows some people outside. Please tell us what you can see in the photograph. Candidate A, you just listen. |
| [PAUSE FOR YOU TO ANSWER] | |
| Examiner: | Thank you. |

### Part 3

## Track 47

| Examiner: | Now, in this part of the test you are going to talk about something together for about two minutes. I'm going to describe a situation to you. A teacher is just about to teach an English lesson. Here are some things she could take to the classroom to use in her English lesson. Talk together about the different things she could take and say which one would be best. All right? Now talk together. |
|---|---|
| Candidate A: | OK, would you like to start? |

[PAUSE FOR YOU TO ANSWER]

| | |
|---|---|
| Candidate A: | I think that's a good idea because she can cut out photographs or articles and give them to the students. I'm not sure that one mobile phone is useful. Only one person can use it. And I don't think the pencils are important. The students will probably have their own. |

[PAUSE FOR YOU TO ANSWER]

| | |
|---|---|
| Candidate A: | Not much really. The laptop and the pair of headphones are like the mobile phone. If there's only one, it's difficult for all the students to use them. The TV could be a good idea though. The teacher could show an English programme or a video. Which one do you think is best, the TV or the magazine? |

[PAUSE FOR YOU TO ANSWER]

| | |
|---|---|
| Candidate A: | OK, I think you're right. Let's say the magazine. |
| Examiner: | Thank you. |

## Part 4

## Track 48

| | |
|---|---|
| Examiner: | Candidate A, what do you like to do in lessons? |
| Candidate A: | I enjoy watching videos on TV and then having a discussion with other people in the class, especially if it's an interesting subject. |
| Examiner: | And what about you, Candidate B? |

[PAUSE FOR YOU TO ANSWER]

| | |
|---|---|
| Examiner: | Candidate B, what do you think makes a good teacher? |

[PAUSE FOR YOU TO ANSWER]

| | |
|---|---|
| Examiner: | And how about you, Candidate A? |
| Candidate A: | In my opinion, the teacher must know the subject very well. But I agree, they also need to be able to explain what they know to the students, so they understand. |
| Examiner: | Candidate B, do you like working on computers at school? |

[PAUSE FOR YOU TO ANSWER]

| | |
|---|---|
| Examiner: | And what about you, Candidate A? |
| Candidate A: | We don't have many computers at my school, so we don't get the opportunity to use them. But I like working on my laptop at home. |
| Examiner: | Thank you. That is the end of the test. |

## TEST 7    LISTENING

## Part 1

## Track 49

*Preliminary English Test for Schools, Listening.*
*There are four parts to the test. You will hear each piece twice.*

*We will now stop for a moment.*
*Please ask any questions now, because you must not speak during the test.*
*Now look at the instructions for Part 1.*
*For each question, choose the correct answer.*
*Look at Question 1.*

**1**    *When is the concert?*

| | |
|---|---|
| Boy: | Hiya, it's Chris. I've just ordered the tickets for the concert. They're supposed to be arriving on the 7th. That's only a day before the event on the 8th and I'm a bit worried about them arriving on time. I was wondering if you fancy coming with me to the concert hall. I'm not doing anything on the 6th so we could go then and get the tickets from their office. Let me know if you can make it. |

*Now listen again.*

**2**    *What did the boy's mother enjoy doing at the party?*

| | |
|---|---|
| Boy: | Do you think everyone enjoyed the party last night? |
| Girl: | I think so. Your mum seemed to be having a great time. Whenever I saw her, she was chatting to someone different. |
| Boy: | I know. I was trying to get her to have a dance but she's not very keen on dancing. But the food she made was delicious, wasn't it? |
| Girl: | Yes, but she told me she wasn't eating any of it as she's on a diet. |

*Now listen again.*

**3**    *What was the weather like on the journey to the football match?*

| | |
|---|---|
| Girl: | How was your game on Saturday? Did you win? |
| Boy: | It was OK, and yes, we did win. It was so windy and it was pouring with rain on the way and I wasn't really looking forward to getting wet. |
| Girl: | I know, I saw it and was thinking of you. |
| Boy: | But to be honest, once we started playing it improved. We didn't get much sunshine but just a few showers now and again. |

*Now listen again.*

**4**    *What time does the exam start?*

| | |
|---|---|
| Teacher: | Can I have your attention, please? I've now got the time for your English exam tomorrow. We've decided to have it just after lunch and you need to make sure you're in the restaurant at 12.30 so the exams officer can come and give you any important last-minute information. We were hoping to start at 1.30 but it looks like it will have to be half an hour earlier at 1.00 as someone needs the room after us. Good luck everyone. |

*Now listen again.*

**5**  *What is the girl's mother doing?*

Daughter:  Dad, where's Mum? I need my pocket money so I can go out with my friends.

Father:  She's in town doing some shopping. She's taking her driving test tomorrow and she wants something nice to wear for it.

Daughter:  She must be so nervous. She was telling me how well her driving lesson had gone yesterday. I hope she passes.

Father:  Me too. Anyway, I can give you your pocket money. How much do you need?

*Now listen again.*

**6**  *What size of shirt does the boy need?*

Woman:  Hello. Can I help you?

Boy:  Yes, I was given this shirt as a birthday present, but it doesn't fit me. It's too large.

Woman:  OK. Have you got the receipt, please?

Boy:  Yes, here you are. It's a medium, which is what I normally wear but it's definitely too large on me, so I'll change it for a smaller one.

Woman:  OK. If you go and get the size you need and come back, I'll exchange it for you.

Boy:  Thanks.

*Now listen again.*

**7**  *What did the father do that was wrong?*

Brother:  Dad's not very happy about that fine, is he?

Sister:  I know, but it's his own fault. At least he doesn't use his mobile phone. I think that's really dangerous when you're driving.

Brother:  I know. From now on we'll have to remind him to wear his seat belt, won't we?

Sister:  Definitely. That's the second time he's been caught not wearing it. Luckily, he's a very careful driver.

Brother:  That's true. We always have to tell him not to drive so slowly, don't we?

*Now listen again.*

*That is the end of Part 1.*

## Part 2

## Track 50

*Now look at Part 2.*
*For each question, choose the correct answer.*
**8**  *You will hear two friends talking about school dinners.*

Girl:  Don't you eat in the school restaurant anymore? I haven't seen you there for a while.

Boy:  I go there sometimes. I was behind you in the queue the other day but you didn't see me.

Girl:  You should have shouted! Are you going there today? If you are, I'll look out for you.

Boy:  Not today. I'm not fond of the Monday or Tuesday menu. I know I should be eating healthy dinners but they don't have my favourites today, like pizza or burgers. I've asked my mum for sandwiches a couple of days a week.

*Now listen again.*

**9**  *You will hear two friends talking about their plans for the weekend.*

Boy:  What are you doing on Saturday? I'm planning a trip into town with some of the others.

Girl:  I can't join you this weekend. I'm going to be too busy to go to the shopping centre.

Boy:  Come out with us! Lots of us are going. You'll have fun.

Girl:  I know, I was talking to some of them earlier. I'd love to come but I won't have time unfortunately. We've got some relatives coming round and my mum wants me to help tidy the house and be around when they arrive.

Boy:  OK. Maybe next weekend then.

*Now listen again.*

**10**  *You will hear a brother and sister talking about where they want to sit in their mother's car.*

Boy:  Right, I think it's my turn to sit in the front. You were in the front seat last time we went out.

Girl:  Actually, I think you had the front seat last time. You said you were feeling sick and didn't want to sit in the back.

Boy:  Well, that journey doesn't count. Let's ask Mum to decide when she comes.

Girl:  Mum won't want to waste her time trying to sort it out. You can have the front seat on the way to the shops and I'll have it on the way back. Fair?

Boy:  I suppose so.

*Now listen again.*

**11**  *You will hear two friends talking about a school party.*

Girl:  I'm staying late at school today to help them organise the hall for the party tonight. Are you coming?

Boy:  To the party yes, but I haven't got time to help out, I'm afraid. I'm going to go home first to get something to eat. There wasn't a lot of food at last year's party and I don't suppose there'll be any more to eat this year.

Girl:  I'm looking forward to it though. It should be good fun.

| Boy: | Me too. It always makes me laugh when the teachers get up to dance. |

*Now listen again.*

**12** *You will hear two friends talking about a laptop.*

| Boy: | That's a lovely laptop. Is it new? |
| Girl: | Yes, my mum and dad bought it for me for school. I really like it. They had the programs I need for my studies installed on it when they bought it as well, which was kind of them. |
| Boy: | What a great present! I need another one as well. Would you recommend this one? |
| Girl: | I prefer it to the one I had before. That was so slow to start it used to really annoy me. It wasn't too expensive either, so I'm happy with it. |

*Now listen again.*

**13** *You will hear two friends talking about the weather.*

| Girl: | Have you seen the weather forecast for the weekend? It's going to pour with rain. I'm not sure I want to go to the park in that. |
| Boy: | It's not looking very good, is it? I know we were going to have a picnic but maybe that's not a good idea. I'd rather not stay at home though. |
| Girl: | Well, what about the cinema? |
| Boy: | I don't know. I still fancy going to the park but I just don't want to get wet. Why don't we leave it until the day and see what the weather's like? We can decide what to do then. |

*Now listen again.*

*That is the end of Part 2.*

## Part 3

## Track 51

*Now look at Part 3.*
*For each question, write the correct answer in the gap.*
*Write one or two words or a number or a date or a time.*
*Look at Questions 14 to 19 now. You have 20 seconds.*
*You will hear a girl called Sarah talking about one of her interests.*

| Sarah: | OK, well, as part of my class presentation on hobbies and interests let me tell you about how I spend my time. For the past 18 months I've been working as a volunteer at the local leisure centre. It's not something I ever imagined myself doing but I absolutely love it. |
| | It was my mum who persuaded me to find out about what was on offer. I don't think I would have gone otherwise. The first thing I did was work with some other kids to serve food to older people for a birthday party one of them was |

celebrating at the centre. I really enjoyed it, especially getting to know some of the other volunteers.

That was a while ago and since then I've done lots of different things. I help run holiday groups for children who are off school. I've been on trips with them and done more activities with older visitors to the centre. At the moment, I'm working with teenagers on an art project.

I've discovered I really enjoy it. It's not like work. If I was getting paid for it then I think it would be different. It would feel like a job. But just giving up my time to help the centre and other people feels good. I suppose I spend about 16 hours a month volunteering, but I'd be happy to do more if I had the time.

The best thing about being a volunteer for me is that it has made me more confident. I've made lots of friends and I love helping out on projects. I would definitely recommend it as it can be really good fun. Not only that, I think the experience I've gained will be useful when I go for interviews for jobs.

*Now listen again.*

*That is the end of Part 3.*

## Part 4

## Track 52

*Now look at Part 4.*
*For each question, choose the correct answer.*
*Look at Questions 20 to 25 now.*
*You have 45 seconds.*
*You will hear an interview with a boy called John Edwards, who is talking about camping.*

| Woman: | Hello John. You've agreed to talk to us about your interest in camping. Where did that start? |
| John: | I've always loved being outside. I'm always looking out of the window at school wondering what's going on or where I'd like to be. It's not that I don't like school, but I just don't feel as comfortable inside as I do outside. I think that's because when I was little, I used to go camping every year with my parents and absolutely loved it. |
| Woman: | What is it that makes camping special for you? |
| John: | Getting out of the tent early in the morning and seeing the sun come up and the fields around just makes me feel fantastic. It's difficult to explain, but you feel it's how life is supposed to be, not waking up in a room with central heating and cut off from the natural world. |

| | |
|---|---|
| Woman: | Do you go camping with your friends or just your family? |
| John: | I've got a few friends I go with sometimes at weekends. Other friends don't like the idea of camping. I keep telling them they should try it at least once as I know they'd have a great time, but I haven't managed to persuade them yet. But I'll keep trying. |
| Woman: | Is there anything about camping you don't like? |
| John: | When the weather's nice, putting up the tent when you arrive is great fun, especially if there are a few of you to help. But if it's raining and windy it isn't very nice, but it can't be avoided. But when you've finished and you get inside out of the rain, it feels good. |
| Woman: | If you had the choice of a holiday in a tent or a hotel, what would you choose? |
| John: | A tent for sure. I spend all my time in the city, surrounded by cars and people and pollution. I suppose checking into a hotel is exciting and having food made for you has its advantages, but the food you cook out in the open air tastes even better. In fact, that's one of my favourite things about camping. |
| Woman: | So have you got another camping holiday planned this year? |
| John: | Not yet. The friends I mentioned before are keen to go away for a weekend, but we haven't decided yet. I'll certainly end up going with my parents in the summer, but they haven't arranged anything yet. |

*Now listen again.*

*That is the end of Part 4.*

*You now have six minutes to write your answers on the answer sheet.*

*That is the end of the test.*

## TEST 7    SPEAKING

### Part 1

## Track 53

| | |
|---|---|
| Examiner: | Good evening. Can I have your mark sheets, please? I'm James Salter and this is Liz Macleod. |
| Examiner: | What's your name, Candidate A? How old are you? |
| Candidate A: | My name's Gerard Dubois and I'm 14 years old. |
| Examiner: | And what's your name, Candidate B? How old are you? |
| [PAUSE FOR YOU TO ANSWER] | |
| Examiner: | Candidate B, where do you live? |
| [PAUSE FOR YOU TO ANSWER] | |

| | |
|---|---|
| Examiner: | And Candidate A, what about you? |
| Candidate A: | I come from Lyon in France but I've been living and studying in London for six months because my parents are working in London. |
| Examiner: | Candidate A, what's your favourite kind of weather? |
| Candidate A: | I definitely prefer sunny weather. It can get cold where I live in France and I like it when it's warm. |
| Examiner: | And Candidate B, what about you? |
| [PAUSE FOR YOU TO ANSWER] | |
| Examiner: | Candidate A, do you prefer travelling by bus or by train? |
| Candidate A: | I think I prefer the train. You can stand up and walk around to stretch your legs but on a bus you have to sit still all the time. |
| Examiner: | What about you, Candidate B? |
| [PAUSE FOR YOU TO ANSWER] | |
| Examiner: | Thank you. |

### Part 2

## Track 54

| | |
|---|---|
| Examiner: | Now I'd like each of you to talk on your own about something. I'm going to give each of you a photograph and I'd like you to talk about it. Candidate A. Here is your photograph. It shows some people on a train. Please tell us what you can see in the photograph. Candidate B, you just listen. |
| Candidate A: | In this photograph you can see a lot of people standing on a train. There are at least ten of them in the photo and it looks very crowded. The man on the right is smiling and talking on the phone. There's a woman in the middle reading the newspaper and a man next to her also is looking at the paper. I think they must know each other. They're both wearing suits. There's a boy on the left wearing headphones and in the background there are lots of other people looking towards the camera. I think they're all either going to work or going back home at the end of the day. |
| Examiner: | Thank you. |
| Examiner: | Candidate B. Here is your photograph. It shows a family. Please tell us what you can see in the photograph. Candidate A, you just listen. |
| [PAUSE FOR YOU TO ANSWER] | |
| Examiner: | Thank you. |

## Part 3

## Track 55

| | |
|---|---|
| Examiner: | Now, in this part of the test you are going to talk about something together for about two minutes. I'm going to describe a situation to you.<br>A family with young children are thinking about getting a pet. Here are some pets they could get. Talk together about the different pets they could get and say which one would be best.<br>All right? Now talk together. |
| Candidate A: | OK, would you like to start? |
| [PAUSE FOR YOU TO ANSWER] | |
| Candidate A: | Well, I quite like dogs but I know some people aren't fond of them so let's forget that one. I really don't like snakes and I don't think they are very popular pets. Do you agree? |
| [PAUSE FOR YOU TO ANSWER] | |
| Candidate A: | I think a fish is a bit boring. My favourite choice would be either the cat or the rabbit. I'm not keen on the bird really. |
| [PAUSE FOR YOU TO ANSWER] | |
| Candidate A: | Yes, I agree. Let's say the cat. |
| Examiner: | Thank you. |

## Part 4

## Track 56

| | |
|---|---|
| Examiner: | Candidate A, do you have any pets? |
| Candidate A: | No, not at the moment. We used to have a cat but she was very old and died a while ago. My parents don't want to get another one. |
| Examiner: | And what about you, Candidate B? |
| [PAUSE FOR YOU TO ANSWER] | |
| Examiner: | Candidate B, do you ever go to the zoo to see animals? |
| [PAUSE FOR YOU TO ANSWER] | |
| Examiner: | And how about you, Candidate A? |
| Candidate A: | I haven't been to a zoo but we do have a small city farm in my area. It just has a few animals like chickens and rabbits, that kind of thing. I like going there. |
| Examiner: | Candidate B, do you have a favourite animal? |
| [PAUSE FOR YOU TO ANSWER] | |
| Examiner: | And what about you, Candidate A? |
| Candidate A: | I don't really have a favourite. I like all animals. I don't like spiders though or any insects like that. |
| Examiner: | Thank you. That is the end of the test. |

## TEST 8    LISTENING

## Part 1

## Track 57

*Preliminary English Test for Schools, Listening.*
*There are four parts to the test. You will hear each piece twice.*
*We will now stop for a moment.*
*Please ask any questions now, because you must not speak during the test.*
*Now look at the instructions for Part 1.*
*For each question, choose the correct answer.*
*Look at Question 1.*

**1**    *What does the girl want to eat?*

| | |
|---|---|
| Girl: | Hi, Mum. I'm still in town with my friends at the moment. Can we have a takeaway for dinner tonight? You've cooked pasta for the past three nights and I feel like something different. Plus, it means you can relax! I fancy pizza and there's a good restaurant on the way home. The fish and chip shop's closed tonight so that's not possible. Call me back and let me know. I don't mind getting it, but you will pay me back, won't you? |

*Now listen again.*

**2**    *Why doesn't the boy want to go to the cinema?*

| | |
|---|---|
| Girl: | We're all going to the cinema on Saturday. Are you coming? |
| Boy: | No, I'm not going to bother this time. I think I'll spend the evening at home. |
| Girl: | Oh, come on. It'll be fun. |
| Boy: | No, it's a really long film, I've heard – nearly three hours. I don't mind that at all, but your friends are always talking, and I find it hard to concentrate. I'm going to stay at home, watch TV and order something to eat. But enjoy yourself and tell me all about it afterwards. |

*Now listen again.*

**3**    *What time does the boy want his mum to collect him?*

| | |
|---|---|
| Boy: | I'm going to Tim's house now. |
| Mother: | OK, have a nice time. How are you getting there? |
| Boy: | Tim's dad's coming to collect me. He said he'd be here at 6.00. Is there any chance you could come and get me later? I don't want to ask his dad for another lift. |
| Mother: | OK, what time? |
| Boy: | Well, I want to get back in time for the football at 10.00, so can you be there for about 8.30? That'll give me time to do some homework before it starts. |

*Now listen again.*

**4**  *How much is the school trip?*

Teacher:  If you're going on the school summer trip to Barcelona, we've had an email from the hotel. You'll need to pay us by Friday so we can book it and reserve the rooms. It's not quite as expensive as we'd thought. The letter we sent your parents said it was going to be £185. However, we've since been offered a discount and it's now £155 in total. So that's £125 for the hotel for seven nights and the rest for the coach ticket.

*Now listen again.*

**5**  *Which TV programme is on at the moment?*

Girl:  Hiya Kate. It's Gill here. I'm just wondering if you're free and want to come round. My dad's watching this gardening programme on TV and I'm really bored. We can go up to my room and listen to some music. There's a police drama on later that my dad will probably want to watch but the football is on after that so we could watch that before you go home. Call me back and let me know if you want to come. Please say yes!

*Now listen again.*

**6**  *Which day has the most exams?*

Girl:  Have you seen the exam timetable? They emailed it to me this morning.

Boy:  Yes, it's not too bad, is it?

Girl:  No, there aren't any terrible days. Last week the teacher said we had three on Thursday, but it looks like there's just one in the morning.

Boy:  Yes, Wednesday's the busiest with one in the morning and another in the afternoon. I'm really not looking forward to Friday though. Just the chemistry exam in the morning I know, but I hate chemistry.

*Now listen again.*

**7**  *Which item of food or drink does the girl want now?*

Daughter:  Hi, Dad. You OK?

Father:  Yes, I'm fine. Have you had a good day at school?

Daughter:  It was OK. But I haven't eaten since breakfast so I'm making myself a sandwich. Do you want one?

Father:  No thanks. Anyway, your dinner will be ready in a little while. Why don't you wait?

Daughter:  It's OK, I'm really hungry. I'll make you a cup of tea while I'm in the kitchen.

Father:  Thanks. But just make sure you eat your dinner, won't you?

*Now listen again.*

*That is the end of Part 1.*

**Part 2**

**Track 58**

*Now look at Part 2.*
*For each question, choose the correct answer.*

**8**  *You will hear a brother and sister talking about a quiz show on TV.*

Boy:  Shall we watch that quiz show on the other channel? You know, the one we saw advertised.

Girl:  You can if you want. I'll do some work.

Boy:  Oh, come on. Let's watch it together. I want to see if I can beat you.

Girl:  No, honestly. I'm getting bored with quiz shows. Anyway, I don't think the questions are very easy on that one. We probably won't get any answers correct between us. No, you watch it if you want. There's nothing else on I'm interested in so the TV is all yours.

*Now listen again.*

**9**  *You will hear two friends talking about opening a bank account.*

Girl:  Is it right you've opened a bank account?

Boy:  Yes, it's great. You can create little pots or sections for different things like holidays or birthday presents and transfer some of your money to each pot.

Girl:  Don't your parents have to agree to it?

Boy:  I'm 16 so I can set one up myself. If you're 15 or under they have to share the account.

Girl:  OK, I might have a look myself.

Boy:  The app isn't too difficult to use either. I've never been good at saving money but I'm hoping this will help.

*Now listen again.*

**10**  *You will hear two friends talking about the girl's birthday.*

Boy:  It's your birthday soon and I still haven't bought you a present. What would you like?

Girl:  That's kind of you but you don't have to get me anything, you know that.

Boy:  Of course I'm going to get you something. Come on. What would you like?

Girl:  Well, it's nice to have something to open if I don't know what it is. Ask my sister what she thinks I'd like but tell her to keep it secret. I was going out for a meal with my family, but we've decided to stay at home instead. So why don't you come round?

*Now listen again.*

**11** *You will hear two friends talking about doing a presentation at school.*

Girl: Right, so how are we going to organise the presentation? I think we should both have our own jobs to do.

Boy: Well, you said you would be happy to give the presentation so shall I work on the content?

Girl: Actually, I'd find it easier if I worked on the content as well. Trying to talk through someone else's work can get a bit confusing.

Boy: But that means you're doing most of the work, doesn't it?

Girl: Remember we need the questionnaires. Why don't you write them and give them out at the end when I've finished?

*Now listen again.*

**12** *You will hear two friends talking about a concert.*

Boy: I really enjoyed that concert. What about you?

Girl: It was fantastic, wasn't it? The lights and the special effects were unbelievable. It was a good idea of yours to pay extra for seats, even though they were quite expensive. I'm sure it was difficult for the people at the back to see anything.

Boy: I know, it was great to be right at the front near the stage.

Girl: They didn't play many of their really famous songs, which was a pity, but all in all I thought it was a very good night.

*Now listen again.*

**13** *You will hear two friends discussing what to do in the afternoon.*

Boy: Shall we still go out somewhere after school?

Girl: Yes, but shall we see what the others are doing first? It would be nice if there were a few of us.

Boy: OK, but I want to go somewhere even if it's just you and me. My parents are getting home late from work today so there'll be nobody in when I get home.

Girl: If nobody else wants to come, you can come round to my house. My mum will make dinner and she'll take you home afterwards.

Boy: OK, that's sounds like a great idea.

*Now listen again.*

*That is the end of Part 2.*

## Part 3

## Track 59

*Now look at Part 3.*
*For each question, write the correct answer in the gap. Write one or two words or a number or a date or a time. Look at Questions 14 to 19 now. You have 20 seconds. You will hear a boy called Tom Ducker giving a presentation at school about a research project.*

Tom: OK, so my group decided to do some research into what people think about shopping online. We wrote a questionnaire which had two parts. The first part had ten questions, which just needed yes/no answers. The second part had questions where they could give longer answers.

We wanted to find out if people prefer shopping online. But as we were doing the research in the shopping centre, we wanted to ask people what they enjoyed about being there as well. We thought it would be interesting to find out what they thought the advantages and disadvantages were in each case.

So, there were five members in my group and altogether we interviewed about 50 people. We decided to focus on two different types of person: people below the age of 21 and people over 60. We chose these two groups as we thought they would have a different attitude towards the Internet.

We were quite surprised by the results. We thought older people would prefer the shopping centre compared to buying things online and that younger people would be the opposite. But in fact, that wasn't the case. Older people spent as much time shopping online as the younger people we spoke to, especially when buying things for their homes. Older people said they weren't keen on going to shopping centres as they found them noisy and too crowded. They preferred shopping in quieter places. The younger people however, loved the busy centres and often met up with friends to go shopping there.

We discovered that older people are really keen on doing their weekly food shop online and having it delivered. Younger people seem happier to buy clothes online and will happily send things back if they don't like them or they don't fit.

*Now listen again.*
*That is the end of Part 3.*

## Part 4

# Track 60

*Now look at Part 4.*
*For each question, choose the correct answer.*
*Look at Questions 20 to 25 now.*
*You have 45 seconds.*
*You will hear an interview with a girl called Tina Steel,*
*who went abroad to study Spanish.*

| | |
|---|---|
| Man: | Tina, you're at school at the moment aren't you, but you decided to spend your summer holiday studying in Spain. |
| Tina: | That's right. I'm doing an important Spanish exam next year during my final year at school and I want to go to university to study Spanish if I do well. I wanted to make sure I made a good start to the school year. I decided going to Spain would help me practise the language far more than being at home in the UK. |
| Man: | I see. So, where did you go? |
| Tina: | I decided to do a course in Madrid. I'd been there once on holiday and liked it. My mum and dad helped me find a language school and we also found a family I could live with. Mum and Dad obviously wanted to make sure I was safe and had somewhere nice to live while I was there. The family were recommended by the school, so that put their minds at rest. |
| Man: | How long did the course last? |
| Tina: | It was a four-week full-time course and I was in a class full of people my age from all over the world. It was fantastic. None of us knew very much Spanish but, unfortunately, most of them knew English very well and we often used that to talk together, but I didn't mind too much. |
| Man: | How was the course? |
| Tina: | I enjoyed it. The teachers were lovely. They made us work hard but the course wasn't cheap so I felt that I was getting my money's worth. I certainly learnt a lot in the lessons. The school was modern and right in the city centre, so at lunchtimes and after the lessons had finished we could walk around the shops and have a coffee. |
| Man: | And what about the family? |
| Tina: | They were the perfect family to live with. They had a daughter my age, Ana. We became good friends while I was there. The mum and dad were really kind and were always checking to see if I was OK or needed anything. They told me that I should relax and generally behave as if I was a member of the family. |
| Man: | So was it worth spending your summer holiday studying? |
| Tina: | Absolutely. I enjoyed the course and the family were lovely. If I go again, I'll probably do a shorter course at the school. I spoke Spanish with the family all the time and I could have booked a four-week stay with them and just done one or two weeks at the school. But I feel my Spanish has improved so much and I'm confident about my studies next year. |

*Now listen again.*

*That is the end of Part 4.*

*You now have six minutes to write your answers on the answer sheet.*

*That is the end of the test.*

## TEST 8     SPEAKING

## Part 1

# Track 61

| | |
|---|---|
| Examiner: | Good afternoon. Can I have your mark sheets, please? I'm Keith Fletcher and this is Lucy Webber. |
| Examiner: | What's your name, Candidate A? How old are you? |
| Candidate A: | My name's Miguel Sánchez and I'm 14 years old. |
| Examiner: | And what's your name, Candidate B? How old are you? |
| [PAUSE FOR YOU TO ANSWER] | |
| Examiner: | Tell me about where you live, Candidate B. |
| [PAUSE FOR YOU TO ANSWER] | |
| Examiner: | Who do you live with, Candidate B? |
| [PAUSE FOR YOU TO ANSWER] | |
| Examiner: | Candidate A, what about you? Where do you live? |
| Candidate A: | I come from Spain. I live in Barcelona, quite near the city centre. |
| Examiner: | Who do you live with, Candidate A? |
| Candidate A: | I live with my parents and my sister and my grandfather. |
| Examiner: | Candidate A, what do you enjoy eating for lunch? |
| Candidate A: | During the week when I'm at school I eat in the school restaurant and my favourite snack is pizza. |
| Examiner: | Candidate B, what about you? |
| [PAUSE FOR YOU TO ANSWER] | |
| Examiner: | Have you got a favourite day of the week, Candidate B? |
| [PAUSE FOR YOU TO ANSWER] | |
| Examiner: | Candidate A, what about you? |

| Candidate A: | I'm the same. I love Friday because it's the start of the weekend. I try to get my homework finished as soon as I get home so I can relax. |
| Examiner: | Thank you. |

## Part 2

## Track 62

| Examiner: | Now I'd like each of you to talk on your own about something. I'm going to give each of you a photograph and I'd like you to talk about it. Candidate A. Here is your photograph. It shows some people in a classroom. Please tell us what you can see in the photograph. Candidate B, you just listen. |
| Candidate A: | OK, so this photograph shows some people in an art class. There are three people in the photo, there's a boy nearest the camera, his teacher is next to him and there's a girl in the background. The boy's painting a picture and the teacher is either giving him some advice or telling him what she likes about his work. I think she's saying something nice as she's smiling, and the boy seems pleased. It's difficult to see what his painting is about but it looks as if he's enjoying himself. I can't see what the girl in the background is doing because we can only see her back. |
| Examiner: | Thank you. Candidate B. Here is your photograph. It shows two people with some flowers. Please tell us what you can see in the photograph. Candidate A, you just listen. |
| [PAUSE FOR YOU TO ANSWER] | |
| Examiner: | Thank you. |

## Part 3

## Track 63

| Examiner: | Now, in this part of the test you are going to talk about something together for about two minutes. I'm going to describe a situation to you. A girl of 18 is going away to a university in another city. Her parents are trying to decide what to buy for her. They want to get her something useful. Here are some things they could give her. |

| | Talk together about the different things they could give their daughter and say which one would be best. All right? Now talk together. |
| Candidate A: | OK, all of these things are useful, what do you think? |
| [PAUSE FOR YOU TO ANSWER] | |
| Candidate A: | That's true. If she's sharing accommodation, they might already have one or she can eat in the university canteen. And what about the TV? |
| [PAUSE FOR YOU TO ANSWER] | |
| Candidate A: | No, I agree. And I think that's the same for the clock. So that leaves the money and the radio. Which of these would be the best present? |
| [PAUSE FOR YOU TO ANSWER] | |
| Candidate A: | Well, it depends how much money, doesn't it? But I think the daughter would like to be able to choose what she needs and buy it herself. |
| [PAUSE FOR YOU TO ANSWER] | |
| Examiner: | Thank you. |

## Part 4

## Track 64

| Examiner: | Candidate A, if you go to university do you think you will move away from home? |
| Candidate A: | I think so. My brother is at university and he's having a great time sharing an apartment with his friends. |
| Examiner: | And what about you, Candidate B? |
| [PAUSE FOR YOU TO ANSWER] | |
| Examiner: | Candidate B, what things do you think are important to have in your own room? |
| [PAUSE FOR YOU TO ANSWER] | |
| Examiner: | And how about you, Candidate A? |
| Candidate A: | Yes, I agree. It would be good to have friends round to watch TV together. But it doesn't need to be in my room. |
| Examiner: | Candidate B, is it better to live on your own as a student or to share accommodation? |
| [PAUSE FOR YOU TO ANSWER] | |
| Examiner: | And what about you, Candidate A, what do you think? |
| Candidate A: | Well, I agree. I wouldn't like to move into somewhere with people I didn't know. Some of them could become friends but I'd prefer to live with friends I know. |
| Examiner: | Thank you. That is the end of the test. |

# Sample answer sheets

### Cambridge Assessment
English

| Candidate Name | | Candidate Number | |
| Centre Name | | Centre Number | |
| Examination Title | | Examination Details | |
| Candidate Signature | | Assessment Date | |

Supervisor: If the candidate is ABSENT or has WITHDRAWN shade here  ○

## Preliminary Reading Candidate Answer Sheet

**Instructions**
**Use a PENCIL (B or HB)**
Rub out any answer you want to change with an eraser.

**For Parts 1, 2, 3, 4 and 5:**
Mark ONE letter for each answer.
For example: If you think A is the right answer to the question, mark your answer sheet like this:

**Part 1**

| | A | B | C |
|---|---|---|---|
| 1 | ○ | ○ | ○ |
| 2 | ○ | ○ | ○ |
| 3 | ○ | ○ | ○ |
| 4 | ○ | ○ | ○ |
| 5 | ○ | ○ | ○ |

**Part 2**

| | A | B | C | D | E | F | G | H |
|---|---|---|---|---|---|---|---|---|
| 6 | ○ | ○ | ○ | ○ | ○ | ○ | ○ | ○ |
| 7 | ○ | ○ | ○ | ○ | ○ | ○ | ○ | ○ |
| 8 | ○ | ○ | ○ | ○ | ○ | ○ | ○ | ○ |
| 9 | ○ | ○ | ○ | ○ | ○ | ○ | ○ | ○ |
| 10 | ○ | ○ | ○ | ○ | ○ | ○ | ○ | ○ |

**Part 3**

| | A | B | C | D |
|---|---|---|---|---|
| 11 | ○ | ○ | ○ | ○ |
| 12 | ○ | ○ | ○ | ○ |
| 13 | ○ | ○ | ○ | ○ |
| 14 | ○ | ○ | ○ | ○ |
| 15 | ○ | ○ | ○ | ○ |

**Part 4**

| | A | B | C | D | E | F | G | H |
|---|---|---|---|---|---|---|---|---|
| 16 | ○ | ○ | ○ | ○ | ○ | ○ | ○ | ○ |
| 17 | ○ | ○ | ○ | ○ | ○ | ○ | ○ | ○ |
| 18 | ○ | ○ | ○ | ○ | ○ | ○ | ○ | ○ |
| 19 | ○ | ○ | ○ | ○ | ○ | ○ | ○ | ○ |
| 20 | ○ | ○ | ○ | ○ | ○ | ○ | ○ | ○ |

**Part 5**

| | A | B | C | D |
|---|---|---|---|---|
| 21 | ○ | ○ | ○ | ○ |
| 22 | ○ | ○ | ○ | ○ |
| 23 | ○ | ○ | ○ | ○ |
| 24 | ○ | ○ | ○ | ○ |
| 25 | ○ | ○ | ○ | ○ |
| 26 | ○ | ○ | ○ | ○ |

**Continues over ➡**

2150

**For Part 6:**
Write your answers clearly in the spaces next to the numbers (27 to 32) like this:

Write your answers in CAPITAL LETTERS.

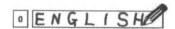

| Part 6 | Do not write below here |
|---|---|
| **27** | 27 1   0    ○   ○ |
| **28** | 28 1   0    ○   ○ |
| **29** | 29 1   0    ○   ○ |
| **30** | 30 1   0    ○   ○ |
| **31** | 31 1   0    ○   ○ |
| **32** | 32 1   0    ○   ○ |

2150

## Cambridge Assessment
English

| Candidate Name | | Candidate Number | |
|---|---|---|---|
| Centre Name | | Centre Number | |
| Examination Title | | Examination Details | |
| Candidate Signature | | Assessment Date | |

Supervisor: If the candidate is ABSENT or has WITHDRAWN shade here ○

## Preliminary Listening Candidate Answer Sheet

### Instructions
**Use a PENCIL (B or HB).** Rub out any answer you want to change with an eraser.

**For Parts 1, 2 and 4:**
Mark one letter for each answer. For example: If you think **A** is the right answer to the question, mark your answer sheet like this:

**For Part 3:**
Write your answers clearly in the spaces next to the numbers (14 to 19) like this:

Write your answers in CAPITAL LETTERS.

**Part 1**

| | A | B | C |
|---|---|---|---|
| 1 | ○ | ○ | ○ |
| 2 | ○ | ○ | ○ |
| 3 | ○ | ○ | ○ |
| 4 | ○ | ○ | ○ |
| 5 | ○ | ○ | ○ |
| 6 | ○ | ○ | ○ |
| 7 | ○ | ○ | ○ |

**Part 2**

| | A | B | C |
|---|---|---|---|
| 8 | ○ | ○ | ○ |
| 9 | ○ | ○ | ○ |
| 10 | ○ | ○ | ○ |
| 11 | ○ | ○ | ○ |
| 12 | ○ | ○ | ○ |
| 13 | ○ | ○ | ○ |

**Part 3**

| | | Do not write below here |
|---|---|---|
| 14 | | 14 1 0 ○ ○ |
| 15 | | 15 1 0 ○ ○ |
| 16 | | 16 1 0 ○ ○ |
| 17 | | 17 1 0 ○ ○ |
| 18 | | 18 1 0 ○ ○ |
| 19 | | 19 1 0 ○ ○ |

**Part 4**

| | A | B | C |
|---|---|---|---|
| 20 | ○ | ○ | ○ |
| 21 | ○ | ○ | ○ |
| 22 | ○ | ○ | ○ |
| 23 | ○ | ○ | ○ |
| 24 | ○ | ○ | ○ |
| 25 | ○ | ○ | ○ |

# Answer key for the Reading and Listening papers

This is the Answer key for the Reading and Listening papers of Tests 1-8.

## TEST 1
### Paper 1 Reading Test

**Part 1**
1 A
2 B
3 A
4 A
5 C

**Part 2**
6 F
7 E
8 G
9 C
10 D

**Part 3**
11 D
12 B
13 A
14 D
15 C

**Part 4**
16 F
17 C
18 A
19 H
20 D

**Part 5**
21 B
22 D
23 C
24 A
25 B
26 D

**Part 6**
27 who

**28** with
**29** as
**30** out
**31** was
**32** the

### Paper 2 Listening Test

**Part 1**
1 C
2 C
3 B
4 A
5 B
6 B
7 A

**Part 2**
8 B
9 C
10 C
11 A
12 A
13 B

**Part 3**
14 11.30
15 main road
16 gym
17 secretary
18 30 minutes
19 hall

**Part 4**
20 C
21 B
22 B
23 A
24 C
25 B

# TEST 2

## Paper 1 Reading Test

### Part 1
1  B
2  B
3  A
4  B
5  C

### Part 2
6  G
7  E
8  C
9  A
10 F

### Part 3
11 C
12 A
13 B
14 D
15 B

### Part 4
16 F
17 H
18 A
19 E
20 C

### Part 5
21 B
22 D
23 A
24 B
25 C
26 D

### Part 6
27 these
28 There
29 they
30 on
31 as
32 how

## Paper 2 Listening Test

### Part 1
1  B
2  C
3  B
4  B
5  C
6  A
7  B

### Part 2
8  C
9  A
10 B
11 C
12 C
13 B

### Part 3
14 sandwiches
15 studio
16 tidy
17 6/six people
18 members
19 club newspaper

### Part 4
20 B
21 B
22 C
23 B
24 A
25 B

# TEST 3
## Paper 1 Reading Test

### Part 1
1 A
2 C
3 B
4 B
5 A

### Part 2
6 F
7 C
8 E
9 A
10 G

### Part 3
11 B
12 C
13 C
14 B
15 A

### Part 4
16 E
17 B
18 H
19 C
20 F

### Part 5
21 B
22 D
23 C
24 A
25 B
26 D

### Part 6
27 them
28 who
29 had
30 was
31 It
32 At

## Paper 2 Listening Test

### Part 1
1 B
2 B
3 B
4 A
5 B
6 C
7 C

### Part 2
8 A
9 C
10 A
11 B
12 A
13 B

### Part 3
14 2/two hours
15 cold drink
16 2/two groups
17 cafe
18 15 minutes
19 paying

### Part 4
20 A
21 C
22 A
23 B
24 C
25 A

# TEST 4

## Paper 1 Reading Test

### Part 1

1  B
2  A
3  B
4  A
5  C

### Part 2

6  D
7  B
8  H
9  A
10 G

### Part 3

11 B
12 C
13 A
14 B
15 B

### Part 4

16 B
17 G
18 D
19 A
20 E

### Part 5

21 A
22 C
23 A
24 D
25 B
26 D

### Part 6

27 the
28 it
29 of
30 even
31 in
32 which

## Paper 2 Listening Test

### Part 1

1  C
2  B
3  A
4  A
5  B
6  A
7  B

### Part 2

8  A
9  C
10 B
11 C
12 A
13 B

### Part 3

14 19/19th July
15 music videos
16 entrance
17 school gate
18 schoolwork
19 table tennis

### Part 4

20 C
21 A
22 C
23 A
24 B
25 A

# TEST 5

## Paper 1 Reading Test

**Part 1**

1 C
2 A
3 C
4 A
5 A

**Part 2**

6 D
7 C
8 F
9 G
10 A

**Part 3**

11 A
12 B
13 B
14 C
15 B

**Part 4**

16 G
17 F
18 A
19 D
20 B

**Part 5**

21 C
22 A
23 D
24 B
25 A
26 B

**Part 6**

27 in
28 had
29 the
30 it
31 so
32 that/which

## Paper 2 Listening Test

**Part 1**

1 A
2 C
3 C
4 C
5 A
6 C
7 C

**Part 2**

8 C
9 C
10 B
11 A
12 C
13 B

**Part 3**

14 12/12th June
15 volunteers
16 map
17 7.30
18 information sheet
19 questionnaire

**Part 4**

20 C
21 A
22 B
23 C
24 B
25 A

# TEST 6

## Paper 1 Reading Test

### Part 1
1  C
2  A
3  A
4  B
5  C

### Part 2
6  D
7  F
8  E
9  H
10 B

### Part 3
11 D
12 C
13 B
14 C
15 A

### Part 4
16 F
17 B
18 H
19 E
20 A

### Part 5
21 A
22 D
23 C
24 A
25 B
26 D

### Part 6
27 than
28 were
29 to
30 have
31 some
32 that

## Paper 2 Listening Test

### Part 1
1  A
2  B
3  A
4  B
5  C
6  C
7  B

### Part 2
8  B
9  C
10 B
11 C
12 A
13 A

### Part 3
14 keep fit
15 professional
16 position
17 3/three
18 13/13th August
19 reception desk

### Part 4
20 C
21 B
22 C
23 A
24 A
25 B

# TEST 7
## Paper 1 Reading Test

**Part 1**
1  A
2  C
3  B
4  B
5  A

**Part 2**
6  F
7  C
8  H
9  D
10 A

**Part 3**
11 D
12 C
13 A
14 C
15 B

**Part 4**
16 E
17 H
18 B
19 D
20 G

**Part 5**
21 B
22 A
23 B
24 D
25 C
26 A

**Part 6**
27 by
28 than
29 as
30 have/need
31 It
32 until

## Paper 2 Listening Test

**Part 1**
1  C
2  A
3  C
4  B
5  C
6  A
7  B

**Part 2**
8  C
9  C
10 A
11 C
12 B
13 A

**Part 3**
14 18/eighteen
15 birthday party
16 art project
17 16/sixteen
18 confident
19 interviews

**Part 4**
20 A
21 B
22 B
23 A
24 C
25 B

# TEST 8

## Paper 1 Reading Test

### Part 1
1 A
2 A
3 B
4 C
5 C

### Part 2
6 G
7 C
8 H
9 A
10 G

### Part 3
11 A
12 C
13 C
14 B
15 A

### Part 4
16 G
17 C
18 A
19 E
20 D

### Part 5
21 D
22 A
23 B
24 D
25 C
26 C

### Part 6
27 it
28 which/that
29 to
30 be
31 and
32 the

## Paper 2 Listening Test

### Part 1
1 A
2 C
3 B
4 B
5 A
6 A
7 B

### Part 2
8 C
9 B
10 A
11 A
12 B
13 A

### Part 3
14 yes/no / yes, no / yes – no
15 shopping centre
16 60/sixty
17 home/homes
18 crowded
19 food

### Part 4
20 C
21 B
22 A
23 C
24 C
25 A

# Model answers for the Writing papers

These are the model answers for the Writing papers of Tests 1–8.

## TEST 1

## Part 1

### Question 1

> Hi Carole,
> Thanks for writing so quickly. I'm really looking forward to seeing you too. It's been ages since we last saw each other.
> I've decided I'm going to get the train. It's a bit more expensive than the coach but it's much quicker and I'll get there earlier. The train arrives at 3.30. I'm so pleased you're coming to meet me as I've never been to your city before.
> Please thank your mum for offering to cook for me. Tell her I eat everything except fish.
> We have such a lot to talk about it I think it would be nice to stay in my first evening if that's OK with you.
> See you soon!

## Part 2

### Question 2

I like to go to my local park. It's huge and has lots of secret corners that nobody ever goes to. There are always lots of birds singing and there's no noisy traffic to spoil the atmosphere. I usually go after school, often on my own but sometimes with friends if we want somewhere to go before we go home.

I really like going there whenever I feel stressed or I have problems I want to think about. It's very peaceful and I always feel so much better after I've been sitting there for an hour or two. It's definitely one of my favourite places.

### Question 3

I looked out of the window at the people passing by. We were on holiday and we'd just unpacked our suitcases and were looking around the place we were staying in. The apartment was opposite the beach and you could see people swimming in the sea. My sister and I waited for Mum and Dad to get ready so we could go to the beach. I'd also seen a man selling ice creams along the road and couldn't wait to get one. Finally, everyone was ready. Before we left my mum insisted we put some sun cream on and then we ran outside to enjoy the first day of our holiday.

## TEST 2

## Part 1

### Question 1

> Hi Robert,
> Good to hear from you. And thanks for your kind words! No, we haven't played yet. The first game is next Sunday and I'm captain!
> I'm happy to help you with your project. We always sit together to eat. My mum never lets us eat while we watch the TV, not at dinnertime, anyway. I like it this way because we can all talk about our day.
> Yes, we go out to eat sometimes, probably about once a month. My brother and I like to have a burger but Mum and Dad prefer to go to an Italian restaurant that's near our house.
> I'm free on Saturday if you want to chat online.
> Looking forward to speaking soon!

## Part 2

### Question 2

I've been dancing for about four years and it is definitely my favourite interest. I go to a dance school near my house. It's close enough for me to walk so I go there on my own after I've done my homework. I'm now in the oldest group and so sometimes the woman who owns the dance school asks me to help with the younger girls and boys. We spend most of the time preparing for different dance competitions or for a show that parents can come to see. To be honest, I prefer it when my mum and dad aren't in the audience as I feel a bit shy when my family come to watch.

### Question 3

I decided to open the smallest present last of all. It was a special birthday because I was 13. I had become a teenager and I had quite a few presents from my family and friends. I was sitting on my mum and dad's bed with my little brother, who was offering to get each present for me from the floor. I knew what some of the presents were, but I had no idea what was in the small box that was wrapped so carefully. After I'd opened the other gifts, my brother gave me the little box and when I opened it I found a beautiful necklace from my mum.

# TEST 3

## Part 1

### Question 1

Dear Mrs Horton,
Thanks for your email. I'm really pleased to hear about the homework club and I'm very interested in attending.
If possible, I would like to have some help with maths. I've already told my maths teacher that I find some parts of maths difficult so it would be good to have some extra help.
I go to dance classes on Wednesdays after school so I can't attend anything on that day. However, I'm free the other days.
I play football on Saturday afternoons but if I can be home in time to get ready, I would be interested in coming to homework club on Saturday mornings too.
Best wishes

## Part 2

### Question 2

I don't watch many TV programmes, but I always make sure I see 'Bake Off'. This is a competition that takes place once a year. We see different people baking various cakes and each week one of them loses and has to leave the show. Lots of my friends watch it and we often talk about it at school.
I like it for two reasons. First of all, once we get to know the people who are taking part, we start to have a favourite, the person we want to win. This makes the programme quite exciting. Also, you can learn a lot about baking and I sometimes try to make some of the cakes myself.

### Question 3

I read the email and couldn't believe it! It was from somebody I'd met on a school trip to Germany. We were visiting a school in Berlin and got to know the teenagers who were studying there. I sat next to Ernst and we quickly made friends. We gave each other our contact details when I left but I didn't expect to hear from him again.
In the email he told me about his plans for the summer holiday. I was so excited when he said he was coming to my country for a holiday with his mum and dad. He came last week and we spent two very happy days together – it was great to see him again and show him my town!

# TEST 4

## Part 1

### Question 1

Hi Mike,

Thanks for writing back so soon. Yes, it'll be great to see you too. I've got so much to tell you about and I'm sure you've got news for me too!

I'm having the party at home. My parents said it would be OK as there aren't too many people coming.

I'd love to see you before it starts. I'll have lots of things to do but it would be great if you were here. If you don't mind, you could help me get everything ready.

It's very kind of you to offer to bring some food. We don't really need anything but you could always bring a cake!

See you before the party!

## Part 2

### Question 2

My mobile phone is definitely the most important thing I own. I bought the one I have at the moment about a year ago. My mum and dad gave me half of the money towards it and I used my pocket money to pay the rest.

Like everybody else, I use it for lots of different reasons. The main thing is texting my friends. I do this all day long. I also use it a lot to watch videos and to listen to music. It's funny that even though it's a phone I don't often use it to speak to people. But for everything else, it's the most important thing I own.

### Question 3

I sat down and looked around me. It was my first day at secondary school and the classroom was full of strangers. I had hoped I would know some children from my previous school but I didn't recognise anybody in the room. The boy sitting next to me looked friendly and I asked him his name. He was called Jonathon and I found out that we both supported the same football team and liked the same music. When the lesson began we had to be quiet but at break time we went to the canteen together and carried on talking. I was so pleased I met him as it made my first day at school enjoyable and stopped me feeling nervous.

# TEST 5

## Part 1

### Question 1

Hi Kate,

Good to hear from you. My family are all looking forward to seeing you – you're very welcome to stay with us. It will be great to be able to spend the whole weekend together!

I'm very happy to come and meet you at the station – it's not very far from my house. I can say hello to your dad there too!

It's nice that he's meeting a friend. I think they would have a good meal in a restaurant called Giotto's – it's friendly with a nice atmosphere, an interesting menu and it's not too expensive.

Yes, I'd love to see your photos of the school party, because mine weren't very good.

Looking forward to seeing you soon!

Love,

## Part 2

### Question 2

I'm lucky because I live very close to the city centre and there are lots of shops that interest me. But there's one shop I always look forward to going to and that's Maisie's.

Maisie's is a clothes shop that also sells beautiful pieces of jewellery and other things that girls my age love. It's only a small shop but there are so many interesting things and you can spend ages looking around. The staff are also very helpful, and they don't try to get you to buy anything. I like it so much I go there almost every weekend with my friends.

### Question 3

It was Monday morning and the start of a new year at school. It was my final year and I was looking forward to going back, although I'd had a very good time during the holiday. I was going in early with a couple of friends to welcome some of the younger children who were starting at the school this year. I put on my school uniform, had some breakfast and then left home to meet my friends at the bus stop. They were already there when I arrived and were talking to some of the new children. They looked so young and nervous and I decided I would try to make their first day as enjoyable as possible.

# TEST 6

## Part 1

### Question 1

> Dear Mr Talbot,
> Thank you for your email. I think it's a very good idea to have an International Day. I'm really looking forward to it.
> As I come from Paris it will be easy for me to find photographs of the city. I will bring as many as I can.
> I will be happy to talk about them. I will ask Maurice if he wants to join me and we can do the presentation together.
> Thank you for offering to provide a computer to help with the presentation. However, I think I will just put the photographs on the wall and talk about them that way.
> Best wishes

## Part 2

### Question 2

There are lots of different kinds of food that I like, especially meals from other countries. However, my favourite is pasta.

There are so many different kinds of pasta and I don't have a favourite because they all taste so nice. We have a pasta meal at home about two or three times a week and I do the cooking one evening. On Wednesday my parents come home later than usual so I get the chance to do it. We like to eat together around the table, so I try to get it ready for around 7.00 p.m. when my mum and dad come home from work.

### Question 3

It was 8.30 and I was late for school. It seemed my alarm clock hadn't gone off. I didn't have time for a shower, so I jumped out of bed and put my uniform on. I was a little surprised that nobody was downstairs, but I ran into the kitchen anyway to get a biscuit for breakfast. It was raining outside so I rushed to the cupboard to get my coat. I put it on and went to the front door. Then I heard my mum at the top of the stairs saying, 'What have you got your school uniform on for? It's Sunday!'

# TEST 7

## Part 1

### Question 1

> Hi Chris,
> Don't worry about after school. I saw you getting into your dad's car, so I knew I didn't need to wait for you.
> I've got no plans for Saturday so I'd love to go into town with you. I'd prefer to go to the cinema as there are a few good films on at the moment. But if other people would rather have a meal, I'm happy to do that too. If that's what everyone wants to do, I'd love a pizza!
> Shall I meet you at the station? It's easier for you to go there than to come to my house first.
> Looking forward to seeing you on Saturday.
> See you soon!

## Part 2

### Question 2

I like a lot of different sports but my favourite one is football. I watch it all the time on TV and often go to see a game with my dad. I love the atmosphere of a big match and if my team wins it makes it a great day.

I also play football for my school team. I enjoy it more than sports like running or gymnastics because I'm part of a team and we all get on well. The best thing of all is playing another school. My friends and I go on the coach together and we get excited preparing for the game.

### Question 3

I checked every pocket but my keys weren't there. Then I remembered I had left them in my jacket the night before! It was 4 p.m., my parents were at work and I knew I wouldn't be able to get in until they got home at 6 p.m. Luckily, it was a warm, sunny afternoon so I decided to go to the park for an hour. I bought something to eat and drink on the way and found a nice place to sit when I got to the park. I really enjoyed being on my own and relaxing after a hard day at school and I felt quite pleased I had forgotten my keys.

# TEST 8

## Part 1

### Question 1

> Dear Miss Evans,
> Thanks for your email. Yes, I am very excited about the trip and would like to go. I have asked my parents and they have said it is OK.
> It is very kind of the school to make sure we have something to eat but I will bring my own lunch, probably just sandwiches.
> I went to the science museum with my mum and dad last year and it is very interesting. I think everyone will enjoy it more than walking around a lot, especially if the weather isn't very good.
> I've told my dad that we need to be collected and he said he will definitely be there at 7 p.m.
> Best wishes

# Part 2

## Question 2

I'm lucky because I enjoy a lot of the subjects I study at school but my favourite is Art. Of course, I've been drawing and painting since I was a child but I've been doing Art properly at school for about three years.

We have Art on Thursday afternoon, which is a nice day of the week. The weekend is just one day away, and everyone is feeling in a good mood. The Art class is very relaxing and completely different to other subjects, where you have to do lots of reading and writing. The Art teacher is very helpful and spends time with every student, answering our questions and offering her advice. I'm quite good at it too and I enjoy taking some of my paintings home to show my parents.

## Question 3

It was late and I felt really tired. I had an essay to write for homework and I really didn't feel like doing it. But I had to give it to my teacher the next day. I thought about doing it in the morning before school, but I knew that probably wasn't a good idea.

So I went upstairs to my room and got my books out of my bag and started work. Fortunately, I found the topic interesting and I managed to get the essay completed quite quickly. It felt wonderful when I finally got into bed for a good night's sleep.

# Model answers for the Speaking papers

The model answers for the Speaking papers of Tests 1-8 are highlighted in grey here. You can listen to these model answers online at: **www.collins.co.uk/eltresources**

## Test 1

## Speaking Part 1

05a

| | |
|---|---|
| Examiner: | Good afternoon. |
| | Can I have your mark sheets, please? |
| | I'm Simon Rickard and this is Cathy Irving. |
| | What's your name, Candidate A? How old are you? |
| Candidate A: | My name's Joshua Kulig and I'm 13 years old. |
| Examiner: | And what's your name, Candidate B? How old are you? |
| Candidate B: | My name's Evi Khomyakova and I'm 14 years old. |
| Examiner: | Candidate B, where do you live? |
| Candidate B: | I live in Moscow. I live with my mum, dad and two sisters. We have an apartment in the city centre. |
| Examiner: | And Candidate A, where do you live? |
| Candidate A: | I live in Switzerland. I live with my family in an apartment in a small village near the mountains. |
| Examiner: | Candidate A, have you got any hobbies or interests? |
| Candidate A: | I'm learning to play the piano. I go to classes after school and I also practise at home. |
| Examiner: | Candidate B, what do you do to relax? |
| Candidate B: | I enjoy listening to music and reading books. I also go to art classes because I'm keen on painting and drawing. |
| Examiner: | Candidate A, tell me about your family. |
| Candidate A: | My mother works as a teacher in a big school and my father is a police officer. I haven't got any brothers or sisters but my cousins live in the same village. |
| Examiner: | Candidate B, tell me about your favourite subject at school. |
| Candidate B: | Well, I like English and we've got a very nice teacher. I also like maths and I think that's really my favourite subject. I think it's very useful too. |
| Examiner: | Thank you. |

## Speaking Part 2

06a

| | |
|---|---|
| Examiner: | Now I'd like each of you to talk on your own about something. I'm going to give each of you a photograph and I'd like you to talk about it. |
| | Candidate A. Here is your photograph. It shows people out shopping. |
| | Please tell us what you can see in the photograph. |
| | Candidate B, you just listen. |
| Candidate A: | This photograph shows a family out shopping. There are four people in the family – mum, dad and their two children, a boy who looks about five years old and a girl who's a little bit older. I think they're paying for their shopping in a supermarket. They're standing at the checkout and on the left of the photo you can see a man's arm. He works at the checkout and he's taking something from the little boy. There's some fruit – bananas and apples and a small orange – by the checkout. I think the man has said something funny because the family are all laughing, It's a very happy photograph. |
| Examiner: | Thank you. |
| Examiner: | Candidate B. Here is your photograph. It shows some young people in a classroom. |
| | Please tell us what you can see in the photograph. |
| | Candidate A, you just listen. |

Candidate B: This photograph is of a classroom with a small group of students working at their desks. The girl sitting nearest to the camera is the main person in the photograph. She has long blonde hair and is wearing a T-shirt. She looks about 13 or 14 years old. There's a boy sitting behind her in a checked shirt and behind him is another girl. There are three other people in the photo – a boy and a girl sitting next to each other at the back, and one we can't really see at the front. The ones at the back are near the window and the sun is shining on them both. They're all working very hard and making notes from books.

Examiner: Thank you.

# Speaking Part 3

07a

Examiner: Now, in this part of the test you are going to talk about something together for about two minutes. I'm going to describe a situation to you.
A girl is going on holiday with her parents. She wants to buy something to eat on the journey.
Here are some things she could buy to eat on the journey.
Talk together about the different things she could get and say which one would be best.
All right? Now, talk together.

Candidate A: So, we need to choose something that she can eat on the journey to her holiday. All of these things are OK apart from the ice-cream. That wouldn't last very long. What do you think?

Candidate B: Yes, I agree. Actually, I don't think any of the sweet things are a very good idea. The cake and the chocolate are very sweet and she could get travel sick.

Candidate A: Yes, that's true even though they're my favourite things. I think the chips are like the ice cream. They need to be eaten quickly. Cold pizza isn't really very nice either, is it?

Candidate B: No, I don't like cold pizza. So that just leaves the fruit and the sandwich. When I go on a long journey, I always feel hungry, so I think I would prefer to have a sandwich instead of an apple. What about you?

Candidate A: Yes, I agree. The family can stop somewhere to get something to eat if they want, can't they. Especially if it's a long journey. But yes, let's say the sandwich is the best thing to buy, shall we?

Candidate B: Yes, let's say that.

Examiner: Thank you.

# Speaking Part 4

08a

Examiner: Candidate A, do you like going on long journeys?

Candidate A: Sometimes, yes. I like travelling in my mum's car because we listen to music and sing some songs. It's always a lot of fun.

Examiner: And what about you, Candidate B?

Candidate B: I'm the same. I prefer to travel by car. It can be a little boring waiting for a train at the station and maybe a bit stressful if the trains are cancelled. I like the car much better for a long journey.

Examiner: Candidate B, what do you like to take with you on a journey?

Candidate B: Well, I love to read and so a book would be great. But the problem is I get travel sick when I read in a car, so I don't take one anymore.

Examiner: And how about you, Candidate A?

Candidate A: I like to read as well, maybe not a book but a magazine. Of course, I also like to take my phone. I can message my friends, listen to music, watch videos, that kind of thing.

Examiner: Candidate B, is it better to travel during the day or late at night?

Candidate B: When I go on holiday with my parents, we often travel in the evening. My dad says it's much quicker because there's not so much traffic.

Examiner: And what about you, Candidate A?

| Candidate A: | I think it's better to travel at night as the roads are quieter. But maybe it's more difficult for the driver if it's dark. Also, the driver might feel more tired if it's later in the day. |
|---|---|
| Examiner: | Thank you. That is the end of the test. |

## Test 2

## Speaking Part 1

🎧
13a

| Examiner: | Good morning.<br>Can I have your mark sheets, please?<br>I'm Sarah Hunt and this is Donald Edmondson.<br>What's your name, Candidate A? How old are you? |
|---|---|
| Candidate A: | My name's Anniek Tindermann and I'm 15 years old. |
| Examiner: | And what's your name, Candidate B? How old are you? |
| Candidate B: | My name's Daniel Herzog and I'm 14 years old. |
| Examiner: | Candidate B, where do you live? |
| Candidate B: | I live in Germany. We live in a little village near Berlin. |
| Examiner: | And who do you live with, Candidate B? |
| Candidate B: | I live with my mother and younger sister. |
| Examiner: | Candidate A, where do you live? |
| Candidate A: | I come from the Netherlands. I live in Amsterdam. |
| Examiner: | And who do you live with, Candidate A? |
| Candidate A: | I live with my mum, dad and brother. |
| Examiner: | Candidate A, do you like studying English? |
| Candidate A: | Yes, I do. I find it very hard sometimes, especially grammar, but I'm looking forward to being able to speak English well. |
| Examiner: | Candidate B, what about you? |
| Candidate B: | I also like studying English. The older students have all of their lessons in English and I can't wait to be good enough to do that too. |
| Examiner: | Candidate A, tell us about a teacher you like. |
| Candidate A: | I like several of the teachers at my school but I think my favourite is my art teacher. She's good at helping us learn how to draw and paint and our lessons are always fun. |
| Examiner: | Candidate B, how do you get to school every day? |
| Candidate B: | In the summer I sometimes walk to school but it's quite a long way and I have to get up very early. In the winter I always catch the bus – it's quick and easy and I don't have to get up so early! |
| Examiner: | Thank you. |

## Speaking Part 2

🎧
14a

| Examiner: | Now I'd like each of you to talk on your own about something. I'm going to give each of you a photograph and I'd like you to talk about it.<br>Candidate A. Here is your photograph. It shows people eating dinner.<br>Please tell us what you can see in the photograph.<br>Candidate B, you just listen. |
|---|---|
| Candidate A: | This photograph has been taken in a family kitchen. It's a beautiful room, with nice white furniture. There are five people sitting around a table. I think it might be a mother, father and three girls although the oldest daughter looks almost the same age as the mother. They're all laughing and looking at the youngest daughter. We can't see her face, but it looks like she's about ten years old. They're all having dinner, but I can't see what it is they're eating. They all have a plate in front of them and there are two dishes in the centre of the table with more food. |
| Examiner: | Thank you.<br>Candidate B. Here is your photograph. It shows someone with a laptop. |

Please tell us what you can see in the photograph.
Candidate A, you just listen.

Candidate B: This photograph shows a teenage boy who is sitting outside with his laptop. He's wearing a black jacket, white shirt and jeans. I think he might be listening to music because he's also wearing a big pair of white headphones. But as he's also using the laptop, he might be listening to something for his studies. It looks like he's either singing along to music or concentrating on something. There's a building behind him. It looks like it might be a school so perhaps he's having a break and getting ready to go back to his lessons.

Examiner: Thank you.

## Speaking Part 3

🎧 15a

Examiner: Now, in this part of the test you're going to talk about something together for about two minutes. I'm going to describe a situation to you.
A girl is going on a walking trip with her school. She is trying to decide what to take with her.
Here are some things she could take.
Talk together about the different things she could take and say which one would be best.
All right? Now talk together.

Candidate A: So, the girl is going on a trip with her school. What do you think she should take? I'm not sure a map is necessary. Won't the teachers know where to go?

Candidate B: Yes, that's true. Unless the trip is about using a map. But she probably doesn't need that. And why does she need an alarm clock? She'll have an alarm clock on her phone if she needs one.

Candidate A: Yes, and if it's just one day, she won't need one, will she? The walking boots might be useful as they're going walking. I think they're important.

Candidate B: Yes, and also the backpack. If she's taking food she'll need something to carry it in. But I don't think the suitcase is necessary. It would be difficult to carry. What do you think?

Candidate A: Yes, I agree. So, that leaves the mobile phone and the umbrella. I don't think it's useful to have an umbrella on a walking trip, do you? And I think it would be good to leave her mobile phone at home so she can relax and not be checking for messages.

Candidate B: That's true. What do think is the most important, the walking boots or the backpack? I prefer the walking boots as she can carry things in her pockets.

Candidate A: Yes, I agree. Let's say the walking boots.

Examiner: Thank you.

## Speaking Part 4

🎧 16a

Examiner: Candidate A, have you been on a school trip recently?

Candidate A: No, not for quite a long time. We went to a museum last year. I enjoyed it but it was only a morning trip and we had to go back to school in the afternoon.

Examiner: And what about you, Candidate B?

Candidate B: My school has a lot of trips. We went to visit a factory a few weeks ago. They made cars there and we were able to see everything and talk to some of the people who worked there.

Examiner: Candidate B, is there anywhere you want your school to take the students?

Candidate B: Well, I would like to go to the seaside for a few days. We live a long way from the coast so I don't go very often with my family. I know we would have a great time on a school trip to the sea.

Examiner: And how about you, Candidate A?

Candidate A: I'd like to go to another country. Maybe for a whole week. I know some of the older students in our school do trips like that in the summer.

| | |
|---|---|
| Examiner: | Candidate B, do you often take photos when you go on a trip with your friends? |
| Candidate B: | I always forget to take them. I'm usually having so much fun I don't think about getting my phone out. But I think it's a good idea because you have a memory of the day. |
| Examiner: | And what about you, Candidate A? |
| Candidate A: | I take lots of photos and videos on my phone. I love to show them to everyone when we get back. I delete the ones I don't want and keep the others on my laptop. |
| Examiner: | Thank you. That is the end of the test. |

## Test 3

## Speaking Part 1

21a

| | |
|---|---|
| Examiner: | Good evening. |
| | Can I have your mark sheets, please? |
| | I'm Richard Burns and this is Christine Morton. |
| Examiner: | What's your name, Candidate A? How old are you? |
| Candidate A: | My name's David Dominguez and I'm 14 years old. |
| Examiner: | And what's your name, Candidate B? How old are you? |
| Candidate B: | My name's Marcia Calvo and I'm 15 years old. |
| Examiner: | Candidate B, where do you live? |
| Candidate B: | I live in Spain. I live in a town not far from Madrid. |
| Examiner: | And Candidate A, where do you live? |
| Candidate A: | I come from Portugal. I live with my family in Coimbra. |
| Examiner: | Candidate A, what do you like to do at weekends? |
| Candidate A: | I like to meet my friends in the town centre. We go to the park to play football or walk around the shops. |
| Examiner: | Candidate B, what about you? |
| Candidate B: | I'm the same. I meet my friends and we often go to the cinema. I also go to my dance class on Sunday, which I really enjoy. |
| Examiner: | Candidate A, tell us about your favourite time of the year. |
| Candidate A: | I like the summer best. I like the weather in the summer and of course I like being on holiday! I often go and stay with my cousins, who live near the sea. We swim every day and we have a lot of fun together. |
| Examiner: | Candidate B, tell us what you use your mobile phone for most. |
| Candidate B: | Well, I use my mobile phone for a lot of things, but I don't use it to phone people very often. I've got lots of apps on my phone and I often use them. My favourite one is a running app – it tells me how far and how fast I've run when I'm training. |
| Examiner: | Thank you. |

## Speaking Part 2

22a

| | |
|---|---|
| Examiner: | Now I'd like each of you to talk on your own about something. I'm going to give each of you a photograph and I'd like you to talk about it. |
| | Candidate A. Here is your photograph. It shows people taking part in sport. |
| | Please tell us what you can see in the photograph. |
| | Candidate B, you just listen. |
| Candidate A: | In this photograph there are some boys playing football. I think it's football, although you can't see the ball as it's not in the picture. There are four boys altogether. Two of them are wearing white shirts. One of these boys is in the centre of the photo and has the number 5 on his shirt. The other two have dark shirts with the numbers 35 and 9 on the front. They all look about 14 or 15 years old. They're playing outside, probably in a park, and you can see the goal in the background. It looks like a lovely sunny day and the boys are enjoying themselves. |
| Examiner: | Thank you. |
| Examiner: | Candidate B. Here is your photograph. It shows people making a film. |

Please tell us what you can see in the photograph.
Candidate A, you just listen.

Candidate B: This photograph shows three teenagers making a film. There are two boys and one girl, she's the person who's being filmed. One of the boys is holding a mobile phone, which is what they're using to film the girl. The other boy has the square black thing that they use when the director tells people to start filming. They're all wearing casual clothes. The girl's wearing a black top and jeans, the boy filming has a striped T-shirt on and the other boy is wearing a grey top. They're standing outside in a field and there are lots of trees in the background.

Examiner: Thank you.

# Speaking Part 3

23a

Examiner: Now, in this part of the test you're going to talk about something together for about two minutes. I'm going to describe a situation to you.
An aunt is trying to decide what to get her eight-year-old nephew for his birthday. Here are some things she could give him.
Talk together about the different things she could give him and say which one would be best.
All right? Now talk together.

Candidate A: Would you like to start?

Candidate B: OK, well, I think they're all good ideas but maybe we should say which ones are not so good first. I don't think the cake is useful. He'll probably get one from his parents. What do you think?

Candidate A: Yes, that's a good point. So no cake. I don't think sweets are a good idea either. His mum or dad might not want him to eat lots of sweet things. What about the toy car? He might like that.

Candidate B: Yes, I think the car is a better idea than the books. And I agree about the sweets. What about colouring pencils? Young children love to draw, don't they?

Candidate A: Yes, they do. So, that just leaves the camera and the money. Are these a good present?

Candidate B: I'm not sure. The camera might be expensive, and I don't think a young child should have a camera. Money isn't very exciting, is it? Not for a young child.

Candidate A: No, I agree. So, do you think the toy car or the colouring pencils?

Candidate B: I think the toy car would be the best present.

Candidate A: Yes, let's say the toy car.

Examiner: Thank you.

# Speaking Part 4

24a

Examiner: Candidate A, have you bought anyone a present recently?

Candidate A: Yes. It was my brother's birthday a few weeks ago and I bought him a video game. We went shopping together and he chose it.

Examiner: And what about you, Candidate B?

Candidate B: The last present I bought was for my teacher when she left our school. She was lovely and all the class were sad when she decided to leave so some of us got her some flowers.

Examiner: Candidate B, what's the best present you've ever received?

Candidate B: My mum and dad bought me a laptop when I started secondary school a few years ago. It was the first computer I'd ever had and I loved it.

Examiner: And how about you, Candidate A?

Candidate A: When I was 13 my dad took me to my first football match. It was a big game and the atmosphere was fantastic. I'll never forget it because our team won.

Examiner: Candidate B, what do you prefer, giving or receiving presents?

Candidate B:     I love to buy presents for my friends and relations and I love seeing them happy when they open them. But I also like receiving them too, so I can't really decide which one I prefer.

Examiner:        And what about you, Candidate A?

Candidate A:     I'm the same. I enjoy going shopping for presents for my mum and dad or my friends, but I get very excited when they buy me presents. So, I think I like giving and receiving them.

Examiner:        Thank you. That is the end of the test.

## Test 4

## Speaking Part 1

Examiner:        Good morning.
                 Can I have your mark sheets, please?
                 I'm Angela Spencer and this is David Williams.

Examiner:        What's your name, Candidate A? How old are you?

Candidate A:     My name's Tania Mestres and I'm 14 years old.

Examiner:        What's your name, Candidate B? How old are you?

Candidate B:     My name's Tom Strauss and I'm 15 years old.

Examiner:        Candidate B, where do you live?

Candidate B:     I live in Vienna. That's the capital of Austria.

Examiner:        And who do you live with, Candidate B?

Candidate B:     I live with my parents and my two brothers – and we've got a very old cat too.

Examiner:        And Candidate A, where do you live?

Candidate A:     I come from Brazil. I live in an apartment in São Paulo.

Examiner:        And who do you live with, Candidate A?

Candidate A:     I live with my parents and my twin sister.

Examiner:        Candidate A, what do you enjoy doing in your free time?

Candidate A:     I play the guitar and I love to practise when I don't have anything else to do. I also like reading and listening to music.

Examiner:        And Candidate B, what about you?

Candidate B:     I enjoy doing sports. I do gymnastics at school and often stay after lessons to practise. I also like seeing my friends at the weekend.

Examiner:        Candidate A, tell us what you did last weekend.

Candidate A:     Yes, I had a great time last weekend. My cousins came to our house and we had a big party with them on Saturday night.

Examiner:        Candidate B, tell us about your last holiday.

Candidate B:     We went skiing in the mountains for our last holiday. My parents are very good at skiing and my sister and I love skiing too. We went with some friends and we had a lot of fun.

Examiner:        Thank you.

## Speaking Part 2

Examiner:        Now I'd like each of you to talk on your own about something. I'm going to give each of you a photograph and I'd like you to talk about it.
                 Candidate A. Here is your photograph. It shows two people sitting together.
                 Please tell us what you can see in the photograph.
                 Candidate B, you just listen.

Candidate A:     In this photograph there are two people. I think it's a father and his daughter or it could be her grandfather. They are both sitting at a table and laughing about something. I imagine the man is helping the girl with her homework because they are both holding a book or some sheets of paper. There's also a cup on the table with one or two pens or pencils in it, so I definitely think they are working. The man's wearing a light-coloured jumper and glasses. The girl has lovely curly hair and has a jumper on. They look very happy to be together.

Examiner: Thank you.

Examiner: Candidate B. Here is your photograph. It shows three people sitting together. Please tell us what you can see in the photograph. Candidate A, you just listen.

Candidate B: In this photograph there are three people. They're sitting outside on something and I think they might be in a park. A boy is in the middle of the photograph and there are two girls, one on his left and the other on his right. The boy is working on a laptop and the two girls are looking at the screen. They're all laughing so I don't think they're working. They might be watching a video or something like that. I can see two backpacks on the ground so they might be at school or on their way home. It looks like they are all good friends.

Examiner: Thank you.

## Speaking Part 3

31a

Examiner: Now, in this part of the test you are going to talk about something together for about two minutes. I'm going to describe a situation to you.
A teenager has the day off school and he's trying to decide what to do.
Here are some things he could do.
Talk together about the different things he could do and say which one would be best. All right? Now talk together.

Candidate A: OK, all of these things are good fun, what do you think?

Candidate B: Yes, but is he on his own? He can't play chess if there's nobody with him so is that a good idea?

Candidate A: Yes, that's true. He can do all the other things on his own. I think the TV is the worst idea. If he wants, he can watch TV programmes on the laptop.

Candidate B: Yes, I agree. Most people use their mobile phone when they're bored, don't they? Do you think he'll want to use that?

Candidate A: Yes, the mobile phone or the laptop. But if he plays the guitar, I think that's one of the best things he can do. What do you think?

Candidate B: Definitely. The guitar or the book. The cards are also good fun, but he might get bored after a little while. So, the guitar or the book. Which one is best?

Candidate A: I think the guitar. That's my choice.

Candidate B: OK. The guitar is our choice then.

Examiner: Thank you.

## Speaking Part 4

32a

Examiner: Candidate A, what do you like to do if you're bored?

Candidate A: I'm afraid I just watch videos or text my friends on my phone. If there's something good on TV I watch that.

Examiner: And what about you, Candidate B?

Candidate B: I like to read. I'm always reading novels or magazines. I also like to go out for long walks when I have nothing to do, and I go running too.

Examiner: Candidate B, do you watch much TV?

Candidate B: I probably watch TV most days. I have my own TV in my bedroom and I usually put it on when I finish studying. But not for too long. Just to relax for half an hour.

Examiner: And how about you, Candidate A?

Candidate A: Yes, I watch a lot of TV. My sister and I have our favourite programmes and we sometimes sit together to watch them.

Examiner: Candidate B, do you prefer to relax or be active when you don't have anything to do?

Candidate B: Usually I prefer to be active. I like going for long walks and I go running at least once a week, but I also like doing gymnastics and other sports.

| Examiner: | And what about you, Candidate A? |
|---|---|
| Candidate A: | I'm not a very active person. I enjoy playing the guitar but most of the time I just go on my phone or watch TV. That's how I relax. |
| Examiner: | Thank you. That is the end of the test. |

## Test 5

## Speaking Part 1

🎧 37a

| Examiner: | Good morning. |
|---|---|
| | Can I have your mark sheets, please? |
| | I'm William Castle and this is Ros Walker. |
| Examiner: | What's your name, Candidate A? How old are you? |
| Candidate A: | My name's Boris Volovik and I'm 13 years old. |
| Examiner: | And what's your name, Candidate B? How old are you? |
| Candidate B: | My name's Susanne Segato and I'm 14 years old. |
| Examiner: | Candidate B, where do you live? |
| Candidate B: | I'm living in London at the moment because my parents are working here but I come from France. |
| Examiner: | And who do you live with, Candidate B? |
| Candidate B: | I live with my family – that's my parents and my younger brother, who is ten. |
| Examiner: | And Candidate A, what about you? Where do you live? |
| Candidate A: | I live in St Petersburg, in Russia. I live in an apartment not very far from the river. |
| Examiner: | And who do you live with, Candidate A? |
| Candidate A: | I live with my mother, my father and my two sisters. |
| Examiner: | Candidate A, what food do you like to eat? |
| Candidate A: | I like anything really. I enjoy pasta, pizza and also fast food like burgers. |
| Examiner: | And Candidate B, what about you? |
| Candidate B: | I'm a vegetarian although I do eat fish. My mother is a really good cook and I like eating her meals. |
| Examiner: | Candidate A, do you prefer being in the city or the countryside? |
| Candidate A: | I prefer being in the city. I like walking around the shops and having different things to do. |
| Examiner: | What about you, Candidate B? |
| Candidate B: | I also prefer to be in the city. I like going to the countryside occasionally, but the city is more interesting. |
| Examiner: | Candidate A, tell us about your favourite day of the week. |
| Candidate A: | I like Saturdays best. We don't have to go to school and so I often meet my friends and we do things together. Sometimes we play football, sometimes we watch a film together – we try to have fun! |
| Examiner: | Candidate B, tell us what your favourite meal of the day is. |
| Candidate B: | Well, I don't eat much at breakfast because I'm often in a hurry before school. I think my favourite meal of the day is dinner in the evening when I sit down with my family and we talk about the day. |
| Examiner: | Thank you. |

## Speaking Part 2

🎧 38a

| Examiner: | Now, I'd like each of you to talk on your own about something. I'm going to give each of you a photograph and I'd like you to talk about it. |
|---|---|
| | Candidate A. Here is your photograph. It shows people doing something together. Please tell us what you can see in the photograph. |
| | Candidate B, you just listen. |
| Candidate A: | In this photograph I can see a man and a teenage boy. They're probably father and son. The boy is wearing a T-shirt and the man has a light-coloured shirt on. They're both looking at a model ship. It looks like one of those ships that you make yourself |

by sticking small pieces together. They've finished making it and now it looks like they're painting it. The boy is holding a paintbrush and there are some paints on the table in front of him. Perhaps they're talking about what colour the ship should be.

| | |
|---|---|
| Examiner: | Thank you. |
| Examiner: | Candidate B. Here is your photograph. It shows some young people outside. Please tell us what you can see in the photograph. Candidate A, you just listen. |
| Candidate B: | This photograph shows a group of children running along the road. There's a bus in the background and I think they're running to get on it as it is stopped. The children look about 13 or 14 years old and there are four of them in the photo. All the children have backpacks so I imagine they have just finished school and want to get home, or they could also be going on a school trip. I think it's summertime because some of the children are wearing T-shirts and none of them have a jacket or a coat. |
| Examiner : | Thank you. |

## Speaking Part 3

39a

| | |
|---|---|
| Examiner: | Now, in this part of the test you are going to talk about something together for about two minutes. I'm going to describe a situation to you. A teenager wants to do some sport with her friends. Here are some sports she could do with her friends. Talk together about the different sports she could do with her friends and say which one they would enjoy most. All right? Now talk together. |
| Candidate A: | OK, would you like to start? |
| Candidate B: | Yes, OK. All of these sports are good fun. But I'm not sure golf is a good choice. You need special equipment and sometimes it's hard to find somewhere to play. |
| Candidate A: | Yes, I agree. I don't think they want to go running either. That seems a bit too serious and isn't really fun. What do you think? |
| Candidate B: | I agree with you. Swimming is always good fun but maybe some of the friends can't swim. If they all have bikes they could go cycling. What do you think? |
| Candidate A: | Yes, cycling's a good idea. And so is football. You don't need any equipment for that, only a ball and somewhere to play. I don't think dancing is a good idea. I don't like dancing anyway. |
| Candidate B: | What about tennis? Maybe some of them can't play tennis, and you need somewhere to play. |
| Candidate A: | Yes, I agree. So what do we think? |
| Candidate B: | Well, I think it's either football or cycling. I prefer cycling so that's my choice. What about you? |
| Candidate A: | I like cycling too, so yes, let's say cycling. |
| Examiner: | Thank you. |

## Speaking Part 4

40a

| | |
|---|---|
| Examiner: | Candidate A, do you like playing sports? |
| Candidate A: | Sometimes, yes. I like playing football with my friends after school and we play basketball as well sometimes. |
| Examiner: | And what about you, Candidate B? |
| Candidate B: | Yes, I'm keen on swimming and I go three or four times a week. I also like to go cycling at the weekend when the weather is nice. I like cycling round the city. |
| Examiner: | Candidate B, do you do any sports at school? |
| Candidate B: | We have a class once a week. Sometimes we do gymnastics. The boys and girls do that together. Then we have football and netball games as well. |
| Examiner: | And how about you, Candidate A? |
| Candidate A: | Yes, it's the same in our school. My school also has a very good basketball team and some of us practise that in lessons. |

| | |
|---|---|
| Examiner: | Candidate B, do you prefer doing a sport on your own or with other people? |
| Candidate B: | I like playing with other people. It's more fun if you're with your friends and it's exciting if you can play in a team against another team. |
| Examiner: | And what about you, Candidate A? |
| Candidate A: | I agree. I prefer team sports. I try harder when I know my friends need me to play well. |
| Examiner: | Thank you. That is the end of the test. |

## Test 6

## Speaking Part 1

| | |
|---|---|
| Examiner: | Good morning. |
| | Can I have your mark sheets, please? |
| | I'm Catherine Huntingford and this is Mark Davies. |
| Examiner: | What's your name, Candidate A? How old are you? |
| Candidate A: | My name's Esther Lenherr and I'm 13 years old. |
| Examiner: | And what's your name, Candidate B? How old are you? |
| Candidate B: | My name's Gianni Karman and I'm 14 years old. |
| Examiner: | Candidate B, where do you live? |
| Candidate B: | I live in Rome. I live in a flat in the city centre. |
| Examiner: | And who do you live with, Candidate B? |
| Candidate B: | I live with my mother and father and my sister and my grandparents. |
| Examiner: | And Candidate A, where do you live? |
| Candidate A: | I come from Zurich in Switzerland but at the moment I'm living in Manchester in the UK. |
| Examiner: | And Candidate A, who do you live with? |
| Candidate A: | I live with my parents and my brother and sister. |
| Examiner: | Candidate A, what's your favourite way of travelling? |
| Candidate A: | I really like cars and they are my favourite way of travelling. I like sitting in the front seat next to my dad and looking out of the window. |
| Examiner: | Candidate B, what about you? |
| Candidate B: | I quite like travelling by train. My parents don't have a car, so we usually travel by train if we go out anywhere. |
| Examiner: | Candidate B, tell me how often you eat in a restaurant. |
| Candidate B: | Probably about once a month. My mum and dad take me and my sister out if we have something to celebrate, like working hard at school. |
| Examiner: | And Candidate A, what about you? |
| Candidate A: | We have lots of restaurants near my house in Zurich but they're quite expensive, so we don't go there very often, but we sometimes go out in Manchester. |
| Examiner: | Thank you. |

## Speaking Part 2

| | |
|---|---|
| Examiner: | Now, I'd like each of you to talk on your own about something. I'm going to give each of you a photograph and I'd like you to talk about it. |
| | Candidate A. Here is your photograph. It shows people sitting on a sofa. |
| | Please tell us what you can see in the photograph. |
| | Candidate B, you just listen. |
| Candidate A: | In this photograph I can see a man and a woman. I think they're at home, sitting on the sofa and watching TV in the living room. There's a football match on and the man is enjoying it. I can't see his face because he's looking at the TV and we can only see the back of his head, but I imagine he's interested in the game. The woman has turned away from the TV and is looking in our direction. She looks very bored and probably doesn't like football. I think she'd like to do something else or watch a different programme. |
| Examiner: | Thank you. |

| Examiner: | Candidate B. Here is your photograph. It shows some people outside. |
|---|---|
| | Please tell us what you can see in the photograph. |
| | Candidate A, you just listen. |
| Candidate B: | This photograph shows three people outside on some steps. Nearest to us is a woman standing still and talking on the phone. She has long dark hair and is wearing trousers and a white blouse. Then there's a man on the left going down the steps. He's drinking something and is dressed in casual clothes. Finally, in the background there's another man walking up the steps. He's also dressed in casual clothes and is carrying a bag. I think it's lunch time and these people are having a break from work, or maybe the building in the background is a station and they're waiting to catch a train. |
| Examiner: | Thank you. |

## Speaking Part 3

🎧 47a

| Examiner: | Now, in this part of the test you are going to talk about something together for about two minutes. I'm going to describe a situation to you. |
|---|---|
| | A teacher is just about to teach an English lesson. |
| | Here are some things she could take to the classroom to use in her English lesson. Talk together about the different things she could take and say which one would be best. |
| | All right? Now talk together. |
| Candidate A: | OK, would you like to start? |
| Candidate B: | Yes, OK, well the teacher can use all of these things in an English lesson, can't she? What about the magazine? |
| Candidate A: | I think that's a good idea because she can cut out photographs or articles and give them to the students. I'm not sure that one mobile phone is useful. Only one person can use it. And I don't think the pencils are important. The students will probably have their own. |
| Candidate B: | Yes, that's true. And the camera isn't very useful either, is it? She can take photos of the students but what can she do with the camera to help her teach? |
| Candidate A: | Not much really. The laptop and the pair of headphones are like the mobile phone. If there's only one, it's difficult for all the students to use them. The TV could be a good idea though. The teacher could show an English programme or a video. Which one do you think is best, the TV or the magazine? |
| Candidate B: | Well, I think they're both a good idea but, actually, I like the magazine best. The students will only be sitting still watching the TV but they could do lots of talking if they have different things from the magazine to use. |
| Candidate A: | OK, I think you're right. Let's say the magazine. |
| Examiner: | Thank you. |

## Speaking Part 4

🎧 48a

| Examiner: | Candidate A, what do you like to do in lessons? |
|---|---|
| Candidate A: | I enjoy watching videos on TV and then having a discussion with other people in the class, especially if it's an interesting subject. |
| Examiner: | And what about you, Candidate B? |
| Candidate B: | Yes, I'm the same. I like having discussions. I prefer working in small groups because you get more chance to talk about the subject. |
| Examiner: | Candidate B, what do you think makes a good teacher? |
| Candidate B: | I think it's important that they are able to explain things clearly and make sure everybody understands the lesson. |
| Examiner: | And how about you, Candidate A? |
| Candidate A: | In my opinion, the teacher must know the subject very well. But I agree, they also need to be able to explain what they know to the students, so they understand. |
| Examiner: | Candidate B, do you like working on computers at school? |

Candidate B:   Sometimes, yes. We use them a lot to help us practise English. But I get bored after a while and I like to talk with my friends as well when we have discussions.
Examiner:   And what about you, Candidate A?
Candidate A:   We don't have many computers at my school, so we don't get the opportunity to use them. But I like working on my laptop at home.
Examiner:   Thank you. That is the end of the test.

## Test 7

## Speaking Part 1

53a

Examiner:   Good evening.
            Can I have your mark sheets, please?
            I'm James Salter and this is Liz Macleod.
Examiner:   What's your name, Candidate A? How old are you?
Candidate A:   My name's Gerard Dubois and I'm 14 years old.
Examiner:   And what's your name, Candidate B? How old are you?
Candidate B:   My name's Magdalena Gruber and I'm 15 years old.
Examiner:   Candidate B, where do you live?
Candidate B:   I live near Vienna in Austria. I live in a village with my mum and dad.
Examiner:   And Candidate A, what about you?
Candidate A:   I come from Lyon in France but I've been living and studying in London for six months because my parents are working in London.
Examiner:   Candidate A, what's your favourite kind of weather?
Candidate A:   I definitely prefer sunny weather. It can get cold where I live in France and I like it when it's warm.
Examiner:   And Candidate B, what about you?
Candidate B:   I don't mind really. I don't like it when it's too hot as it makes me feel exhausted. Actually, I quite like the snow. We have a lot of snow in winter where I live.
Examiner:   Candidate A, do you prefer travelling by bus or by train?
Candidate A:   I think I prefer the train. You can stand up and walk around to stretch your legs but on a bus you have to sit still all the time.
Examiner:   What about you, Candidate B?
Candidate B:   Yes, I'm the same. I prefer being on a train. Sometimes the buses where I live are crowded and sometimes you have to wait a long time for the bus to come.
Examiner:   Thank you.

## Speaking Part 2

54a

Examiner:   Now, I'd like each of you to talk on your own about something. I'm going to give each of you a photograph and I'd like you to talk about it.
            Candidate A. Here is your photograph. It shows some people on a train.
            Please tell us what you can see in the photograph.
            Candidate B, you just listen.
Candidate A:   In this photograph you can see a lot of people standing on a train. There are at least ten of them in the photo and it looks very crowded. The man on the right is smiling and talking on the phone. There's a woman in the middle reading the newspaper and a man next to her also is looking at the paper. I think they must know each other. They're both wearing suits. There's a boy on the left wearing headphones and in the background there are lots of other people looking towards the camera. I think they're all either going to work or going back home at the end of the day.
Examiner:   Thank you.
            Candidate B. Here is your photograph. It shows a family.
            Please tell us what you can see in the photograph.
            Candidate A, you just listen.

| Candidate B: | In this photograph we can see some people celebrating something outside. It looks like a group of neighbours having a street party because it's on a quiet road with houses in the background. There's a table on the pavement which is full of drinks and cakes and some children are serving food. I think this must be a party that the young people have organised because most of the people in the photo are quite young. It's probably in America because I can see the American flag on the table. It's a sunny day and everyone looks very happy to be there. |
| --- | --- |
| Examiner: | Thank you. |

## Speaking Part 3

55a

| Examiner: | Now in this part of the test you're going to talk about something together for about two minutes. I'm going to describe a situation to you. A family with young children are thinking about getting a pet. Here are some pets they could get. Talk together about the different pets they could get and say which one would be best. All right? Now talk together. |
| --- | --- |
| Candidate A: | OK, would you like to start? |
| Candidate B: | Yes, OK. Can I start by saying I don't like dogs so I wouldn't choose one of them? What about you? |
| Candidate A: | Well, I quite like dogs but I know some people aren't fond of them so let's forget that one. I really don't like snakes and I don't think they are very popular pets. Do you agree? |
| Candidate B: | Yes, I agree. I don't really like mice and as the children are quite young they could hurt a mouse if they don't hold it properly. What about the fish? |
| Candidate A: | I think a fish is a bit boring. My favourite choice would be either the cat or the rabbit. I'm not keen on the bird really. |
| Candidate B: | OK, so a cat or a rabbit. I think the young children would like them both but a cat is easier to take care of I think. What do you think? |
| Candidate A: | Yes, I agree. Let's say the cat. |
| Examiner: | Thank you. |

## Speaking Part 4

56a

| Examiner: | Candidate A, do you have any pets? |
| --- | --- |
| Candidate A: | No, not at the moment. We used to have a cat but she was very old and died a while ago. My parents don't want to get another one. |
| Examiner: | And what about you, Candidate B? |
| Candidate B: | No, we've never had pets. I'd love to have a cat but my father doesn't like cats so it isn't really possible. |
| Examiner: | Candidate B, do you ever go to the zoo to see animals? |
| Candidate B: | Yes, I've been lots of times. We have one near where I live. I love going and I spend ages there looking around. |
| Examiner: | And how about you, Candidate A? |
| Candidate A: | I haven't been to a zoo but we do have a small city farm in my area. It just has a few animals like chickens and rabbits, that kind of thing. I like going there. |
| Examiner: | Candidate B, do you have a favourite animal? |
| Candidate B: | I love really big animals like elephants and giraffes. I always go straight to see them when we visit the zoo as I think they're so beautiful. |
| Examiner: | And what about you, Candidate A? |
| Candidate A: | I don't really have a favourite. I like all animals. I don't like spiders though or any insects like that. |
| Examiner: | Thank you. That is the end of the test. |

## Test 8

### Speaking Part 1

61a

| | |
|---|---|
| Examiner: | Good afternoon. |
| | Can I have your mark sheets, please? |
| | I'm Keith Fletcher and this is Lucy Webber. |
| Examiner: | What's your name, Candidate A? How old are you? |
| Candidate A: | My name's Miguel Sánchez and I'm 14 years old. |
| Examiner: | And what's your name, Candidate B? How old are you? |
| Candidate B: | My name's Amy Guillard and I'm 14 years old. |
| Examiner: | Tell me about where you live, Candidate B. |
| Candidate B: | I come from France. I'm from Bordeaux but I'm living in Paris at the moment because my parents are working there. We live in a small flat. |
| Examiner: | Who do you live with, Candidate B? |
| Candidate B: | I live with my parents and my brother. |
| Examiner: | Candidate A, what about you? Where do you live? |
| Candidate A: | I come from Spain. I live in Barcelona, quite near the city centre. |
| Examiner: | Who do you live with, Candidate A? |
| Candidate A: | I live with my parents and my sister and my grandfather. |
| Examiner: | Candidate A, what do you enjoy eating for lunch? |
| Candidate A: | During the week when I'm at school I eat in the school restaurant and my favourite snack is pizza. |
| Examiner: | Candidate B, what about you? |
| Candidate B: | At the weekend I like going to a café near where I live and I meet my friends for a sandwich or a burger. |
| Examiner: | Have you got a favourite day of the week, Candidate B? |
| Candidate B: | Yes, it's definitely Friday. I usually see my friends on Friday evening and we can all look forward to the weekend. |
| Examiner: | Candidate A, what about you? |
| Candidate A: | I'm the same. I love Friday because it's the start of the weekend. I try to get my homework finished as soon as I get home so I can relax. |
| Examiner: | Thank you. |

### Speaking Part 2

62a

| | |
|---|---|
| Examiner: | Now, I'd like each of you to talk on your own about something. I'm going to give each of you a photograph and I'd like you to talk about it. |
| | Candidate A. Here is your photograph. It shows some people in a classroom. |
| | Please tell us what you can see in the photograph. |
| | Candidate B, you just listen. |
| Candidate A: | OK, so this photograph shows some people in an art class. There are three people in the photo, there's a boy nearest the camera, his teacher is next to him and there's a girl in the background. The boy's painting a picture and the teacher is either giving him some advice or telling him what she likes about his work. I think she's saying something nice as she's smiling, and the boy seems pleased. It's difficult to see what his painting is about but it looks as if he's enjoying himself. I can't see what the girl in the background is doing because we can only see her back. |
| Examiner: | Thank you. |
| | Candidate B. Here is your photograph. It shows two people with some flowers. |
| | Please tell us what you can see in the photograph. |
| | Candidate A, you just listen. |
| Candidate B: | There are two people in this photograph. I think it's a grandmother and her granddaughter because the woman on the right of the photo is quite old and the girl on the left is probably only about five or six years old. I think they may be in the |

grandmother's garden and they're doing some gardening. The woman is holding a pot and the little girl is putting a plant in it. They both have a flower in their hair. It looks like one of the flowers from the plant. The girl is concentrating very hard on the job she's doing and the grandmother looks very happy to be spending time with her granddaughter.

Examiner: Thank you.

## Speaking Part 3

63a

Examiner: Now, in this part of the test you are going to talk about something together for about two minutes. I'm going to describe a situation to you.
A girl of 18 is going away to a university in another city. Her parents are trying to decide what to buy for her. They want to get her something useful.
Here are some things they could give her.
Talk together about the different things they could give their daughter and say which one would be best.
All right? Now talk together.

Candidate A: OK, all of these things are useful, what do you think?

Candidate B: Most of them are, yes. They don't need to buy her a microwave though, do they?

Candidate A: That's true. If she's sharing accommodation, they might already have one or she can eat in the university canteen. And what about the TV?

Candidate B: I don't really think she would need a TV. She can watch most things on her laptop, can't she? The cushions and the towels would be useful but they're not very exciting presents.

Candidate A: No, I agree. And I think that's the same for the clock. So that leaves the money and the radio. Which of these would be the best present?

Candidate B: I don't think the radio is necessary. The girl can probably use her phone or laptop to listen to music, so that just leaves the money. Is that a good present?

Candidate A: Well, it depends how much money, doesn't it? But I think the daughter would like to be able to choose what she needs and buy it herself.

Candidate B: OK. Let's say the money.

Examiner: Thank you.

## Speaking Part 4

64a

Examiner: Candidate A, if you go to university do you think you will move away from home?

Candidate A: I think so. My brother is at university and he's having a great time sharing an apartment with his friends.

Examiner: And what about you, Candidate B?

Candidate B: I'm not sure. I live in a big city and there's more than one university there. I think I would prefer to live at home when I'm at university unless I move to another city.

Examiner: Candidate B, what things do you think are important to have in your own room?

Candidate B: I think a TV is very important. I spend a lot of time watching videos on my phone, but a TV would be nice for when I want to watch a film.

Examiner: And how about you, Candidate A?

Candidate A: Yes, I agree. It would be good to have friends round to watch TV together. But it doesn't need to be in my room.

Examiner: Candidate B, is it better to live on your own as a student or to share accommodation?

Candidate B: It depends. If you can choose the people you're sharing with, I think that's best. It would be good fun to live with friends.

Examiner: And what about you, Candidate A, what do you think?

Candidate A: Well, I agree. I wouldn't like to move into somewhere with people I didn't know. Some of them could become friends but I'd prefer to live with friends I know.

Examiner: Thank you. That is the end of the test.

# Speaking paper: Additional practice by topic

This section will give you extra practice in the sorts of questions the examiner may ask you in the Speaking test. Listen to the audio and practise answering the questions. Some of the questions mean quite similar things but the words used in the question are different; this gives you more speaking practice and shows you how different questions are formed. Remember that the examiner will choose what questions to ask you and won't ask you lots of questions about the same topic.

When you are practising, try to give a longer answer even if you want to just say *No*. Imagine the question is followed by *Why?* or *Why not?* Doing this will help you make your answer longer. For example, you may not watch films very often, but if the question is *Do you like watching films about the future?* and your real answer is *No*, you can say something like *No, I don't like watching films about the future because I think some of them are frightening.*

Once you are feeling confident, it would be a good idea not to look at the book – just listen to the audio and answer the questions. And keep practising!

When you have practised with the audio a few times, it would be a good idea to work with a 'study buddy'. Take turns to ask each other the questions and answer them, trying to make your answers a bit longer each time. Choose questions about different topics as that is what the examiner will do in the Speaking test.

The questions are grouped under different topic headings: accommodation; books and films; celebrations; clothes; family and friends; food; future plans; hobbies and interests; music; shopping; sport; studying; technology; the environment; the past; travel and holidays.

### Accommodation

65

Now let's talk about accommodation.
Tell us about where you live.
Do you live in a house or an apartment?
How long have you lived in your house or apartment?
Who do you live with?
What's your favourite room where you live? Why?
Is there anything you don't like about where you live?
What kind of place do you think you will live in in the future?
Would you prefer to live in the city or the countryside?
Do you have a garden?
Would you like to live on your own when you're older?
Which room do you spend most time in when you're at home?
Have you ever moved house? Tell us about it.

### Books and films
66

Now let's talk about books and films.
Tell us about books and films.
Are books and films important to you? Why?
Do you read many books?
What sort of books or magazines do you read most?
Do you like reading? Why? / Why not?
What sort of things do you like reading most?
What's the best book you've ever read?
Is there a cinema near where you live?
Do you enjoy going to the cinema? Why? / Why not?
What's your favourite type of film?
How often do you watch films, TV or cartoons?
Are there any films or TV programmes you dislike?

How often do you go to the cinema?
What was the last film you saw?
Do you prefer to see a movie at home or at the cinema? Why?
Have you seen a good film recently? What was it about?
Is there a film you want to see?
Who's your favourite actor?
Are you interested in celebrities?

### Celebrations

Now let's talk about celebrations.
Tell us about celebrations in your life.
Do you like going to parties? Why? / Why not?
When was the last party you went to? Whose party was it?
Tell us about the last party you went to.
What kind of things do people celebrate in your country?
What do you like to do at parties?
How often do you go to a party?
What kind of games can you play at a party?
What can you do to make a party successful?
Do you like to dance when you're at a party?
Have you been to a wedding?
What's the best food to serve at a celebration?
Have you had a party in your house?
Which famous person would you most like to invite to a party?

### Clothes

Now let's talk about clothes.
Tell us about the clothes you like.
What kind of clothes do you usually wear?
How often do you buy new clothes?
Where do you like to shop for clothes?
What are your favourite clothes?
Do you have to wear anything special for school?
Do you have to wear a school uniform? If so, tell us about it.
Do you like to wear the same clothes as your friends? Why? / Why not?
Do you wear any jewellery?
Are you interested in the jewellery other people wear?
Do you like to wear clothes that are in fashion?
What do you like to wear in summer?
Do you like to shop in department stores? Why? / Why not?
Do you buy many clothes online?
What did you wear last weekend?

### Family and friends

Now let's talk about family and friends.
Tell us about your family.
Are you like anyone in your family?
Is there anyone in your family who is very important to you? Why?
What's your favourite family memory?
Is there anything you and your family like to do together?
Tell us about your friends.
How often do you see your friends?
What do you like doing with your friends?
Where do you like going with your friends? Why?

What do you do with your friends when you go out?
Do your friends have the same hobbies as you?
Do your friends live near you?
Did you see any of your friends yesterday?
Where did you meet your best friends?
How do you keep in touch with friends when you can't be together?

## Food

70

Now let's talk about food.
Tell us about the food you like.
What time do you have dinner?
Have you got a favourite meal?
How often do you go to a restaurant?
Do you like to eat healthy food?
How often do you eat fruit?
Do you think it's important to eat three meals a day?
Which meal of the day do you enjoy most?
Can you cook?
Do you enjoy cooking? Why? / Why not?
Do you like to try cooking different meals?
What did you have for breakfast this morning?
Is there any food you dislike?
What did you eat for dinner yesterday?
Do you prefer to eat at home or in a restaurant? Why?
Can anyone in your family cook really well? Tell us what they cook.

## Future plans

71

Now let's talk about future plans.
Tell us about your future plans.
What are you going to do at the weekend?
Are you going to have a holiday soon?
Where do you want to live in the future? Why?
Which country would you like to visit in the future? Why?
How much do you think you will use English in the future?
What are you doing for your next holiday?
Do you think you will work or study in a foreign country in the future?
Where do you think you will work in the future?
Are there any subjects you want to study at college or university?
Is there anywhere you want to visit next year?
Tell us about a job you would like to do in the future.

## Hobbies and interests

72

Now let's talk about hobbies and interests.
Tell us about your hobbies and interests.
Have you got any hobbies?
Are there any hobbies you used to have that you don't do anymore?
Is there a hobby you would like to start?
Are there any hobbies you wouldn't like to do? Why? / Why not?
What are the most popular hobbies in your country?
Do any of your friends have an interesting hobby?
What do you like to do at the weekend?
What do you like to do to relax?
Do you like doing activities alone or with other people? Why?
How often do you do exercise?
What do you do when you get home from school?

## Music

Now let's talk about music.
Tell us about the type of music you like to listen to.
How often do you listen to music?
What kind of music do you like?
Do you listen to music while you're studying? Why? / Why not?
Are you learning any musical instruments at school?
Can you play any musical instruments?
Is there a musical instrument you would like to learn?
Do you like to sing?
Who is your favourite singer?
Do you download songs?
What was the last song you downloaded?
Do you listen to music when you do exercise? Why? / Why not?
Is there a band or singer you would like to see?

## Shopping

Now let's talk about shopping.
Tell us about shopping.
Do you enjoy shopping? Why? / Why not?
Are there many shops near where you live?
Which shops do you go to most often?
Do you like to shop online? Why? / Why not?
What was the last thing you bought?
Do you ever go shopping with your friends?
How often do you buy clothes?
How often do you go to a supermarket?
Do you like shopping in large shopping centres? Why? / Why not?
Do you prefer to shop online or in a real shop? Why? / Why not?
What was the last present you bought for someone?
What would you most like to buy if you had enough money?

## Sport

Now let's talk about sport.
Do you play any sports?
Tell us about the sports you like.
What sports do you like?
How often do you do sport?
What kind of sports do you play?
Where do you play sports?
Is sport important in your life? Why? / Why not?
Do you play sport with your family?
Do you play sport at the weekend?
Do you ever watch sport on TV?
Do you play much sport at school?
Who's your favourite sports team or player?
When did you start playing your sport?
Have you ever played sport in a competition?

## Studying

Tell us about studying.
What subjects do you enjoy studying most at school?
Do you enjoy studying English? Why? / Why not?
How often do you have English lessons at school?

What things do you find easy and difficult about learning English?
Have you got a favourite room to study in at home?
What time of day is your best time for studying?
Do you like to study online? Why? / Why not?
What are the advantages and disadvantages of studying online?
What do you find most difficult about studying?
Do you ever do your homework with friends?
Do you prefer studying alone or with other people?
Which area of English do you find most difficult?
Is the Internet always useful for studying?
Are there any new skills you would like to learn?

## Technology

Now let's talk about technology.
Tell us why it's important to know about technology.
Tell us about the technology you use.
Are you interested in new technology? Why? / Why not?
Do you know much about new technology?
Have you got a smartphone?
Could you live without a smartphone? How long for?
Is it a good idea for children to have mobile phones? Why? / Why not?
Would you like to have the latest mobile phone?
Do you use the Internet to practise English?
What are some of the problems with the Internet?
Does technology make our lives easier? How?
What are your favourite websites?
Do you play computer games?
Do you listen to podcasts? If so, which ones? Why?
Do you have any friends who make podcasts or videos?
Do you listen to podcasts in English?
When do you listen to podcasts?
Do you watch videos online? What kind of videos do you watch online?
Do you watch movies online?

## The environment

Now let's talk about the environment.
Do you do anything to help protect the environment?
What kind of environmental problems are there where you live?
Do you think it's important to recycle things? Why? / Why not?
What kind of things does your family recycle?
What kind of things do you recycle?
Is there a bottle bank in your local area?
Is litter a problem in your area?
How do people deal with litter in your country?
Do you think local people should do more to clean up their streets?
What's the traffic like where you live?
Do you think people should use their car less often? Why? / Why not?
Does your school do anything to help protect the environment?
What do people in your class think about climate change?
Tell us about the wildlife where you live.
What things do people do to help wildlife in your area?

## Travel and holidays

Now let's talk about travel.
Do you like to travel? Why? / Why not?

How do you travel to school?
How often do you travel by car?
Do you ever travel by train?
Do many people cycle in the area where you live?
What form of transport do most people use where you live?
What's your favourite way of travelling?
Have you ever lived in another country?
Would you like to live in another country one day? Why? / Why not?
What do you like to do on holiday?
Do you prefer lying on the beach or sightseeing? Why?
Which country would you most like to visit?
Do you have many tourists where you live?
What's the most interesting place you've ever visited?
Do you like to buy souvenirs?
Are you going on holiday this year?
Have you been on holiday this year?

**The past**

80

Now let's talk about the past.
Tell us about the past.
Where were you born?
Have you always lived in the same place?
How old were you when you started school?
Where did you meet your best friends?
What do you remember about the games you played before you started school?
Which of your friends have you known the longest?
What do you like to do now that you didn't like when you were younger?
How has your town or city changed in the past few years?
What was your favourite TV programme when you were younger?
Can you remember a time when you were really excited?
Can you remember a time when you were really bored?
Can you remember a birthday present you were given when you were younger?